Beijing Jeep

BEIJING JEEP

A Case Study of Western Business in China

JIM MANN

WestviewPress

A Division of HarperCollins*Publishers*

Copyright © 1997 by Westview Press, A Division of HarperCollins Publishers, Inc.

Published in 1997 in the United States of America by Westview Press, 5500 Central Avenue, Boulder, Colorado 80301-2877, and in the United Kingdom by Westview Press, 12 Hid's Copse Road, Cumnor Hill, Oxford OX2 9JJ

Library of Congress Cataloging-in-Publication Data
Mann, Jim, 1946–
    Beijing Jeep : a case study of Western business in China / Jim Mann.
        p.   cm.
    Originally published: New York : Simon and Schuster, 1989.
    Includes bibliographical references (p.   ) and index.
    ISBN 0-8133-3327-X(pbk.)
    1. American Motors Corporation. 2. Jeep automobile.
3. Automobile industry and trade—China. 5. Joint ventures—United States.
6. Joint ventures—China. 7. United States—Foreign economic
relations—China. 8. China—Foreign economic relations—United
States. I. Title
HD9710.U54A6574   1997
338.8'87292222—dc21   96-51810
                                                                                              CIP

The paper used in this publication meets the requirements of the American National Standard for Permanence of Paper for Printed Library Materials Z39.48-1984.

10   9   8   7   6   5   4   3   2   1

*In memory of
my brother Ron,
who died at home
while I was stationed
in China*

Contents

Contents

Acknowledgments

The idea for this book originated aboard American Airlines 77, the daily nonstop from Washington to Los Angeles, and it is to this flight that I owe my first unsolicited words of gratitude.

In the late winter and spring of 1984, I was commuting monthly from coast to coast, from my daily work in the *Los Angeles Times* Washington bureau to the newspaper's headquarters in Los Angeles. At that time, I was preparing to leave for China for a three-year tour as the newspaper's resident correspondent in Beijing.

Like countless other hurried Americans, I find those five-hour transcontinental flights to be among the longest, quietest, unbroken stretches of free time I have for concentrated work. And so, on those coast-to-coast flights, I would regularly pull out my language books, eagerly studying the Chinese words that might help me when I began my new assignment.

There, aboard American 77, on every trip in those early months of 1984, the same ritual would unfold. As I began to study Chinese, a seatmate would watch me with my books. Sooner or later he or she would strike up a conversation: Is that Chinese or Japanese you're studying? Why?

The conversation might start in any of a number of ways. But it would almost always end the same way. "I've always wanted to do business in China," my airline seatmate would confide. "I've been thinking of trying to get something started there myself. Maybe someday soon, I'll be studying Chinese, too. . . . "

After several of these airplane encounters, I began to realize that, in those months of early 1984, the American business interest in China was virtually limitless. There were, indeed, few companies, entrepreneurs, lawyers, or investors who weren't thinking, dreaming, or scheming about getting something started in China. What would happen to them? How successful would they be?

During my three years as a *Times* reporter in China, from mid-1984 through mid-1987, I attempted to keep track of the development of China's business dealings with the West. And in the two years since my return to Washington, I have continued these efforts, both from the United States and on two return trips to China.

The second return visit to China was during May and June 1989. I was reporting in Beijing for my newspaper when the tanks and troops of China's People's Liberation Army shot and killed their way into Tiananmen Square on the night of June 3–4, 1989. That event was a milestone, not only for the Chinese Communist Party's relations with the Chinese people and for China's general dealings with the outside world, but also for the attitudes of the Western business community toward China. It also marked a dramatic—and frightening—end to the work on this book.

The book is based in large part on personal interviews I conducted, mostly in China and in the United States, but also in Hong Kong, Taiwan, and Moscow. A few of the interviews will have to remain confidential, at the requests of the people who granted them. Although the book and the views it expresses are entirely my responsibility, I would like to acknowledge and thank the following people for their time, insights and help:

Robert O. Anderson, Arthur E. Bates, Valery I. Biryukov, Rory Callahan, Nicolas Chapuis, Chen Xulin, Jim Cherfoli, Warren Christopher, Tod O. Clare, Bradley G. Clark, Fred P. Clark, Jerome Alan Cohen, David Edinburgh, Lyn Edinger, Charles W. Freeman, Jr., Barry I. Friedman, John Frisbie, Lauren Giglio, Ronald Gilchrist, Robert Goodwin, Vladimir N. Gorshkov, John Guiniven, Mike Hammes, Han Xu, Harry Harding, He Chunlin, Murray Hudson, Arthur W. Hummel, Jr., Kerry Ivins, Darryl N. Johnson, Richard Johnston, Thorkild Juul-Dam, Arthur Kobler, Harry S. Langerman, Nicholas Lardy, Kenneth Lieberthal, Winston Lord, Viatcheslav F. Lukjanchuk, Wilhelm Meier, Shankar Menon, Stephen E. W. Mulder, Michel Oksenberg, Charles Parton, Hervé Pauze, Ralph A. Pfeiffer, Jr., Dwight Porter, Donald St. Pierre, Yuri N. Sapounov, Shyam Saran, Hulan Saren, Lynn C. Saunders, Ed Schulze, Melvin W. Searls, Jr., Shao Ligong, Troy E. Simmons, Jerry L. Sloan, Richard H. Solomon, Robert Steinseifer, Su Jinzhui, Roger Sullivan, C. B. Sung, David S. Tappan, Jr., W. Paul Tippett, Marvin S. Traub, P. Jeffrey Trimmer, Hector Veloso, George V. Wood, Leonard Woodcock, Wu Xinhui, Takashi Yamamura, Wu Zhongliang, Zhang Jizhang, Zhou Kaiying.

The parts of this book concerning the Beijing Jeep joint venture are also aided by the confidential minutes of the joint venture's board of directors; by the detailed contract signed in 1983; and by copies of the secret agreement that the Chinese and American sides negotiated in 1986. I thank those people who enabled me to obtain these valuable documents.

Throughout the course of the narrative, I have attempted as often as possible to reconstruct the actions, perceptions, and motivations of both Westerners and Chinese. While in China I interviewed Chinese officials; attended Chinese briefings; talked with Chinese cadres at Beijing Jeep and other, similar operations; and met Chinese workers in random encounters on the streets, in stores, even while ice-skating on a winter day. I was helped by some Chinese sources who will have to remain nameless. As the world has recently witnessed, China is not yet so open that its people can talk freely without fear of retaliation upon themselves or their families.

However, in the end it would be presumptuous, indeed ridiculous, to claim that I had as much access to Chinese thoughts and perceptions as to Western ones, or that I learned as much about the inner workings of the Chinese side of Beijing Jeep as I learned about the American side. This account, then, inevitably reflects a Western point of view. A full and complete account of China's perspective on the Western businesses remains to be written. I hope that it will be, and that the political climate in China will be such that it can be written in a spirit of free and open inquiry.

In researching and writing this book, I have had the help of many different people, all of whom deserve my warmest thanks.

At the *Los Angeles Times*, foreign editor Alvin Shuster and his assistants, Simon Li and Linda Mathews, contributed invaluable help and advice to me during my three years in China; and Washington bureau chief Jack Nelson, deputy bureau chief Richard T. Cooper, and editor Joel Havemann all provided support and encouragement during the writing of this book in Washington. In addition, Washington librarians Aleta Embry and Abebe Gessesse aided in obtaining research materials.

While I was in Beijing, Tamara Perkins and Cheng Yafei helped keep me going, and Diane Atkinson Shen and Maureen Ulevich did the laborious work of transcribing tape recordings. Back in the United States, the Gerald R. Ford Presidential Library made an invaluable contribution by providing a travel grant that enabled me to examine the library's files on China and on the formation of the National Council for U.S.-China Trade (now the U.S.-China Business Council). Attorney Edward James also supplied crucial help and advice, both while I was in China and after my return to the United States.

At Simon and Schuster, I am most grateful to my editor, Alice Mayhew, who grasped the idea for this book from the beginning and encouraged it along at every step of the way; and to her attentive and talented assistant, David Shipley, who provided invaluable help and suggestions with the manuscript.

I owe an extraordinary message of thanks to a close friend and remarkable journalist, Steve Luxenberg, who read the manuscript carefully on his own and had the insight to understand, sometimes better than I did, how the narrative fit together. Another good friend, Richard Hornik, also served as helpful reader of the manuscript.

By far the greatest thanks go to my wife, Caroline Dexter, and my children, Elizabeth and Teddy Mann, who supported and tolerated this book and the long hours it took over the past five years.

Washington, July 1, 1989

Prologue

Invite Chinese officials to Las Vegas? Why not? To the corporate executives of the American Motors Corporation, it seemed like a perfectly good idea, although nobody now remembers thinking about it too much.

In the summer of 1985 American Motors had just begun to produce its Cherokee Jeeps in China. American Motors executives had made countless trips to Beijing, and a few AMC employees were already living there. Several Chinese officials of the Beijing Automotive Works—AMC's partner in China, one of the gargantuan state-owned industrial enterprises operating under China's socialist system—had visited the American company's headquarters outside Detroit and had toured other major American cities as well.

Over the previous six years virtually all business dealings between the leaders of this struggling American corporation and the high-level cadres of the Chinese *danwei*, or work unit, had been either in Beijing or in the Detroit area. Now it was time for another series of meetings between the two sides: the Chinese and Americans were trying to decide how to come up with the money needed to upgrade the auto plant in Beijing.

American Motors suggested what the Americans thought would be an interesting change of scene. The meeting with the Chinese delegation was scheduled in mid-August, at approximately the time AMC was staging its annual dealer show, this time in Las Vegas. The show was a big affair in which AMC unveiled its new model cars and trucks to all its North American dealers. For AMC, as for other American auto manufacturers, the dealer show was an epic production, one on which the company spent lavishly to impress the dealers. At this 1985 show, AMC was planning to unveil

its new Comanche truck, which the American company also hoped
to introduce eventually in China. Why not show AMC's new
Chinese partners how the Comanche was launched at home? Why
not let them see one of the most spectacular events in AMC's
domestic sales operations? Under China's centrally planned economy, the leaders of the Beijing Automotive Works were accustomed to selling a fixed, predetermined number of cars to the state
each year for eventual allocation to other state enterprises. The
Chinese auto manufacturers didn't have to worry about sales; that
wasn't their problem. The Americans had begun to preach to their
Chinese partners about the importance of marketing and the methods of introducing new models. Why not let them witness firsthand
a bit of Western-style marketing? Why not show them how it was
done in America?

So Wu Zhongliang, the senior Chinese official at AMC's venture in Beijing, and seven other Chinese auto officials in the company were invited to AMC's dealer show in Las Vegas. There they
began a series of meetings with their counterparts from AMC. The
sessions were held at Las Vegas's MGM Grand Hotel. On the way
into and out of each lunch, dinner, or meeting, the Chinese officials
would have to go by the slot machines, the roulette wheels, and
the blackjack tables located throughout the hotel. The dollars were
flowing one way and another, and so were the usual high rollers
and loose women—women who, so the Chinese expression goes,
mai xiao, sell their smiles. It was a scene that left the Chinese
delegation wide-eyed. A couple of them stood by the gaming tables
with the slow, unembarrassed stare one sees on the streets in
China. Some of Vegas's high rollers stared back, wondering who
these oddly dressed foreigners might be.

Wu Zhongliang couldn't believe the gambling. Even three
years later he would recall how Americans had been gambling in
Las Vegas at breakfast. Wu himself, a graying, middle-aged state
bureaucrat, had been born in Shanghai in 1931 and educated at
missionary schools, including St. John's University of Shanghai.
There had been gambling back in Shanghai then, plenty of it, but
only for foreigners and rich Chinese, and it was exactly the sort of
thing the Communists had wanted to suppress through their successful revolution. Since the liberation of Shanghai in the spring of
1949, there had been nothing like this in any public place in China.
The scene at the MGM Grand's gaming tables was reminiscent of

the Maoist propaganda movies about life on Taiwan. Wu's best friend at AMC, Tod Clare, the vice president for international affairs, sought to ease Wu's discomfort by inviting Wu to join him in a night of gambling, but Wu politely refused. Gambling, he said, was just not for him. He and the rest of the Chinese delegation had come to work, not to gamble.

Because the company had more than 1,500 dealers, American Motors usually held these annual conventions in two shifts. Half of the dealers would come for two days; they would leave, and the other half would come for the next two days. But in 1985, as it prepared to launch its new Comanche truck, AMC wanted to make a particularly big splash. The company arranged to have a one-night overlap in which all the AMC dealers would gather for dinner and a show in the MGM Grand's huge rectangular banquet room. The Chinese delegation was invited to this special occasion, AMC's biggest dealer show ever.

The night started out calmly enough. The dealers seemed to be drinking quite a bit, but the ceremonies themselves seemed quite staid. A bandstand played soft music, while the car dealers and their wives, husbands or companions ate filet mignon. AMC's new president, Jose Dedeurwaerder—who had been installed the previous year by the management of Renault, AMC's parent company —gave a speech to the dealers, extolling both their work and the quality of the new AMC cars and trucks they would be selling.

As the dealers were finishing their desserts, the house lights were brought down and the music was brought to a crescendo. Two red AMC Comanche trucks cruised onto the floor of the dining room. On the back of each was a girl in a bikini who tossed beach balls around the room and onto the tables. The two Comanches rolled up to the bandstand at the far end of the room, and out from the cabins came the Beach Boys, the rock group selected especially for its appeal to AMC's middle-aged dealers.

American Motors had been sponsoring the Beach Boys' national tour that summer. In Las Vegas, for the benefit of their corporate sponsor, the Beach Boys gave it their all. The ninety-minute show was filled with all the old favorites, their car songs, "409" and "Little Deuce Coupe" and all the rest. The dealers, with a few drinks under their belts, stood and stomped and clapped. They began dancing on the floor and then on the chairs and the tables.

In the center of this raucous scene was the Chinese delegation, its members sitting together silently at one round table. Before long, Chairman Wu rose from his table, expressionless, and walked out of the room. He was followed by other Chinese officials. A few younger officials in the Chinese delegation stayed, and one of them, a young woman in a modest skirt, summoned the courage to dance on one of the chairs for a few minutes. (Later, AMC officials in China reported that she had been punished; she was taken off her assignment at the car factory and given nothing to do for two years.)

When daylight and sobriety returned, the top leaders of AMC and the Chinese enterprise resumed their business meetings. They were trying to settle some serious financial questions: Where would they find the cash to make expensive but necessary improvements, such as an engine plant, at the Chinese factory? Chinese officials were suggesting that AMC should invest more capital in the new joint venture. AMC officials replied that the American company was in a precarious financial condition and could not spare additional capital for the Chinese venture.

A few days after the Beach Boys concert, Jose Dedeurwaerder, American Motors' president, came to one of these sessions. Soon after he entered, he was given a stern dressing-down by Chairman Wu.

"This is terrible," Wu told him. "You tell us American Motors doesn't have enough money, that you can't invest any more in China. But you're spending money on all this *foolishness*."

"You don't understand," replied Dedeurwaerder. "This is just the way things are done in the United States. In fact, this is why we wanted your delegation to come here, so that you could see what you have to do in marketing and sales promotion in the automobile business."

Wu reproached Dedeurwaerder the next day with the same lecture. AMC was wasting money on this dealer show; why couldn't it invest more money in China?

Now Dedeurwaerder lost his temper. "Listen," he said, "I won't tell you how to run your Communist system if you won't tell me how to run my company." The AMC president stormed out of the room and refused to take part in any further meetings. He told aides at AMC he never wanted to see Chairman Wu again. Indeed, Dedeurwaerder never visited his company's China project; on a couple of occasions, he cancelled plans made by his staff for him to visit Beijing.

Later, American Motors officials would admit that the Las Vegas meeting had been a disaster. If there was anything they had learned about China, they said, it was this: Don't take the Chinese to Las Vegas.

Three years later Chairman Wu recalled that American Motors had confessed to spending $1 million, *one million dollars*, on that dealer show.

Introduction

Even if some Chinese received them warmly, there were always more who met them with indifference, deception or hostility. Each adviser had sought to control China's destiny in some fashion; the dawning realization that such would not be the case was a serious disappointment.

—Jonathan Spence, *To Change China*

On the afternoon of June 6, 1989, the scene at Beijing's Capital Airport was one of bedlam. In front of the All Nippon Airways counter, Japanese businessmen waited in long lines, hurrying to buy tickets in time for the takeoff of the next plane to Tokyo. Their children lay on the floor, sleeping with their heads on hastily packed luggage. Some in the crowd had spent the previous night at the airport. Others had just arrived there after paying extravagant sums to any Chinese taxi driver who would risk the drive to the airport through the barricaded streets of Beijing.

At nearby ticket counters, American representatives from companies like Westinghouse and General Electric sought to arrange flights from Beijing to wherever else in East Asia they could buy a plane ticket. They tried the Cathay Pacific flight to Hong Kong, or, if that was full, the Singapore International Airlines flight to Singapore, or the Thai International plane to Bangkok. It didn't matter where, as long as the planes took them out of Beijing, a city with gunfire on the streets.

Downtown Beijing was in the sort of chaos that is a businessman's worst dream. For several days tens of thousands of troops from China's People's Liberation Army patrolled the streets, carrying AK-47 automatic weapons, occasionally firing them at errant residents of Beijing, more often unloading volleys of ammunition high into the air in an effort to terrorize the city into submission.

Some of those volleys pierced windows in the big brown high rise called the CITIC (Chinese International Trust and Investment Corporation) building, the principal office building for foreign companies in Beijing. When John Frisbie, head of the China office for the U.S.-China Business Council, the main trade group for American companies in China, went to his office on the twenty-second floor of the CITIC building to retrieve his passport in preparation for leaving the country, he discovered that bullets had come through the outside window and into his office ceiling. Other companies with offices in the CITIC building, such as Wang Computer, also found bullet holes in their windows.

More bullets struck the facades of the Beijing, Jianguo, and Beijing-Toronto hotels—three of the city's best-known enclaves for foreigners, where, over the years, thousands of Western businessmen had slept, ate, hoped, and worried. Just off Tiananmen Square, Chinese troops for a time occupied the bland plastic interior of Kentucky Fried Chicken, the fast-food restaurant that had served, since its opening in 1987, as a symbol to the rest of the world of China's supposed eagerness to Westernize.

All through that week, the second week of June 1989, foreign businessmen fled China for their own safety. The exodus was so large that national airlines such as British Airways, Qantas, and Lufthansa brought in extra jumbo jets to Beijing or Shanghai to help get their nationals out of China.

On the previous Saturday night, the night of June 3–4, Chinese troops had driven into the heart of Beijing in order to recapture Tiananmen Square from the youthful demonstrators for democracy who had occupied the square for most of the previous six weeks. The soldiers fired indiscriminately into crowds, killing, by most estimates, a few thousand people.[1] The regime of Deng Xiaoping succeeded in repressing the prodemocracy movement that had swept across China that spring—but at extraordinary costs to China's political stability and international standing. For more than a week after the Tiananmen massacre, residents of Beijing and virtually every other large city in China blocked streets, demonstrated, and burned trucks and even a railway train in outrage over the massacre in Beijing. For weeks after that China's huge security apparatus arrested, jailed, and in some cases executed those who had been involved in the nationwide protests; the regime also fired and sometimes arrested intellectuals who had pressed for changes in China's political system.

Once safely aloft on their flights out of China, the foreign business-men had a quick drink or two, rejoicing in their escape from the immediate fear and the danger. Aboard one Cathay Pacific flight from Beijing to Hong Kong on that frenetic Tuesday afternoon, a relieved Hong Kong businessman recounted how he had been stuck for two days in the Minzu Hotel, just off Tiananmen Square, with troops firing outside the hotel's front door and no food inside. "There was not even a bowl of rice, nothing," said the business-man. He had escaped only with the quiet help of some loyal Chinese friends.

On that same Cathay Pacific flight, Timothy L. Hooper, the chief representative in China for Britain's Standard Chartered Bank —which has five branches and four other representative offices in China—grumbled that he had not wanted to leave the country that day. The British embassy had been insistent, Hooper said, and his company could not afford to lose the cooperation of embassy offi-cials. "We were quite prepared to stay," said Hooper. "But we got rung up by the British embassy Monday night saying your depen-dents should leave, and they called this [Tuesday] morning and told everyone to leave."

Standard Chartered Bank had been in China since the mid-nineteenth century, Hooper reflected. In one way or another, the British bank had survived the Taiping Rebellion, the Boxer Rebel-lion, the fall of the Qing dynasty, the warlord era of the early twentieth century, the anti-Japanese war, and the Communist revolution of 1949, always managing eventually to return to China. So Hooper knew his company would survive the turmoil of 1989, too. He himself planned to go back to Beijing when the situation cooled down.

Nevertheless, as a result of the massacre, Hooper was deeply pessimistic about the prospects for foreign businesses in China. As the Cathay Pacific flight descended through the clouds to the bright lights of Hong Kong, Hooper rendered his judgment: it would take years for China to recover from the damage it had just done to itself. "This will set them back five to ten years," Hooper mused. "China is a new area of the world to explore, and people aren't going to do that now. They'll go off and explore other areas."

Like Hooper, thousands of other Western business executives found themselves reevaluating their companies' prospects in China following the events of the spring of 1989. China, it turned out, was not as safe and stable as they had thought. The assumption in the West had been that under the leadership of Deng Xiaoping, China had put political purges and ideological campaigns behind it in its drive for modernization. Now, in 1989, the power struggles at the top of the Chinese leadership seemed little better than in the days of the Cultural Revolution. When confronted with calls for democracy and a threat to its own power, Deng and his allies at the top levels of the Chinese Communist Party were resorting to the techniques of conventional Stalinism.

The businessmen had misjudged. China's Communist Party leadership had not changed quite as much as they had believed throughout the previous decade. The business hopes for China had been much too high. To some degree, executives had deluded themselves about the extent of change in China because of their own eagerness to sell to the most populous country in the world. And to some degree, the Western companies had been misled by their own governments—by leaders such as President Reagan, who, after a five-day visit in 1984, characterized China as a "so-called Communist" country.

Correspondingly, at least some senior Chinese leaders felt that they had misjudged, too: that their own expectations of what Western businesses might do for China had also been unrealistic. After the massacre, when the U.S. Congress threatened to impose broad economic sanctions against China, President Yang Shangkun quickly retorted: "China is not afraid of that. China has to rely on itself for development."[2] It was a revival of the old view that China didn't need the West and shouldn't rely on it.

At no other time in the twentieth century have the institutions of Western capitalism sought to do business with and inside a Communist state to the extent that they did in China during the 1980s. After the Russian Revolution of 1917, and particularly since the division of Europe following World War II, it had become common-place to think of communism and capitalism as two separate worlds—sometimes, after China and the Soviet Union took competing paths in the early 1960s, as three separate worlds. The private corporations that dominate the economies of the United States, Western Europe, and Japan had remained largely isolated from the centrally planned economies of the Communist nations. To be sure, there were brief, occasional, and highly publicized flirtations: Armand Hammer selling his pencils to Lenin; Pepsi-Cola and other Western companies exploring prospects in Moscow and Eastern Europe during the détente of the early 1970s; Japanese and West European companies buying and selling goods within the narrow confines of China's semiannual Canton Trade Fair. For the most part, however, these were transactions in which the Western corporations and Communist governments met merely to conclude a sale or a trade. Western companies were rarely permitted to set up ongoing manufacturing and service operations inside the borders of a Communist state or to invest their own capital in the state-run enterprises of a centrally planned Communist economy.

What China had done during the 1980s was unprecedented. In its effort to modernize the nation as rapidly as possible, the Communist Party leadership headed by Deng Xiaoping not only permitted but invited, indeed encouraged, Western corporations to join hands with Chinese state enterprises. Motivated largely by the centuries-old Western desire to penetrate and capture the vast China market, Western companies heeded Deng's call. By the beginning of 1989 more than five thousand foreign-owned companies had invested in China. The numbers of these foreign businesses in China and the scope of their business operations far exceeded anything seen in Moscow at the height of détente or in even the reforming socialist economies of Hungary or Yugoslavia. It was a grand experiment, not just for China but for the rest of the world; and it suggested at least the possibility of dramatic change in the relationship between private capital and Communist states. By the late 1980s, Soviet leader Mikhail S. Gorbachev was starting to imitate the example of economic reform set by China. Like Deng, Gorbachev began seeking to attract Western capital and to encourage the creation of joint ventures between foreign companies and Soviet state enterprises.

. . .

Nevertheless, even before the massacre at Tiananmen, the Chinese experiment had begun to produce a considerable degree of disappointment on both sides. China never managed to attract as much foreign investment as it had hoped. The foreign companies that set up operations in China did not obtain the massive sales or the low-cost production of which they had dreamed. Executives sent to work inside the Middle Kingdom by Western businesses like American Motors ran up against the enormous frustrations of daily life there: the delays, the bureaucracy, the often exorbitant and unpredictable prices, the sudden changes in government policy, the not infrequent requests for changes in the terms of signed contracts. Chinese officials were themselves frustrated by the impatience and willfulness of foreigners—foreigners who were never quite satisfied with the answer that this was the way China had always worked, foreigners who did not always want to do what was in the interests of China.

The Chinese have an old saying that describes well the uneasy business relationships that developed when the Western companies entered China. *Tong chuang yi meng*, the slogan went: "Same bed, different dreams."

For the most part, the Western corporations starting up in China were dreaming about a market of one billion people. This was the same dream that has beguiled Western companies since the Industrial Revolution, since one British writer declared more than 150 years ago: "If we could only persuade every person in China to lengthen his shirttail by a foot, we could keep the mills of Lancashire working round the clock." The products had changed —the West now wanted to sell the Chinese personal computers, Jeeps, baby food, shampoo, razor blades, Tampons, and Ritz crackers—but the dreams were essentially the same.

China had its own dreams, which also date back to the nineteenth century. China wanted to try once again to obtain the technology it needs to modernize and to catch up with the West and with Japan, its East Asian neighbor with Western technology. In 1860 the Chinese scholar Feng Guifen wrote, "There ought to be some people of extraordinary intelligence who can have new ideas and improve on Western methods. At first they may learn and pattern after the foreigners; then they may compare and try to be their equal; and finally they may go ahead and surpass them—the way to make ourselves strong actually lies in this."[3] After 120 years of turbulent history, China was still trying to fulfill these dreams.

The ultimate question was whether two partners with such different dreams could last for long in the same bed. Would the alliance of Western corporations and Chinese socialism work, or were the two sides incompatible? Could $100,000-a-year executives from nations of wealth and abundance blend into a single management team with $75-a-month cadres from a nation of poverty and scarcity? Could private corporations whose aim is to maximize profits join together with the industrial subunits of a socialist state geared toward maximizing output, control, and social order?

By the late 1980s the relationship between the Western businesses and China was clearly beginning to cool. Board chairmen and chief executive officers of Western companies were no longer so awed by the business prospects in China. China, for its part, had begun to reexamine the extent to which it could rely on the private corporations of the West to provide the capital and technology needed for its economic development. Dramatic as it was, the Tiananmen massacre merely accelerated a phenomenon that was already under way: the gradual, progressive disillusionment with China on the part of the Western business community.

The purpose of this book is to recount what happened through that period of more than a decade in which Western companies went hunting for business in China, signed contracts, started up operations, and then, often, became increasingly frustrated and disenchanted there. I have chosen to tell this story primarily through the eyes of the executives and other employees in one particular company, the American Motors Corporation, which in 1983 agreed to set up a new joint venture to manufacture Jeeps in Beijing.

That joint venture, Beijing Jeep, became in many ways the bellwether joint venture between the West and China. It was the first major manufacturing joint venture set up after China opened its doors to foreign investment. The 1983 announcement of the creation of Beijing Jeep was front-page news in the United States, raising false hopes that the deal would blaze a new path for the American automobile industry in its effort to compete with Japan. The difficulties that American Motors later confronted—culminating in a highly public financial crisis in the spring of 1986—served as the catalyst for an outpouring of Western disenchantment with the business conditions in China. Beijing Jeep was the most closely watched business venture between China and the West, the one most regularly visited by political leaders such as then Vice President George Bush and then Communist Party General Secretary Zhao Ziyang.

I do not mean to argue that American Motors' experiences were typical in all ways of all foreign companies setting up shop in China. Indeed, as the later chapters of this book make clear, American Motors' joint venture, Beijing Jeep, eventually became a special case, a "model" joint venture whose favored treatment made it decidedly atypical. Yet throughout the 1980s, AMC served as the trailblazer for the unprecedented business dealings between Western corporations and the Chinese state. What happened to AMC may serve to illuminate both the difficulties confronting Western businesses in China and, more broadly, the general pattern of interaction between a private corporation and a Communist economic system.

This is a narrative, a reporter's reconstruction, of what took place when a private, profit-oriented Western corporation sought to do business inside the People's Republic of China.

1

Outside Looking In

Tod Clare had worked in Hong Kong during the bad old days, from 1961 to 1965, when a businessman for an American company couldn't go to China, couldn't buy anything directly from the Chinese, couldn't even really talk openly about doing business with China. The United States recognized Chiang Kai-shek's Nationalist regime on Taiwan, and American businessmen were supposed to follow suit. Any action that suggested acknowledgment of the existence of Mao Tse-tung's government in Beijing was out of bounds.

Clare thought being in Hong Kong then was like a gigantic game of blindman's buff. China wasn't supposed to exist, but you knew it was there. You saw pictures of China. You saw the population of Hong Kong—four million people, many of whom had escaped from China during the Japanese invasion of China in 1937, the Communist revolution of 1949, or another of China's twentieth-century upheavals. From Hong Kong's New Territories, or from a yacht out on a sail from Hong Kong's magnificent harbor, you could see the high green hills of China's Guangdong Province. On the other side were the rice paddies from which many of Hong Kong's energetic workers had fled. On a quiet Sunday, the only day of the week when Hong Kong was not fully engaged in the frenetic pursuit of money, you could go right up to the Chinese border in the New Territories and peer across. Clare had done it himself; he had looked at the border guards in the green uniforms of the People's Liberation Army and, like thousands of others before and after him, had thought to himself that he was looking at a sleeping giant.

In the early 1960s Clare was working for Cummins Engine Company, which had its Far East headquarters in Hong Kong. For

Clare, it was a wonderful time. He was single. His car came with a Chinese driver who polished its wheels every day, spoke by spoke. His apartment came with a Chinese maid, or amah. Living in Asia was the fulfillment of a dream that had started during his college days at Stanford. Clare had majored in international relations, and his special interest had been the Far East. In a political science seminar, all his classmates had chosen subjects relating to Europe; that had seemed to be the way to get ahead in the years right after World War II, when the United States found itself the dominant political and financial power on the other side of the Atlantic. But Clare had opted out; when his classmates wrote about France's political parties, he studied Japan. From Palo Alto, Asia just seemed more interesting to Clare than Europe.

Clare's job at Cummins's Hong Kong office was to set up a regional operation for Southeast Asia. The early 1960s were the heyday of the licensing business, when all an American company had to do was go out and license its name and technology to foreign businesses. As he traveled around the region, he discovered very quickly that the best businessmen and entrepreneurs—in fact, the entire merchant class of many Southeast Asian countries—were Chinese. They were Filipinos, but they were the Chinese Filipinos; they were Malays, but the Chinese Malay. Like many other Americans, Clare had thought the expression "overseas Chinese" referred primarily to the Chinatowns of the United States, like the one in San Francisco. Instead, he saw virtually every country in Asia had a large Chinese community, and that these overseas Chinese had tremendous economic power in every country. So great was their energy that at times it seemed to Clare as though the nations of Southeast Asia would simply collapse without their communities of overseas Chinese.

When he was home in Hong Kong, Clare also found himself impressed by the diligence and business acumen of the refugees from China. The man who rented Cummins its office came from Shanghai, and so did many of the Chinese with whom Clare did business in Hong Kong. The Cantonese who made up most of Hong Kong's population referred to the Shanghainese as "city slickers," much the way Americans from the southern United States regard New Yorkers. It was clear to Clare and everyone else that the Shanghainese knew their business. Until World War II Hong Kong had been a sleepy little port town, a backwater governed by the British for Britain's global interests, one more pretty little colonial pearl in a chain that included Singapore and Bombay. Those who looked for a cosmopolitan, international city in East Asia settled up the Chinese coast in Shanghai. But after Mao's revolution of 1949, many of Shanghai's leading business families and its most industrious workers moved to Hong Kong, where they quickly began to breathe new spirit into the place. Hong Kong's population grew from 1.5 million at the beginning of World War II to 2.4 million after the peak of immigration from China in May 1950. Shanghai businessmen in Hong Kong moved in on the markets of the British establishment and opened new markets the British had never imagined. British department stores in Hong Kong lost customers to Chinese-owned stores like Wing On—whose owners, the Kwok family, had moved to Hong Kong when their store on Nanjing Road in Shanghai was taken over by the new Communist government and turned into the nondescript Number Ten Department Store.

The more Clare did business with the Chinese, the more he wanted to know China itself. And the more he watched how the Chinese operated, the more he found himself puzzled by problems he found himself unable to explain. Outside China, it seemed as though the Chinese were imbued with a remarkable talent for making money, a stunning entrepreneurial spirit. Yet inside China, the people were little more than servants of a conventional, centrally planned economic system. Outside China, the people were such brilliant independent businessmen that many of them became millionaires; inside China, even the best and the brightest worked as government officials on tiny state salaries. Was there some difference in entrepreneurial talent or in other abilities between those Chinese who left their homeland to go abroad and those who stayed at home? If not, how had the new government managed to suppress those entrepreneurial instincts that seemed so natural to the Chinese outside of China itself? How could these instincts possibly be bottled up, even by Mao's totalitarian regime?

A quarter century later, after watching China reopen its doors and spending a good portion of his career doing business with China, Tod Clare still wasn't certain he knew the answers to these questions.

For the Americans, as for the British, French, Dutch, Portuguese, and other Europeans before them, the impetus for doing business with China had originated centuries earlier with the desire to obtain China's tea and spices, silk and porcelain. That desire had been one of the oldest, most enduring themes of Western commerce; it had been the search for a new and better route to China and India, after all, that had brought Europeans to America in the first place. The Americans had quickly joined the Europeans in the rush to China. In 1784 an American merchant ship named the *Empress of China* sailed from New York Harbor around the Cape of Good Hope to Canton, where it unloaded a cargo of furs, wool, and ginseng and brought back tea, silk, and porcelain. "The Chinese had never heard of us, but we introduced ourselves as a new nation," one American sailor wrote home during that trip.

The problem in those days was that the Westerners wanted far more from China than they had to offer in return. In what was one of the most famous and loftiest rebuffs in the long history of relations between China and the West, the Chinese emperor Qianlong turned aside a British mission to Beijing in 1793 by writing to King George III: "We have never set much store on strange or ingenious objects, nor do we need any more of your country's manufactures." In desperation, British traders began bringing opium to China so that they would have something to offer in exchange for Chinese goods.

The Industrial Revolution had brought about a fundamental change. In the nineteenth century factories in Britain and the United States began producing goods at an astonishing rate and needed new markets to absorb their ever-expanding production. For the first time, the Western drive to do business with China was fueled more by the desire to sell goods to China than to buy goods from China. In the United States, the idea that China's huge population could serve as a prime outlet for American manufactured products reached a plateau at the end of the nineteenth century. In 1898 Secretary of State William R. Day told Congress that American factories were producing a "large excess over home consumption," which required "an enlargement of foreign markets." The most favorable markets for American exports were in underdeveloped areas of the world, Day said, and "nowhere is this consideration of more interest than in its relation to the Chinese Empire." The eagerness for American trade with China had served as one of the principal forces prompting President McKinley's administration to keep possession of the Philippines after seizing it during the

Spanish-American War. U.S. officials working on the peace commission spoke of "the great importance of the Philippines with reference to trade in China." Americans in the Philippines, said one Treasury Department official, would serve as "pickets of the Pacific, standing guard at the entrances to trade with the millions of China and Korea, French Indo-China, the Malay Peninsula and the islands of Indonesia."[1]

But those hopes of a huge Chinese market for American products had gone largely unfulfilled. In the first half of the twentieth century, China had been torn apart by revolution, Japanese invasion, and civil war. Even in the 1930s, when the United States became the leading trading partner of Chiang Kai-shek's Nationalist regime, China never took up more than 2 percent of America's world trade. After the Communist revolution of 1949 and the outbreak of the Korean War, a U.S. trade embargo forced China to turn to the Soviet Union and Eastern Europe for the goods it needed. "The Canton Bus Company, which had always bought British and American [cars and buses], is now using Hungarian vehicles with red and yellow painted body," reported one visitor to China in 1954. "American cars are now rare in China, and imports of spare parts for American cars are almost nil."[2]

In the 1950s, the earliest years of the People's Republic, China had regained peace and economic stability, and it had seemed for a time as if the factories of Eastern Europe might succeed in capturing the huge Chinese market that had so long eluded the mills of Lancashire. In a 1954 article called "From Grey, Black and Blue to Colors," the Hong Kong magazine *Far Eastern Economic Review* marveled at changing fashions in China. Using language reminiscent of *Time* or *Newsweek* in the 1980s, the magazine observed, "Blue, grey and black cadre uniforms have been predominant on the mainland ever since the Communist occupation. Foreign visitors to Peking and other . . . cities had difficulty in judging the sex of the people they met on the streets." But now, the magazine said, the Chinese government was encouraging the population to wear Western-style clothing, even for May Day celebrations. China was importing new textiles from Czechoslovakia and Poland. As a result, "fresh, bright colors are beginning to appear. Workers . . . students and peasant women in the fields are now seen in vivid prints of many colors."[3]

Polish and Czech commercial hopes for China proved no more

lasting than the dreams of the Americans or British. The East-bloc trade and the bright colors on the Chinese streets had both faded with the Sino-Soviet split at the end of the 1950s. After the outbreak of the Cultural Revolution in 1966, China became swept up in domestic turmoil and increasingly isolated from the rest of the world.

On May 31, 1973, some of the most prominent business leaders in the United States convened in the State Room of the Shoreham Hotel in Washington, D.C., for what could fairly be called a summit conference of corporate America.

The menu included vichyssoise, poached salmon steak, and string beans almandine. The open bar offered Cutty Sark Scotch and Gilbey's gin. The tables were covered with green linen. Small flags of the United States and the People's Republic of China served as centerpieces.

Among the speakers were men such as Thornton A. Wilder, chairman of the board of the Boeing Company; Donald Burnham, chairman of Westinghouse Electric; and W. Michael Blumenthal, chairman of the Bendix Corporation. Others who had organized the session included David Rockefeller of the Chase Manhattan Bank and Donald M. Kendall, chairman of Pepsico; and David Packard of Hewlett-Packard Company.

The purpose was to prepare the American business community for the resumption of trade between the United States and China. Since 1969 President Richard M. Nixon had been gradually lifting some of the legal prohibitions on trade with China. The Shanghai communiqué signed during Nixon's 1972 trip to China had called for the two countries to begin working together to facilitate the development of commerce. Since then, Nixon's secretary of commerce, Frederick B. Dent, had been urging American business executives to form an umbrella group that could oversee the effort.

The original plan had been to have Secretary of State Henry A. Kissinger address the corporate leaders on the prospects for business with China. But Kissinger was unavailable. The executives had to settle for one of his lesser-known aides, Under Secretary of State William J. Casey, later to become CIA director. "I view the long-term prospects for large trade with the People's Republic of China as good," Casey told the group. But he added some words of caution, telling the American business leaders not to "expect too much too soon." China, Casey said, "will move at a reasonably slow pace." America's business leaders should not lose their heads in their rush to the Chinese mainland, Casey warned, and should always keep in mind that the new relationship with the People's Republic "is not to be obtained at the expense of our old friends" on Taiwan.

Still, the American business leaders forged ahead with their new organization, the National Council for U.S.-China Trade. At the outset, membership in the organization was confined to American corporations with sales of $50 million or more. Within a year 136 U.S. corporations had joined, paying $2,500 apiece for the privilege, and the group had begun to open its membership to other, smaller American companies also eager to pursue the old dream of doing business in China.[4]

A handful of deals were made in those first years after Nixon's opening to China. In 1973 the M. W. Kellogg Co. of Houston sold China eight ammonia plants for the production of fertilizer, at a price of $200 million. Boeing sold ten of its 707 jet planes and assorted spare parts to the People's Republic for $150 million in what was widely perceived as a political gesture by Premier Chou En-lai to the United States.[5]

In these earliest days, the handful of Americans who moved to China for ongoing business operations rarely got very far. In 1973 Boeing opened an office in Beijing. However, the office was closed three years later and the records were moved to Tokyo after the Boeing representative found that he was denied any access to airline operations and was virtually confined to his hotel room. (When a new Boeing representative, E. E. Bauer, returned in 1980, he found Boeing's office "in suspended animation . . . and covered with a thick layer of abrasive yellow dust."[6])

U.S. trade with China grew from zero at the beginning of the decade to more than $800 million a year in 1973 and 1974, still a relatively modest amount by international standards. Most of this money was taken up by American sales of wheat and other agricultural products to China. In 1975 China cut back on these purchases of American grain, and for the next three years annual trade between the two countries slumped back to levels of about $400 million. The reality was that despite the hopes of the American business community, China was not buying very much from the United States.

The obstacles were largely political on both sides. In the wake of the 1972 opening to China, the Nixon and Ford administrations were not yet willing or politically able to take the next step of restoring diplomatic relations with Beijing. Moreover, many of the legal problems left over after the rupture of relations in 1949 remained unsolved. Chinese assets in the United States were still blocked, and there were a series of outstanding claims by private U.S. citizens against China for financial losses suffered after the Communist revolution. In practical terms, these legal snarls meant that any Chinese government property in the United States could be attached by U.S. claimants. Even the Chinese government's efforts to send art and archaeology exhibits to American museums had State Department lawyers working overtime, trying to prevent a possible seizure by private claimants of the Chinese objets d'art.

On the right wing of the Republican Party, opposition to recognizing the People's Republic remained intense. The internal files of the Ford administration make clear how strong the pressure was. In October 1974, when former Republican National Committee Chairman George Bush was about to leave for China to head the U.S. liaison office there, Secretary of State Kissinger sent a private note to President Ford, telling him to remind Bush of the importance of a "low public profile" in Beijing. Any sign of closer ties with the Communist regime might stir up political trouble in the United States.

On May 28, 1976, at a time when Ford was trying to stave off a tough conservative challenge by Ronald Reagan for the Republican nomination, Senator Barry Goldwater delivered a private ultimatum to the Ford administration. He threatened to announce that he was withdrawing support for Ford unless the administration promised him within a day that it would not establish diplomatic relations with the People's Republic. "It doesn't make any sense to me to forgo our friends on Taiwan," Goldwater wrote to Kissinger. "And I don't intend to stay quiet about it, so please within twenty-four hours let me know what the truth is, and I mean the truth." Kissinger quickly called Goldwater and gave the necessary assurances.[7]

China was also mired in domestic politics. In the final years before Mao's death in 1976, the leadership of the Chinese Communist Party was virtually paralyzed by factional divisions. One group within the party—which would eventually coalesce under the leadership of Deng Xiaoping—emphasized the importance of modern technology and education for advancing China's economy and favored some degree of contact with the West in order to obtain this technology. The other group—which included Mao's wife, Jiang Qing—rejected the importance of Western technology and stressed the need for China to remain "self-reliant."

One typical ideological battle involved China's auto industry. In May 1974 a Communist Party newspaper in Shanghai reported that workers in a car factory there had been enthusiastically criticizing the "revisionist line which had blind faith in foreign things." The workers had learned a lesson about relying on foreigners when they discovered that they were unable to obtain spare parts for an imported tractor truck. "Now they are manufacturing their own tractors, which just shows how unwise it was to follow 'the beaten path of technical development abroad,' " the newspaper said.[8]

The turning point came in the fall of 1976. In China Mao died, and within a month Jiang Qing and the other ultraleftist leaders later branded the Gang of Four were thrown into jail, clearing the way for Deng's rise to power. Meanwhile, in the United States, Jimmy Carter won the presidential election, thus bringing to the White House a Democrat with no political obligation to the right wing of the Republican Party on the issue of breaking with Taipei and establishing diplomatic relations with Beijing.

Even so, it took another two years before conditions were ripe for the two countries to talk seriously about doing business with one another. In the United States, Carter moved first on the Panama Canal treaty and put off establishing diplomatic relations with Beijing until after the 1978 congressional elections. In China, Deng had to first consolidate his control over the Chinese Communist Party.

In 1978 trade between China and the United States jumped to $1.1 billion, more than triple the level of the previous year. China may have been stepping up its purchases from the United States in order to stimulate greater pressure in the American business community for establishing diplomatic relations between the two countries. Carter granted formal recognition to Beijing's Communist regime and cut off official ties with Taiwan on January 1, 1979.

In each of the next two years, the amount of trade between the United States and China doubled, bringing the total to $4.8 billion by 1980. More important, with the establishment of diplomatic relations, the Chinese regime was ready to let American companies set up operations inside China itself. Deng was willing to permit Western companies to work hand in hand with China's state enterprises—even perhaps to invest in China.

In the United States, businessmen like Tod Clare were ready to move.

2

Making the Deal

After his time in Hong Kong, Tod Clare returned to the United States. He went to work for American Motors, rising through the ranks until in 1977 he became vice president of international operations, the head of the company's overseas network. AMC, the nation's fourth-largest car manufacturer, had a tin-roofed plant in Venezuela and a new factory in Egypt. It did a lot of business in the Middle East and, in particular, in Iran, where the upper and middle classes had grown prosperous under the shah.

If you put a suit on the Marlon Brando of *Last Tango in Paris* and cleaned him up a bit, you would come up with someone like Clare. Short and slightly pudgy, he has longish gray hair and brown eyes that convey both toughness and intelligence. His dress is classic Ivy League executive: dark suits, blue Oxford-cloth shirts, and patterned ties. His approach to visitors is direct, the same no-bullshit-here style that Lee Iacocca made famous.

AMC had been formed in 1954 by the merger of two failing car companies, Hudson Motor Car Company and Nash-Kelvinator Corporation. AMC was at its strongest in the years immediately after the merger, under the leadership of George Romney, AMC's president from 1954 to 1962 and later governor of Michigan.

Romney promoted what was, for the American automobile industry, a novel idea—a compact car, the Rambler, which was marketed as an alternative or a supplement to what he scathingly called the "gas-guzzling dinosaurs" of General Motors, Ford, and Chrysler. But even at its height, AMC never grabbed more than 7.5 percent of the American car market, and it never posed any threat to the Big Three.

By the mid-1970s the company was being sustained largely by a single, highly profitable product, the Jeep. In 1970 AMC purchased Kaiser Jeep Corporation from Kaiser Industries, the company that made the famous four-wheel-drive utility vehicles. AMC overhauled the design of the car, gave it a sporty look, and started to market it as a recreational vehicle for private use—a high-priced substitute for the passenger car or station wagon. Marketing was made all the easier by the fame and easy recognition of the Jeep name, which American GIs had given to the funny-looking heavy-duty military vehicle Kaiser's predecessor, Willys-Overland Company, had supplied to the U.S. Army during World War II. The name apparently derived from a comic strip character, Eugene the Jeep, who was believed to have supernatural powers. To the World War II generation, the name was as friendly and familiar as Beetle Bailey. With the exception of Ford, Jeep was arguably the most easily recognized car name in the world.

Even the Chinese knew the name Jeep. China had its own four-wheel military vehicle, called the *jipuche* (jee-poo-chir), or "jeep car." In the 1950s, during the postrevolutionary decade of Sino-Soviet alliance, China had obtained the design for this vehicle from the Soviet Union. The Chinese jeep wasn't redesigned or upgraded for two decades, and by the late 1970s, as China began to talk about modernization, it was only natural for leaders of the state-owned automotive industry to begin looking at the American company that was heir to the original, world-famous Jeep. In those days, as China began to open its doors, it wanted the very best and was going straight for the few Western names it could identify: names like Coca-Cola, Kodak, and Jeep.

At AMC Tod Clare had been eyeing China ever since the Nixon visit. He felt he had a personal interest in the country from his days in Hong Kong. More to the point, as an international car executive, he had a commercial interest in China. After all, the country's population was bigger than Iran, Venezuela, or Egypt, all the other nations in which AMC was operating.

There was competition within the automobile industry, of course. In the late 1970s, in one fashion or another, executives of virtually all the world's leading car manufacturers began streaming to China, full of plans to modernize China's industry and, hopefully, to gain access to the domestic Chinese market.

In June 1978 Henry Ford II visited Beijing and met with then Vice Premier Deng Xiaoping, seeking to pave the way for the sale of Ford trucks to China. *Wen Wei Po*, a Chinese-language news-paper in Hong Kong that supported the Communist regime, pro-claimed that Ford's father "was known to Americans as the king of cars." The paper also speculated, without any evidence, that Ford might also be serving as a secret emissary for President Carter, whose administration was in the midst of negotiations with Beijing over the restoration of diplomatic relations. (In fact, the hard nego-tiations were carried out not by Ford, but by another name familiar to the American automotive industry—former United Auto Work-ers President Leonard Woodcock, who was then head of the U.S. liaison office in Beijing.)

Mercedes-Benz, Fiat, and British Leyland also sent emissaries to check out the business prospects in China. The only auto com-pany Clare felt posed no real competition in China was the world's largest, General Motors. Clare thought they had a third-rate inter-national operation; sure, they had some big plants in Europe, but when you looked around the world, they really weren't very aggres-sive. They wanted to sit back in their offices at home and write orders. When Clare was selling engines for Cummins, his leading American competitor, GM's Detroit Diesel division, was a push-over. You could go into the lumber camps in Borneo selling to the truck owners and find that they had never even seen a Detroit Diesel man in there.

Yet at the time it seemed as though all the talk about the competitive nature of doing business in China was exaggerated. China came to Jeep. China wanted Jeep. Or so it seemed.

Since the time of the Nixon trip, AMC had been putting out feelers to China. Clare thought China seemed a lot like Saudi Ara-bia, where everybody claimed that he was releated to the king and that his blood ties could make millions for your company. During the 1970s, everybody and his brother claimed to have connections to the Chinese leadership. Clare thought he was pretty wise to this routine, and AMC began trying to separate the phonies from those who really knew the China trade.

In 1978, however, before Clare's staff was finished checking everyone out, a Chinese-American named C. B. Sung, the chairman of a consulting firm called Unison International, came to AMC to say he thought China wanted to do business with the makers of Jeep.

Sung seemed different from the other hustlers: he was a prom-

inent business executive, a former vice president of Bendix. Clare
encouraged him to pursue the idea of a Jeep deal on Sung's next trip
to China.

To the AMC people, C. B. Sung was an enigma. On the one hand,
they never quite knew what he had going in China or exactly with
whom he was dealing. On the other hand, he was useful, an Amer-
ican-trained businessman capable of explaining the Chinese to the
Americans and the Americans to the Chinese.

Sung was a Shanghainese, born and educated in that most cosmopolitan of Chinese cities amid the traumas of the anti-Japanese
war and China's civil war. In 1947, at the height of the Chinese
civil war, Sung and his wife fled to the United States, where Sung
earned both a master's degree in engineering from the Massachusetts Institute of Technology and an MBA from Harvard Business
School. For more than twenty years he worked in the Bendix Corporation, rising through the ranks to become the company's vice
president for engineering and research. Sung helped direct the development of high-technology products; at one point he was in
charge of Bendix's aerospace division and its advanced products
development. He became one of the leading Chinese-American corporate executives in the United States.

Sung's wife, Beulah, was a Kwok, a member of the well-to-do
Chinese family that ran the Wing On department stores, first in
Shanghai and later in Hong Kong, where the Wing On chain and
the Kwok family thrive today. Among Beulah Sung's family friends
was Rong Yiren, a Shanghai millionaire who elected to stay on and
work for his country after the Communist takeover. When China
opened its doors to the West, Rong became the Communist regime's chief delegate to the international business community.

In 1973, the year after the Nixon trip to China, the Sungs
returned to China for the first time. They revisited Shanghai and
saw old friends, including Rong Yiren. The trip changed their lives.
Mao, his wife, Jiang Qing, and the radical left wing of the Communist Party were still the dominant force in the leadership. But
China was beginning to make overtures toward the United States,
and Sung was exactly the sort of American it wanted to cultivate:
wealthy, well informed on both business and technology, and eager
to be of help to his native China.

Soon Sung found himself traveling regularly to China to give lectures. At first, before Mao's death in 1976, Chinese officials gave him strict orders to lecture only on narrow subjects of science and technology—a difficult task, since Sung had moved into management and had not been directly involved in scientific research for decades. Sung found himself having to study hard to relearn scientific subjects before giving his lectures in China. He begged for permission to lecture on American management, a subject he was convinced was China's greatest need and on which he could lecture with little preparation. But Communist Party officials told him that all the management techniques China required could be found in Mao's Little Red Book. Finally, in 1977, the year after Mao's death, Sung was told he could begin giving lectures on the subject of management.

Not long after his first trip back to China, Sung quit his job at Bendix and went into business as an entrepreneur, aiming to establish or restructure several small, private manufacturing firms in the United States. But increasingly his life became tied up with Chinese ventures. His wife, Beulah, began importing Chinese goods into the United States. She also founded a new company, Unison (the name was fashioned from the letters *Sino-U.S.*), to represent and advise American companies trying to do business in China. Beulah was a pianist by training; Sung was an experienced businessman. Inevitably it was C. B. Sung who became the principal figure in Unison.

In 1978 Sung was giving one of his standard lectures on management to China's First Ministry of Machine Building, one of the most important bureaucracies in the country's centrally planned economy. Among his students were some cadres, or officials, from the Beijing Automotive Works, the state enterprise responsible for Beijing's decaying jeep factory. Sung was asked to talk about the subject of joint ventures between Chinese enterprises and foreign companies. When he finished, some of the cadres from the automotive enterprise asked him whether he thought it would be possible to find an American partner for the jeep plant.

Sung took the idea back to the United States. From his days at Bendix, he had good contacts in Detroit and the auto industry. One of his neighbors in the Detroit area, in fact, was a fellow Harvard MBA working at AMC. Sung used his connections to obtain an appointment with Clare and offered to become, in effect, the intermediary between AMC and China.

AMC began paying Unison what was to become an annual fee for services as a consultant. Over the coming years Sung served as AMC's paid representative and adviser in dealings with the Chinese, earning fees that would eventually grow to as much as $5,000 to $6,000 a month when work was busy. Yet Sung often played the role of go-between, explaining the official Chinese position to the Americans as well as the American position to the Chinese. Years later some skeptical AMC executives would consider him as much a representative of China as of the American company.

Encouraged by Sung, Clare's international staff at AMC prepared a thick book for the Chinese, a glossy presentation showing how well AMC was operating in countries such as Egypt and Venezuela, training local workers and transferring technology in the process. Sung delivered AMC's book to China in the late autumn of 1978. Not long afterward Sung sent a telex back to AMC's corporate headquarters, giving Clare the go-ahead. China had invited American Motors to send over a team of its executives to Beijing for talks.

On January 6, 1979, Jeff Trimmer, one of Clare's aides in AMC's international division, stepped off a Swissair plane at the Beijing airport, followed by three other junior AMC officials. They were the pioneers, the first American Motors officials to set foot in China. They had been traveling for thirty hours, on flights from New York to Geneva, Zurich, Athens, Bombay, and, finally, Beijing. When they finally arrived, at about 8:30 P.M. in China, there was martial music playing at the airport, and all Trimmer could see in front of him was a large picture of Chairman Mao. He was exhausted, thought of the movie *The Manchurian Candidate*, and wondered whether he would ever get home to America.

But their Chinese hosts welcomed them warmly and served them a huge dinner. And over the next couple of weeks the first, exploratory discussions went well. They were meeting in the unheated reception room of the First Ministry of Machine Building, in a downtown office building. The Americans were so cold that they wore fur-lined boots and long underwear to the meetings. Even those clothes weren't enough, so they wrapped their hands around the regularly refilled tea mugs to warm themselves, all the while trying to pay attention to the talk about jeeps and joint ventures.

Things went so well that after a couple of weeks they sent the word for Clare, their boss, to fly over, too. They were ready to talk about at least the outlines of a deal.

It was still only a few weeks after China and the United States had resumed diplomatic relations. Deng Xiaoping had just consolidated his power in the Chinese Communist Party leadership over Mao's successor, Hua Guofeng, paving the way for China to press ahead with the efforts to modernize its economy. China was also on the verge of launching a short and costly invasion of Vietnam, but Clare and the other AMC executives didn't know that. They cared about selling cars; they wanted to bring about revolutionary changes in the American and Chinese automotive industries; they wanted to score a great strategic masterstroke for American Motors in the global chess game against the Big Three and the Japanese; they wanted to be the first car company to get into China in a big way.

On Clare's first trip to China, he was accompanied by the company treasurer, Kenneth Lawton. The two men traveled in from Detroit via Hong Kong, picking up a Hong Kong businessman who was the friend of an AMC director and who claimed, in the usual fashion, that he could help them win business in China. AMC thought every little contact would help.

Before leaving Detroit, Clare and Lawton went out and bought a half-gallon of Cutty Sark at one of the local discount liquor stores. They didn't know what they were going to face in China, and a bit of Scotch might at least make a winter's evening in Beijing a little warmer. They took turns lugging that particularly heavy bottle in its own bag to Hong Kong, onto a small plane from Hong Kong to Canton, through an exhausting four-hour layover at the Canton airport, and from there on the final leg to Beijing. When they finally arrived at the Beijing Hotel, where they were staying, they looked in a lobby showroom case and saw good Glenfiddich Scotch on display for $6.90 a fifth, about half the price it sold for at the discount stores back home on Maple and Telegraph in Detroit. In the future, Clare resolved, there would be no more toting of half-gallon bottles halfway around the world.

Chinese auto officials adjusted the obligatory sightseeing tours of Beijing to take account of the interests of their AMC guests. Virtually all visitors to the capital city were escorted to the Great Wall, but the AMC executives were allowed to drive there in the

Chinese jeep, the BJ212, as it was called. Clare couldn't believe it; the thing had no springs and drove as if it had ninety pounds of pressure in the tires. On a cold winter day there was nobody around at the Wall, just the AMC people and a car that seemed to them almost as strange and old as the Wall itself.

The AMC executives were also given a special tour of the Beijing Automotive Works, the factory that made the BJ212 and that Chinese officials hoped AMC would help modernize. Clare didn't think it was so bad. He had seen some pretty lousy car plants in his time. When you looked at the Chinese plant, you couldn't judge it by American standards; you had to compare it with Jeep plants like those in Iran, India, and Sri Lanka. In some ways the Chinese plant was great. The layout was good. The plant was made of brick, and it had a good roof. By contrast, the AMC plant in Venezuela had a roof of corrugated tin. Sure, the Chinese plant was poorly tooled, but AMC had a few third-rate operations of its own.

The Chinese assembly line seemed crazy; it looked as though the workers put it up one day, with little thought, and then went to work making cars the next. But there was a certain charm to that, like an old-fashioned cottage industry. AMC could find plenty of conveyor experts to help fix the assembly line. The paint system looked like the worst in the world, but they could rip it out and put in a new one. The electrical supply was good.

At least for the days when the AMC executives were visiting, the people on the assembly line seemed to be working hard. Of course, the AMC officials had no way of knowing how things looked on a routine day, when there were no foreign guests touring the factory. But everything seemed to be in order. Pieces were coming in and going out. Clare thought to himself that the quality was crappy, but that some of it was fixable. There were some simple, obvious steps that could be taken to improve the plant. All in all, the AMC executives were pleased.

They were brought to the end of the assembly line. Clare realized he was standing in a place that looked familiar. Years ago, at a time when ordinary Americans could not travel to China and when the plant making jeeps for the Chinese People's Liberation Army was considered top secret, some visitor had managed to snap a picture of the end of the Chinese jeep assembly line. It was a famous photo in the auto industry, one that had appeared in car publications in the United States and elsewhere around the world;

it was the only picture the AMC executives had ever seen of the inside of any Chinese factory.

Though Clare didn't realize it, the famous picture had been taken during President Nixon's 1972 trip to China. The Beijing Automotive Works was one of the tours offered to the press corps traveling with Nixon—except that the plant in South Beijing had been known then as the Dong Fang Hong ("The East Is Red") Auto Works. Most of the American reporters passed up the trip to the auto plant, because it conflicted with another government-sponsored event thought to be of greater political interest: an interview with a professor at Beijing University who gave them a taste of the ritual self-criticism so common during the Cultural Revolution. The professor confessed that he had once been arrogant but had corrected his ways, thanks to the leadership of the masses and the great Chairman Mao.

Only a small handful of reporters traveling with Nixon went on the tour of the auto plant, among them Bill Ringle of Gannett News Service, Jerry terHorst of the *Detroit News* and author James Michener for *Reader's Digest.* They found that the plant was run by a Revolutionary Committee led by People's Liberation Army Colonel Qing Ping, who had been sent there to restore order and discipline amid the chaos of the Cultural Revolution. The American reporters were told that the Chinese workers received no incentives or bonuses; there was no piecework and no paid overtime. They were shown what Chinese considered many ground-breaking innovations at the plant and were told that all of them were the work of Chairman Mao. It was Mao, for example, who was responsible for the special process by which parts for the Chinese jeep were dipped in antirust coating—or so their Chinese hosts said. The Americans realized that the same antirust process had been used at car plants in the United States for decades.

Now, seven years later and scarcely more than two years after the death of Mao, the AMC executives were being asked to help modernize the jeep plant. Clare, Lawton, and the other AMC officials sat down with Chinese auto officials from the Beijing factory and from the Chinese government's First Ministry of Machine Building. The sessions were held in a small conference room on the ground floor of the Beijing Hotel, where the Americans were staying.

The Chinese representatives seemed to be excited by the prospect of working with the Americans, but Clare thought they were having trouble getting down to specifics. So he decided to help them out. He recalled from his Hong Kong days that Chinese seemed to have a special, almost worshipful fondness for numbers. So finally he told them that the arrangement between AMC and China should be viewed as a three-legged stool. One leg would be the export of jeeps from China to other countries. Another would be the technology AMC would provide for the Chinese jeep. And the third would be the equity that AMC and China would each provide toward the new venture. In order to do business with one another, the two sides would have to reach agreement on all three legs of the stool, Clare said. He kept returning to that three-legged stool, and the Chinese officials got warmer. Clare thought their eyes widened a bit; they seemed to like the idea.

One conflict that quickly arose was AMC insistence on "exclusivity"—that is, on a clause guaranteeing that it should be the sole foreign manufacturer of jeeps, or four-wheel-drive vehicles, inside China. From AMC's point of view, it was hardly an unusual request. If the company was going to start up operations in China, it wanted to be sure it had a preferred position there. But Chinese negotiators such as Rao Bin, the vice minister of the First Ministry of Machine Building, didn't want to put any guarantee of exclusivity in writing; they said the word had negative connotations and would be interpreted as unfriendly by other companies with which China was dealing.

At an impasse, AMC turned to their consultants, the Sungs. Beulah Sung had been sitting in the negotiations along with the AMC executives. Meanwhile, her husband, C. B., was across the street from the Beijing Hotel in a separate office building, working on another business scheme: he was talking to Chinese tourism officials about his plans to develop the Great Wall Hotel, the biggest and most expensive luxury hotel in Beijing. Beulah Sung walked in and interrupted her husband in the middle of his hotel negotiations.

"C. B., I have a critical problem, and I don't think I can resolve it," she whispered. So she and her husband decided to switch places: Beulah Sung sat down in the hotel negotiations (which were themselves stalled), and C. B. moved across the street into the stalemated jeep negotiations.

Sung offered his own solution. If China wouldn't accept the

idea of exclusivity, how about putting the idea in positive terms? Why not say that China would give "100 percent attention" to the AMC venture? That was okay, Chinese officials said, but it was hard to express the idea in Chinese. Finally they settled on the Chinese expression *bu feng xin*—that is, "undivided heart." In other words, China would promise to give the AMC project its "undivided attention." The words sounded nice, and the Chinese accepted them. An AMC lawyer might have quibbled and said this was not exactly the same sort of commitment as exclusivity, but in these first meetings, this first effort by AMC to establish a business relationship in China, AMC was not going to let itself be ruled by lawyers. Second thoughts would come many years later.

Eventually Clare heard himself saying, "Well, why don't I take a try at the first draft of an agreement?" The AMC officials went upstairs to their rooms at the Beijing Hotel, then one of the few hotels where foreigners could stay in the city. There were no secretaries, no copying machines, no supplies or aids of any kind. They found some notepaper and borrowed a portable typewriter. And there at the creaky Beijing Hotel, in guest rooms world famous for bugs of both the crawling and electronic varieties, they put together what they called a memo of understanding between AMC and the Beijing government's automobile enterprise.

Trimmer, an earnest, bespectacled graduate of MIT and Harvard Business School, did the secretarial work, balancing the borrowed typewriter on a hotel radiator, typing out the draft in a two-fingered hunt-and-peck method. He was the only member of the AMC executive team who could type well; the rest were accustomed to relying on secretaries in the corporate offices back home. You do what you have to do, Trimmer thought to himself. No one cares where your degrees are from.

The AMC team discovered belatedly that the draft had coffee stains on it. Nevertheless, on the following day, the morning of January 26, 1979, the AMC executives went downstairs and got the Chinese to agree to their language. American and Chinese officials signed the vaguely worded memo of understanding. It wasn't a contract. What the two sides had done was to agree to investigate the prospects for building new jeeps with American technology in China. The process was supposed to be completed by the end of 1979.

The memo laid out the broad objectives: to improve the quality of the Chinese jeep; to introduce a new family of jeeps made under AMC's direction; and to begin manufacturing parts and components in China for export. The specifics, the details, would all have to be worked out later. In effect, all they had done was to agree to negotiate. But it was an important first step.

Clare was dazzled by the speed with which they had reached the agreement. My God, he had only been in China for seventy-two hours, and boom, crash, everything's fine, it was all done. China was going to be much easier than they expected. Clare thought this was going to be a pushover.

3

Mao Tais and Friendship

It was called "Come to China at Bloomingdale's." On September 24, 1980, the fourteen Bloomingdale's department stores from Boston to Washington launched a special promotion of Chinese fashions, food, and other products. Bloomingdale's main store on the East Side of Manhattan reconstructed one room as a Cantonese town house, another as a garden pavilion. At a shopping center in the New York City suburb of White Plains, a Bloomingdale's store featured what was said to be an authentic Chinese junk. All the stores offered special sales of silk rugs and dresses, embroidered pillowcases, screens, porcelain lamps, rattan furniture, cashmere sweaters, down jackets, and tea.

Bloomingdale's had previously had similar exhibits for India and Israel, but the China promotion was as big as the other two combined. Store officials claimed it was the largest single promotion of Chinese goods ever held in the United States. Bloomingdale's executives boasted that their China promotion was the result of approximately 130 trips to China by Bloomingdale's officials, who had bought goods worth more than $10 million. "We expect China to be a very important future supplier for Bloomingdale's," said Bloomingdale's chairman Marvin S. Traub. In newspaper interviews, Traub's aides praised Chinese-made goods. "Chinese products are competitive with any country in the world," senior vice president Carl Levine told *The New York Times*. "The workmanship is excellent, probably because they haven't yet learned the sloppiness of the Western world."[1]

In the first blush after restoration of diplomatic relations between China and the United States, many Americans were finding China to be both fashionable and accessible. It was a rush, a kind of craze. Nowhere was its impact felt more than in the American

business community. China became the favorite new destination
on the map. Businessmen—particularly the chairmen, presidents,
and vice presidents of international divisions of leading American
corporations—had money available for travel to China and a plausible reason to go. Suddenly the vast market they had been dreaming of for years seemed to be within reach or, if not within reach,
open enough for them to go see it. A business leader was supposed
to think about the future, about his or her company's position in
the twenty-first century. And what could be more important than
gaining a toehold in China at a time when the country seemed
eager to modernize? It was certainly worth an exploratory visit.

China did nothing to discourage the influx of American businessmen. It was eager, indeed desperate, for Western technology,
and the United States was the most technologically advanced country in the world. After World War II, China's neighbor and East
Asian rival, Japan, had rebuilt itself as an economic power with the
help of American technology, often obtained by first inviting the
Americans in for a joint venture and then kicking them out. Why
couldn't China do the same?

Under Deng's leadership, the Chinese Communist Party began
emphasizing to its forty million members the importance of obtaining science and technology from the West, and especially from
the Americans. Gradually the Party began dismantling the severe
ideological restrictions that had been imposed by Mao on business
dealings with the Americans.

In September 1980, the same month the Bloomingdale's ex-
hibit opened in the United States, the *People's Daily*, the official
newspaper of the Chinese Communist Party, published a commentary informing loyal cadres that "the proletariat have more to learn
from the bourgeoisie than from the feudal class, because the bourgeois class built up the economy of mass production. . . . Lenin
once said, 'Whom shall we learn from if not the bourgeois class?' "

The *People's Daily* commentary described the outstanding
contributions of George Washington. "He was commander-in-chief
of the army during the War of Independence in North America.
After the victory, he opposed the establishment of a monarchy, and
refused to be a monarch. After he served as president for two terms,
he resolutely refused to serve in this position any longer. His successor did not depend on his choice, but was to be elected through
a democratic process by the ruling class, that is, the bourgeois class.

To the bourgeois class, bourgeois democracy is genuine, not hypo-
critical."

Like virtually everything else written in the *People's Daily*,
such language had a strong component of domestic Chinese politics: the implied contrast was between George Washington and
Mao, who, after leading the Chinese revolution, refused to give up
the reins of power, acted like a monarch, and tried to choose his
successor. But apart from domestic politics, the essay, and others
like it, conveyed to Chinese officials the message that they were
permitted, indeed encouraged, to do business with the Americans.
The unalloyed enthusiasm in the *People's Daily* commentary contained none of the fear of American culture and politics which
would later emerge in the Chinese press during the regime's "campaign against bourgeois liberalization" in 1987, or, particularly,
after the massive student demonstrations for democracy of 1989.

There were plenty of Americans available. In September 1980,
just as Bloomingdale's was opening its China promotion, *Newsweek* reported, "For much of this month, the lobby of the Beijing
Hotel has seemed very much like an American colonial outpost.
Texas oilmen on a mission to inspect offshore oil fields drawled
enthusiastically over cocktails about the deals they hoped to
clinch. Tired U.S. government officials hovered nearby, waiting to
initial the first Sino-American civil aviation agreement, and a contingent from the Pentagon added a flash of medals and braid as they
swept back and forth from talks on military-equipment sales."[2]

American business executives had been streaming to China in
increasing numbers since 1978, when it became increasingly clear
that China was looking for help from the West. The board chairmen scouting for prospects in Beijing included Armand Hammer of
Occidental Petroleum, Traub of Bloomingdale's, and Donald
Regan, then chairman of the board of Merrill Lynch &Co. and later
President Reagan's Treasury secretary and White House chief of
staff. "Any nation of over 950 million people growing at the rate of
18 million individuals a year is a tremendous market," Regan told
The Wall Street Journal.[3]

The American executives crowded into the Beijing Hotel, the
foreigners-only establishment in the center of the city, just down
the street from the Forbidden City and Tiananmen Square. Their
Chinese hosts—usually officials of a state enterprise anxious to
attract foreign technology and investment—met them at the air-

port, toasted them with potent *mao tai* wine at banquets, and arranged (indeed, insisted upon) tours of Beijing's leading tourist attractions, the Great Wall and the Ming Tombs.

A handful of the most prominent executives would be granted an audience with Deng or one of his top aides. Those businessmen involved in manufacturing, like the auto executives, might be escorted through a plant they were being asked to renovate. Others whose products were less tangible might see little beyond the historical sites and their hotel rooms.

The offices where Chinese conducted their day-to-day affairs, their regular business, were off-limits to foreigners. Instead, business discussions between Chinese and foreigners were held in formal reception rooms, sometimes in a hotel or sometimes inside a Chinese work unit. These reception rooms were eerily detached from China itself. They were usually large enough for a meeting of twenty to twenty-five people, although so oversize that if all the seats were filled, the people at one end of the room were too far away to hear those at the other end. A typical reception room was filled with old, stuffed couches and chairs, each one covered with a white antimacassar. Every couch or chair had a table in front of it for business papers; on the table, in front of each person's place, was a lidded cup of tea. Chinese assistants would refill the teacups so often that the foreigners would eventually be forced to sit uncomfortably through the discussions, wondering whether to be so rude as to ask for a restroom break.

There were usually at least three or four Chinese officials in the meetings and, when translators and representatives of the state ministry and municipal government were added, often eight or more, compared with at most three or four Western business people. It was a setting made for ritual, not one that would contribute to the development of close personal ties. Of course, in establishing such a rigid, artificial environment in which to talk business, the Communist regime of modern-day China was following the example blazed by their predecessors in imperial times. "The various barbarians have come to live at peace and in harmony among us," the imperial clansman Chi Ying wrote in 1844. "We must give them some sort of entertainment and cordial reception; but we are on guard against an intimate relationship in our intercourse with them."[4]

Why were so many of these visiting businessmen willing to

conduct business on turf, and often on terms, that they would not have been willing to accept elsewhere? The business executives of these early days sounded the themes that would be heard again and again through the mid-1980s—themes that China's Communist regime understood well and, in many cases, exploited.

The first and overriding theme was that China was a huge market of limitless potential, the most important undeveloped market in the world. To be sure, some businessmen came to China looking for things to buy, such as silk; and others came hoping to reap the benefits of what they thought might be cheap labor. But the overwhelming number came hoping to sell. Even those companies hoping to cut their production costs by manufacturing in China, like American Motors, were interested mainly because of the possibility of selling their output there. You could find cheap labor elsewhere in the world, but you couldn't find a billion consumers anywhere else.

The second theme was that even if a company couldn't immediately do the kind of business it wanted in China, it would be wise at least to establish a presence there—to open an office, start some small-scale production, give a little technical help to a prospective Chinese partner, do something, anything, to get started. The underlying assumption was that when China was finally ready to hand out real business, it would reward those who had gotten there first.

Theme number three was that since the goal was to develop a long-term market in China, short-term costs didn't matter very much. What did it matter if China doubled and doubled again the prices of hotel rooms, offices, telex machines? Who cared if the duty on an imported car was raised from 80 percent to 120 percent, and from 120 percent to 260 percent, so that even a small $8,000 Toyota sedan would cost around $30,000 after Chinese duty and taxes? So what if it required a Western business to pay Foreign Enterprise Service Corporation (FESCO), the state-owned company that provided translators and other staff, wages that were eight or ten times what the workers themselves actually received? How did you measure these costs against the twenty-first century?

It added up to a revival of the old Western dream about the China market, a dream that continued to entice leading American executives throughout the end of the 1970s and the first half of the 1980s. In early 1984, for example, Ralph A. Pfeiffer, Jr., chairman of the board of IBM's international division, sat over a catered lunch in the second-floor executive dining room of his company's corporate headquarters in Tarrytown, N.Y., and told me how eager he was to develop IBM's sales in China. "Who knows where China will be in fifty years?" he asked. "You never know what would happen if they really got going. Japan's got only one-seventh of China's population. . . . With their [China's] labor force, their resources, and their market, anything could happen." Pfeiffer paused and then laid out, in classic form, the modern-day version of the old Western dream: "If we could just sell one IBM PC for every 100 people in China, or every 1,000, or even every 10,000 . . . " He left the sentence unfinished.

In the United States, businesses anxious to develop a presence in China received encouragement from their own government. Particularly in the late 1970s, the United States was eager to develop strong commercial ties to China to help reinforce the growing strategic relationship between the two countries. China was seen as a friend—not an ally like the NATO countries or Japan, but certainly a partner in what amounted to an entente against the Soviet Union.

After the Iranian revolution, the new regime of Ayatollah Khomeini had closed down the electronic eavesdropping posts in Iran through which the United States intelligence agencies had monitored missile firings in the Soviet Union. Those listening posts were replaced with ones in northwestern China.[5] Senior Carter administration officials such as Zbigniew Brzezinski were particularly eager to develop the new U.S. links to China and to pursue their security implications.

"Our new ties with China are of fundamental importance to the United States, and to the prospects for a peaceful and prosperous world," Deputy Secretary of State Warren Christopher told the U.S. Congress on November 1, 1979, as he urged approval of the first trade agreement between the two countries. "We want to encourage China to play a constructive and stabilizing role in Asia."

The logic of the American executives rushing to China seemed simple and self-evident: If China had a lot of people, then it was a potentially important market. If you wanted to develop the market, you had to be there. And if you wanted to be there, you shouldn't haggle over costs. What could be more obvious?

And yet, upon examination, each one of these assumptions was questionable.

First and most important, the supposedly vast Chinese market was a myth. China was an extremely poor country. Its consumers didn't have the purchasing power and its state enterprises didn't have the foreign exchange necessary to buy large quantities of goods from the West—and it wasn't clear the situation would improve much for decades. One World Bank study estimated that in the mid-1980s, the amount available for consumer spending was less than $100 a year for each person in China—and that even if the Chinese economy were to enter a period of high growth, the figure in the year 2000 would be a little more than $200 per person.

Second, even if China had money to spend, it was not certain that the money would go to the foreign companies that started up operations in China. It was a cliché that the Chinese cared about what they called *guanxi*, connections, rewarding their old friends. Although this was very often true with respect to personal relationships, it was hardly automatic when it came to business dealings. In fact, Chinese enterprises were fully capable of looking at each new business deal afresh; often they sought to buy at the lowest cost and abandoned old business associates whose prices were higher than the lowest bidder. The Western company that had waited patiently in China for a decade might well lose out to a new arrival from abroad who got off the plane with a more attractive price list.

More fundamentally, there was the overriding problem of Chinese protectionism. No one knew whether any foreign company, no matter how good its connections or how low its prices, would really be permitted to sell large quantities of their product in China. On the contrary, as China's supposedly vast market opened up, China's own state enterprises would work hard to corner it for themselves.

Each time a new product from abroad was introduced on a small scale in China, Chinese imitations with greater access to the local market would appear. In the early 1980s Coca-Cola opened Chinese bottling plants but was required to sell most of its product to tourists and other foreigners to help generate the foreign currency necessary to import concentrates from overseas. Within a short time a local Chinese imitation, Tianfu ("Land of Abundance") Cola was being made at a bottling plant in Chongqing, Sichuan Province. Despite Coke's vaunted secret formula, Chinese newspapers said Tianfu was "the same as Coca-Cola in color, smell, and taste, but different in its makeup and contents."[6] Not only that, but the Chinese version was said to have its own magic formula; the drink would help strengthen the liver and the spleen.

Communist protectionism could be at least as potent as its capitalist counterparts, and often more so. When the Chinese regime wanted to favor local products over foreign competition, it had a variety of weapons at its disposal. The government could tell Chinese state enterprises which products to purchase or pressure them to stop buying foreign products by threatening to cut off or raise the prices of their supplies. The Chinese state controlled the transportation and distribution of goods. State enterprises set the wage levels and supplied water and power. Moreover, the state controlled the propaganda apparatus. At one point in 1983 a Chinese magazine published by the Chinese Writers Association launched a broadside attack on Coca-Cola, saying that Chinese who drank the foreign product "succumb to capitalist decadence and harm China's basic national interests to satisfy the profit motive of foreign financial groups. . . . They willingly fulfill the role of slaves for the foreign buyers."

In fact, the foreign business seeking a market in China might run up against not just one brand of protectionism, but several. There was national protectionism: the efforts by the central government and ministries to protect Chinese industries from foreign competition. And then there were the protectionisms of provincial governments, municipal governments, and local governments. The government of Shanghai would do its best to favor the products of factories in Shanghai over those in Beijing, and the government of Fujian Province would make it tougher for products from its neighbor, Guangdong Province, than for goods made inside Fujian. China was not so much a national market as a crazy quilt of overlapping local, provincial, and regional markets—and in each one, authorities could and often did seek to protect local industries from competition by restricting access to their market.

Third, the final assumption of Western business leaders—that if you wanted to establish your company's presence in China, you shouldn't worry too much about costs—was a prescription for future problems. Clearly there would be some point at which costs in China mattered; no one argued that a company should spend $10 billion a year on its China operations now in hopes of a chance at its market in the twenty-first century. It was only a question of how high the costs might be before a Western company would begin to consider whether establishing a corporate presence in China was worth it. When foreign companies came to China with the attitude that short-term costs didn't matter, they created a situation in which, inevitably, a Chinese government desperate for foreign exchange sought to plumb the depths of foreigners' corporate pocketbooks. How much could Western companies be charged for housing, office space, labor, and supplies before they would stop paying? Chinese authorities didn't know for sure, but with Western companies seemingly falling over one another to get into their country, they intended to find out.

Yet American business leaders tended not to examine these assumptions. There was a mystique, a romance, about the China market that transcended all logic and caused the board chairmen and chief executive officers to suspend their normal, everyday business judgments.

In order to see the strength of China's romantic attraction, it is worth considering, for a moment, the contrast between China and India. With eight hundred million people, India is the world's second most populous nation, and some demographers believe that if China's family planning program is successful, India's population will overtake China's in the early part of the twenty-first century. But American business leaders rarely talked or dreamed of getting in position to capture the vast Indian market. The board chairmen and CEOs weren't streaming to New Delhi.

American attitudes toward China were different for several reasons. There were considerations of history and geography. India had been a British preserve, but China had always remained independent. China is directly across the Pacific from the American West Coast, and dating back to the nineteenth century, Americans have viewed it as a natural outlet for American goods. "The Chinese market . . . rightfully belongs to us," the Riverside, New York, Republican Club told Secretary of State John Hay in 1898 as the United States was developing its Open Door policy toward China.[7]

In America's imagination, India was thought to be timeless and changeless, while China was always about to become something different. The missionaries had once hoped China was on the verge of converting to Christianity; and, in similar fashion, after Mao's death American businessmen managed to persuade themselves that China might be ready to abandon Marxism and embrace capitalism. China's authoritarian traditions somehow helped to reinforce these perceptions by conveying the impression, at least overseas, that the country was controllable and could be changed quickly by orders from the top. If Chiang Kai-shek could be converted to Christianity, then perhaps the Chinese nation would become Christian; if Deng Xiaoping would only read Adam Smith, China might someday become a free-market economy.

These underlying assumptions about China's malleability were just as open to question. There were Chinese traditions just as timeless and changeless as anything in India. China's intractable bureaucracy had stymied Mao and Deng just as it had the imperial and republican leaders who went before them. Its provincial and local officials had such remarkable power and independence that they were often impervious to the policy pronouncements of the central government. The Chinese who were sent overseas, and those who were assigned to foreign visitors in China, always seemed much more eager for change than did the rest of the country. In fact, it was far from clear, to say the least, that the Chinese people in the late 1970s and early 1980s were eager to embrace American-style capitalism (with its concomitants of unemployment, bankruptcies, and wide disparities in income) any more than their predecessors of the late nineteenth and early twentieth centuries had been eager for Christianity.

Nevertheless, the notion of a rapidly changing China took hold, particularly in the United States, attracting buyers to Bloomingdale's and American businessmen to Beijing.

It was not just the high and the mighty, the Fords and the Reagans, who were susceptible. The small-time operators and drifters came to China, too. Where else but in China could you find Harry S. Langerman of Miami, Florida, a balding retiree with a white mustache whose business card read "Consultant to the food service industry"? Langerman, who had once run a restaurant called "Langerman's Luau" in Bala Cynwyd, Pennsylvania, came to China in 1984, determined to open up some kind of restaurant or, better yet, a chain of restaurants. He talked to Chinese officials in Beijing, Shanghai, and Shenzhen. He first wanted to open an outlet near the Great Wall but was told that unfortunately there was no water available. This, he acknowledged, "would be a problem." He thought about selling ice cream, then tried out the idea of hamburgers and fried chicken. When I interviewed him in 1986, he had a new idea. "Why not open up an American-style Chinese restaurant, done up with class?" he asked me. He admitted that a Chinese restaurant in Beijing seemed like a classic case of bringing coals to Newcastle but decided this didn't matter. "I have an extensive background in Chinese food," he said. "I figured why subject the Chinese to a food they are not familiar with?"

4

Getting Nowhere

In May 1979, four months after the signing of the Beijing Hotel agreement, Chinese officials from Beijing Auto Works and the First Ministry of Machine Building made their first visit to the United States. AMC's international division served as their hosts and gave them a grand tour.

For three weeks AMC executives like Trimmer and Ron Gilchrist, another of Clare's aides, escorted their Chinese guests not only around Detroit, but to other American cities like New York and Los Angeles. They also took the Chinese delegation to Canada, where some of AMC's operations were located. To Trimmer, the Harvard MBA, it was yet another adventure beyond the realm of the textbooks. You've never lived, he thought, until you've arrived from Canada at the Port Huron border checkpoint at ten o'clock at night and tried to explain to U.S. customs and immigration officials—officials accustomed to waving through American vacationers—that you've got ten people from Communist China inside your bus.

None of the visitors had ever been outside China before. The Chinese couldn't understand how a country as wealthy as the United States could have poverty or homeless people. At one point some of the Chinese saw a beauty contest on television and asked Gilchrist why the American government permitted such a tawdry spectacle. Gilchrist began to see his own country through Chinese eyes, and it looked different.

On that tour of the United States, the AMC people felt they got to know the Chinese officials well. Some of the Chinese—such as Wu Zhongliang, who was in this 1979 delegation—would prove important to AMC's future in China.

Yet whenever the AMC people tried to talk business to the Chinese, they got nowhere.

Clare couldn't understand it. In January everything had gone so smoothly. AMC and the Chinese had negotiated the original memo of understanding with little difficulty, and the Chinese led the Americans to think they might work out a detailed contract by the end of 1979. But suddenly China went quiet on them. For two long years it seemed impossible to make any progress toward negotiating a contract. No matter what the Americans did, they couldn't get a commitment—or, in fact, anything specific—from their new Chinese friends.

Only years later did Clare and others at AMC learn that during this strange hiatus of 1979–80, Chinese auto officials had entered into new, serious discussions with Toyota. China was using the agreement signed with AMC as a lever to get a better deal from the Japanese. Clare could see them waving copies of the Beijing Hotel agreement in the faces of Toyota executives and telling the Japanese they had better come up with something similar, something better, if they did not want to be left out of the China market.

The Chinese ploy didn't work. The Japanese were not going to compete—at least not on the same basis as AMC. They wanted to play by different rules. Japanese manufacturers were eager to sell cars and trucks in China, but they had no interest in setting up manufacturing operations there. If the Chinese wanted to buy Toyotas, fine; Toyota would offer them the lowest prices in the industry. But the cars themselves would be made in Japan.

It was a good illustration of the different objectives of the Americans and the Japanese. The commercial interests of their businessmen were not the same, and neither were the geopolitical strategies of their governments.

Both American and Japanese companies saw China as a vast untapped market, a potentially crucial outlet for future sales. Business executives in both countries wanted to develop sales in China. To that limited extent, the Americans and Japanese were competitors. Yet the Americans were also interested in something else: manufacturing in China to take advantage of what seemed like incredibly low labor costs.

In the early 1980s, when the yen was valued at well over 200 to the dollar, American auto companies were paying wages of roughly $20 an hour including benefits, while their Japanese competitors were paying the equivalent of $12. Making cars in China, where workers were paid the equivalent of 60 cents an hour, might help even out the difference. Even if China charged AMC more for labor costs than the workers themselves were paid, even if there was overstaffing, low productivity, low quality, and innumerable hidden costs, the Americans believed that none of that could counterbalance the difference between $20 an hour and 60 cents.

Furthermore, AMC looked upon China as a base from which to export cars throughout the rest of East Asia, a region in which the sale of four-wheel-drive vehicles was increasing at the rate of about 30 percent a year and which had come to represent close to a third of the world market for these vehicles. From China, the transport costs to places like the Philippines or Thailand would be much lower and the delivery time much quicker than from the American Midwest.

Japan didn't need China as a base for exports in East Asia. Japan was its own base. Furthermore, the Japanese didn't find it in their own interests to have China develop as an industrial competitor. Here, commercial interest converged with geopolitical strategy. To the Americans, China was a potentially important counterweight against the Soviet Union. China's enmity with the Soviets helped to distract Moscow from focusing full attention on Europe and tied down more than fifty divisions of Soviet troops in Central Asia. United States policymakers thought that helping China to develop its industrial base was all to the good.

By contrast, the Japanese were, at best, ambivalent about the prospect. To the extent that China helped distract or fend off the Soviet Union, Japan was delighted. To the extent that China would provide coal, oil, and other natural resources for Japanese factories, that was all to the good. To the extent that the income of Chinese workers went up and they had more money to purchase Japanese consumer goods, that was fine, too. But Japan had no interest in turning over to China the technology and management skills that would enable China (with a population more than eight times that of Japan) to become Japan's rival in East Asia. Such a showdown might come, sometime in the twenty-first or twenty-second century, but the Japanese didn't want to hasten the process. If China needed help in developing a modern auto industry, let it go to AMC. Toyota wasn't interested.

There was another consideration, too. The Japanese business community was wary about the prospects for making money in China. The Japanese kept thinking about Baoshan.

The Baoshan Iron & Steel Works rises up on what must be one of the ugliest river sites in the world. It takes about an hour to get there, traveling north from Shanghai's maze of crowded streets, through suburbs of once rural shacks and cheaply built concrete apartment buildings, and finally through a series of mud flats and open land that make up the south bank of the Yangtze River.

The Yangtze is China's greatest river, the dividing line between north and south China. In the mountains of Qinghai Province, far to the west, the river is as clear and fresh as an Alaskan fishing stream. Farther down in Sichuan Province, the river opens out into the beautiful, mysterious stretch that Western tourists see on their river cruises. But at Baoshan, less than fifty miles from the Yangtze's entrance to the South China Sea, the river is so muddy and slow-moving that it appears to be carrying the silt, waste, and detritus of the entire Chinese nation. At Baoshan, the Yangtze is more than twelve miles wide, and on a gray, cloudy day one can barely see the other side: in the foreground, all that is visible is the depressing yellow brown of the water and a few desultory cargo ships heading for the port of Shanghai.

It was at Baoshan that the international business community had its first collision with the harsh realities of the newly opened China.

In 1977, within a year after the death of Mao Tse-tung, the Chinese leadership had mapped out an elaborate plan for economic modernization. It was China's first shift away from Maoism, away from the belief that the communal effort of one billion people working hard together would itself make the nation great. But in its first abandonment of Mao, the regime had fallen back on some of the economic policies of Josef Stalin: It hoped to advance the economy through massive state investment in heavy industry. China was going to build big, modern factories, with outside help where necessary.

In December 1978 China began construction of a massive iron

and steel plant at Baoshan. The $5 billion project was probably the single biggest and most ambitious venture the Communist regime had ever launched. The location was chosen because it was on the Yangtze, near China's eastern coastline and close to Shanghai, which has the most skilled work force in all of China. However, it soon turned out that in the rush to modernize, China hadn't done the feasibility studies and financial planning that such a project required. In the soft, silty soil along the Yangtze, the pilings put down for the construction of the plant kept sinking into oblivion. Eventually engineers were forced to build the foundation for the factory on expensive sixty-yard-long steel pilings.

China had decided that the Baoshan plan should have the most advanced steelmaking technology available and signed contracts with Japanese and West German companies to obtain this technology. But the modern equipment that China purchased from the foreign companies required a higher grade of iron ore than was available in China. As a result, China discovered that it would have to import ore from other countries, such as Australia and Brazil. A sandbar at the mouth of the Yangtze River prevented the ocean-going ships that carried iron ore from abroad to go directly into Baoshan, so China had to pay the bill for a new port installation at Ningbo, down the South China coast.

As if this weren't enough, the new steel plant sparked off a startling wave of local opposition in Shanghai, the most politically powerful of all Chinese cities. In 1980, during a session of the National People's Congress, China's parliament, delegates from Shanghai complained that the central government in Beijing overlooked the environmental effects of putting the steel mill in Shanghai. Winds from the Yangtze would blow sulfur dioxide from the steel plant south and east into downtown Shanghai. Some delegates also voiced fears that Baoshan would increase water pollution and waste disposal problems in Shanghai.

Authorities in Beijing had second thoughts of their own concerning the Baoshan plant. Their concern was money. Baoshan was merely the most conspicuous of a whole series of ambitious industrial projects that China had launched in the first years after Mao's death. By 1979 China was beginning to realize it couldn't pay the bills. Chinese economists and planners—led by Chen Yun, the veteran Communist Party leader who had dared to criticize Mao's

Great Leap Forward of the 1950s—persuaded the regime to begin scaling back.[1]

In 1980 China announced a temporary freeze on construction of the first phase of the Baoshan steel mill while it reviewed the plans for the project. In addition the regime suspended all plans for the second phase of the mill—thus cancelling contracts that had already been signed with foreign companies for the construction.

It was a stunning blow to the Japanese Nippon Steel Corporation which had signed a $2 billion contract to oversee the first phase of construction and had a commitment from China for another $1.5 billion for the second phase. Other companies that had signed contracts to supply equipment to the plant—including Japan's Mitsubishi Corporation and West Germany's Mannesman-Demag and Scholesman-Siemag—also found themselves out in the cold.

What happened at Baoshan also occurred elsewhere throughout China. Between 1979 and 1982 China launched what could be viewed either as one prolonged period of retrenchment or, perhaps, a series of several different retrenchments. Each time, contracts that had been signed with foreign companies were suspended or canceled.

In 1979 China announced a temporary suspension of twenty-two contracts with Japanese firms, worth approximately $2.5 billion in business. Chinese officials explained that they needed time for a "reassessment" of the economy. In the spring of 1980 Chinese officials informed representatives of the National Council for U.S.-China Trade that nearly all of the one hundred foreign contracts under negotiation would be postponed at least until the following year. Christopher Phillips, the president of the American group, told Chinese trade officials that they ran the danger of losing momentum in their effort to attract U.S. corporations to China, but his warning had little effect.

That summer Chinese authorities suspended several multi-million-dollar industrial projects launched by American companies, including a proposed aluminum plant by the Bechtel Corporation and plans by the Fluor Corporation for what was to have been the world's largest copper mine. In each instance, the American company had already carried out design and engineering studies for the project and was preparing to start construction. Fluor said it had spent $10 million on these preliminary studies.[2] In a public 1980 report on China's economy, the Central Intelligence Agency explained, "The Chinese have concluded that they need more time to digest the $11 billion worth of whole plants purchased in 1972–79 and that they must be more discriminating in making future purchases."

Some of these suspended projects eventually were allowed to go forward. In the case of the Baoshan steel mill, after two years of reexamination China decided to proceed with the plant and to permit the Japanese and West German companies to do some of the work, although not as much as these companies had hoped. Nippon Steel had been counting on installing the blast furnace in the second stage of the project, but Chinese officials announced they would do that job themselves.

In some instances, contracts were simply revoked. The victims in this early stage were more likely to be Japanese and Western European companies than the Americans, who had been relatively slow to conclude deals with China. In late 1980 China canceled major contracts worth $1.5 billion with Japan. West Germany's exports to China were down by 25 percent in 1980 from the previous year, and British, French, and Italian exports were down by almost as much.

To those who dared to complain, Chinese officials explained simply that these actions were an economic necessity. On January 1, 1981, the *People's Daily* told the nation: "Only when sufficient retreat is made in certain fields will it be possible to free the national economy as a whole from the potential danger of inflation."

Many foreigners in Beijing accepted these explanations. "They had to take the steps they have taken," observed Leonard Woodcock, who had become the first U.S. ambassador to China after diplomatic relations were restored. In a February 1981 farewell address as he was leaving Beijing, Woodcock told the American business community to be patient. "There will be business done [in the 1980s]—not massive, but substantial, I believe. And those enterprises that do business on a sensible, mutual-benefit basis in these difficult years will reap the reward, I am confident, when China turns the corner economically."

Not everyone was so philosophical. Japanese and West German companies asked for compensation for their canceled contracts, and in 1981 Japan sent its special trade representative, Saburo

Okita, to China. "This is not only a matter of money, but also of trust," said Okita during his visit. "China has always said it values trust, so if this matter is not dealt with promptly, Japanese industrialists will become alarmed." Okita was urged by Chinese Vice Premier Gu Mu to take the "long, strategic view" and "not focus on this relatively short period of readjustment."[3]

In the end, a few foreign companies received compensation and others were later rewarded with new contracts. But China's retrenchment of the early 1980s had a lasting, sobering impact on the international companies trying to do business with Beijing. In case there was any doubt, China had served notice that it would play by its own rules. A signed contract did not have the same binding effect in China as it had elsewhere. It was merely a statement of intentions—a general, qualified agreement by which a Chinese agency agreed to try to do something, if possible and if nothing else came up after the contract was signed.

Foreign businessmen began to be a bit more cautious in committing money to China. In 1982 the total foreign investment in China fell to less than $50 million, a decline of more than 50 percent from the previous year.

Still, for the Chinese, the experience of the early 1980s had a different meaning. It seemed to show that China could dictate the terms by which international business would be conducted in China. Despite the fury of the companies whose contracts were canceled, there was no mass exodus of foreign businesses. China was still the world's largest untapped market. Companies were willing to accept terms and treatment in China that they would have immediately rejected anywhere else.

True, the foreign companies were investing less money during China's economic retrenchment. Yet almost nobody was willing to leave, to write off China entirely, and newcomers arrived with newly printed business cards each day. China's big chill didn't stop Tod Clare or his team from American Motors from trying to gain a toehold in China, and it didn't stop too many other businessmen, either.

In those first couple of years of meetings with AMC, the Chinese officials and negotiators had their own problems.

American Motors was a private company with authority to make decisions on its own, but the Beijing Automotive Works was a state enterprise. While outsiders commonly imagine a Communist system to be one in which one single, all-powerful decision maker controls everything, the reality in China is often much more complex. In an abstract sense, the government rules or influences nearly everything; yet within the Chinese bureaucracy, different government agencies compete viciously with one another.

One of the Chinese representing the state-owned Beijing Automotive Works in the talks with American Motors, Feng Xiantang, confessed afterward that BAW had more than ten different sections of the Chinese government supervising its negotiating work. At one point none of the ten government agencies was willing to give its official imprimatur, a Chinese seal or chop, for the feasibility study necessary to get the negotiations with the Americans moving again.

During the negotiations with AMC, moreover, the Chinese factory officials were required to report to their leaders in government ministries more than three hundred times, or an average of once every five days. When BAW officials gave these reports, they heard very little in response from their many superiors.

Within BAW, the Chinese auto venture, there was still considerable mistrust of the Americans.

"At that time . . . there were still people involved with [Beijing Auto Works] who had misgivings about entering into a joint venture with foreigners—a result of the mental shackles imposed by years of 'leftist' ideas," a Chinese magazine later acknowledged. "Arguments on the potentially destructive effects of dealing with a capitalist country were debated on all sides."[4]

Frustrating as the slowdown was to Clare and his colleagues, there was nothing particularly unusual about it. It was typical of China's careful, arm's-length handling of foreign businesses, particularly during the 1979–80 period.

China had not really decided how much latitude foreign companies should have inside its borders. At the top, Deng and his allies made a vaguely worded commitment to throw open China's doors to foreign businesses. But there was no consensus on the details, the crucial questions of exactly what kinds of businesses China should attract, in what form they should cooperate with China's state-owned enterprises, and what the rules should be. Within the ranks of the Chinese Communist Party and even at senior levels, in its Politburo, there remained deep suspicion about giving too much to the foreigners who had exploited China in the past.

It might be acceptable for China to buy technology or pay foreign companies to help build a factory, such as at Baoshan. It might be acceptable to carry out trade with the West, buying only what China decided it needed from abroad and selling whatever would earn foreign exchange. But it was a wholly different matter to give foreign companies a foothold inside Chinese industry, to allow foreign companies to start manufacturing operations on Chinese soil. That raised the old and extremely sensitive question of who controlled China, the foreigners or Chinese. Moreover, for the Chinese Communist Party, allowing foreign investment in Chinese industries raised the ideological question of whether the Party might be allowing capitalism to gain a foothold on Chinese soil.

The standard way of attracting foreign investment and letting foreign companies help develop domestic industries was through the joint venture. That was the method employed by China's East Asian neighbors, Taiwan and South Korea, and before them Japan. A foreign business and a local company would sign a deal to work together for a fixed period of time, such as twenty years, each contributing a share of the equity and assuming a share of the management and the profits. For the foreign business, the joint venture provided a means of gaining access to inexpensive labor and to a new market; in China, of course, access to the world's largest market was a factor of far greater consideration than on a small island like Taiwan. For the domestic company, the joint venture was a vehicle for gaining access to the foreign company's technology, management techniques, and operations.

Under Deng's leadership, China passed its first law to permit joint ventures in the spring of 1979. It took nearly a year, until April 1980, before China cleared the way for the first three joint ventures. All three ventures involved tourism, not manufacturing. One of the three was for construction of Sung's Great Wall Hotel, the luxury 1,007-room, $75 million tourist facility in Beijing that Sung had been proposing to Chinese officials at the same time as he helped launch the AMC negotiations. The second was for the Jianguo Hotel, another Beijing project also aimed at the foreign community and tourists. And the third was for a catering service to provide food for international travelers on China's airline, the Civil Aviation Administration of China (CAAC). In each of these joint ventures, Chinese authorities retained at least a 51 percent share, ensuring that the foreign partner would have only a minority interest.

From the Chinese perspective, these joint ventures had two important advantages: they would earn foreign exchange in a relatively short period of time and would provide minimal contact between foreign companies and ordinary Chinese workers. The staff of the hotels could be carefully screened and restricted to those few privileged Beijing residents who had already learned English or some other foreign language. In effect, China was reviving an updated version of the old "comprador" system, under which a few selected Chinese at the port of Canton were assigned to deal with foreign companies and keep them at some distance from the rest of Chinese society.

Arthur W. Hummel, Jr., the career diplomat who succeeded Woodcock and served as U.S. ambassador to China from 1981 through 1985, came to the conclusion that China didn't really want joint ventures, no matter how much Chinese leaders said they did. Hummel was the son of one of America's most prominent sinologists and had been for a time a Japanese prisoner of war in China during World War II. From his vantage point at the American embassy, he observed repeatedly how difficult it was for a foreign company to reach a deal in China.

When it came right down to it, Hummel decided, the Chinese were at best ambivalent about the prospect of allowing foreign investment on a large scale. They weren't sure it was in China's interest. Chinese leaders were too scared about the possibility of foreign exploitation. In particular they feared doing anything that might allow foreign companies to take over too large a share of the Chinese economy. Hummel thought these Chinese fears were preposterous, because China was too vast for foreigners to control. But whether the fears were exaggerated or not, Hummel felt, they were the underlying Chinese attitudes that foreign businessmen would have to confront.

It was part of the more general problem of Chinese xenophobia. In business negotiations, Hummel noticed, nobody on the Chinese side got any brownie points for being nice or helpful to foreigners. No Chinese official would get penalized if a business deal got canceled, but an official might assume substantial risks if a deal went through. Someone else in China could always accuse the official who struck the deal of being too easy with the foreigners. If a Chinese official signed a contract with an American company, a rival Japanese firm might come around later on and suggest that China had given too much to the Americans. And enemies of that Chinese official within his work unit, or elsewhere in the bureaucracy, might begin suggesting that he had been duped by the foreigners. Over and over again, Hummel found that the Chinese negotiators were unwilling to take risks.

Exasperated foreign businessmen began to make jokes about the Chinese evasiveness and stalling. In the earliest days, the Chinese negotiators dealing with foreign businesses were so vague about who they were and which ministries or agencies they represented that a fake Chinese business card made the rounds of the foreign community: it said, in English and Chinese, "The responsible official from the department concerned." The building in Beijing at which many negotiations were conducted was located at Erligou (Chinese for two-mile gully); newly arrived foreigners were warned that this most certainly did not mean "early go."

Even when Chinese officials actually wanted to strike a deal, long delays were often part of their negotiating strategy. Just as Clare found that the Chinese put AMC on hold while they sounded out Japanese car companies, so many other foreign businesses discovered that the Chinese were adroit at playing off rival businesses against one another for protracted periods of time. At one point executives of Westinghouse and other international companies seeking to sell nuclear power plants or equipment to China, such as General Electric and the French firm Framatome, were kept on different floors of the same hotel for several weeks, while Chinese officials walked upstairs and down over and over again, getting different price quotations from each firm.

Sometimes, even when there was no competition at all, Chinese negotiators would test a foreign company's endurance by holding out for the lowest price. China possessed, and exploited to the fullest, the advantage of conducting most of the negotiations on its own turf. At the end of a long, tiresome bargaining session in which no progress had been made, the Chinese negotiator would return to his home in Beijing. The foreign negotiator would go back to his uncomfortable hotel, have another dinner of food to which he was not accustomed, and then struggle with the Chinese phone operator to get a late-night phone call through to his boss or business associates, spouse or lover, back home in the United States, Europe, or Japan.

If the foreign businessman let the Chinese know his stay in China was of an indefinite length, the Chinese would effectively control the pace and timing of negotiations. The impatient businessman would discover, to his frustration, that the only item on tomorrow's agenda was a visit to the Great Wall or the Ming Tombs; and if he complained about this, a Chinese official might act as if this were an affront to China's great cultural heritage. On the other hand, if the visiting businessman announced that he was only in Beijing for four days and had a flight out next Friday, the Chinese hosts might act insulted and suggest that he was taking China less seriously than his competitor from another company.

It was not unusual for a foreign businessman to conclude the negotiations were going nowhere, decide to fly home, and then be approached at the last minute, even at the airport, with a slight shift in the Chinese position that would require him to return downtown for further talks. Nor was it unusual for a Chinese negotiator to press for agreement on an important issue from a jet-lagged traveler at the end of the day, or during the last course of a banquet, after the foreigner had drunk a few too many *mao tais*. Charles W. Freeman, Jr., a diplomat who served as second in command of the U.S. embassy in Beijing in the early 1980s, once called the Chinese "masters at the creative use of fatigue."

So skillful were the Chinese in negotiations that during the early 1980s, lessons on Chinese bargaining stratagems and tactics became a cottage industry throughout the United States and Western Europe. Lawyers and businessmen who had gone through the ordeal—as well as Hong Kong entrepreneurs and hustlers who claimed to have cousins or in-laws in powerful positions inside China—conducted seminars and training sessions, hired themselves out as consultants, and otherwise sought to profit from the uncertainty and perplexity that Western businessmen were experiencing as they tried to cut deals in China. The unintended effect of all these lessons and advice, of course, was often to make the businessman all the more uneasy and unsure of himself as he got off the plane in Beijing.

Even the U.S. government, universities, and think tanks got into the act. Scholars began carrying out studies on the Chinese art of negotiation and to write analyses of Chinese bargaining strategies.

For the benefit of U.S. government officials, Richard H. Solomon, a sinologist who served on Henry A. Kissinger's National Security Council staff and later became an assistant secretary of state in the Bush administration, wrote an article called "Friendship and Obligation in Chinese Negotiating Style." He concluded: "The most fundamental characteristic of dealings with the Chinese is their attempt to identify foreign officials who are sympathetic to their cause, to cultivate a sense of friendship and obligation in their official counterparts, and then to pursue their objectives through a variety of stratagems designed to manipulate feelings of friendship, obligation, guilt or dependence."[5]

The U.S. Air Force commissioned a Rand Corporation study on Chinese negotiating tactics by Lucian Pye, a leading political scientist and sinologist.[6] The air force interest was in helping private American aerospace companies in their negotiations with China, although the study was written in terms general enough to cover any commercial negotiations with the Chinese.

Pye's most important bit of advice to businessmen was to be patient and to be ready for repeated delays. "The Chinese believe that patience is a value in negotiations, particularly with impatient Americans, and they frequently use stalling tactics and delays," he said. "The most elementary rules for negotiating with the Chinese are 1) practice patience; 2) accept as normal prolonged periods of no movement; 3) control against exaggerated expectations and discount Chinese rhetoric about future prospects; 4) expect that the Chinese will try to influence by shaming; 5) resist the temptation to believe that difficulties may have been caused by one's own mistakes; and 6) try to understand Chinese cultural traits, but never believe that a foreigner can practice them better than the Chinese."

That was good advice, but not always easy to follow.

Throughout 1979 and 1980 the AMC executives kept on flying to China, trying without luck to make some progress on a contract. For a while Clare was traveling to Beijing once a month, spending much of his life going to China and back.

Others in the international division did so, too. AMC worked it out so that Beijing was covered for months at a time; there was always someone from AMC in town. Gilchrist won the division's frequent-flyer award; he crossed the Pacific again and again, sometimes remaining in China for up to five weeks on a single trip. While in Beijing, he would be forced to move constantly from antiquated hotel to antiquated hotel, sleeping wherever there was space.

There were no telexes for a company to rent then, no computers, no direct-dial telephones. When Gilchrist wanted to call the United States, he did it from his hotel room, sometimes waiting for hours for an operator to come through with a line. As soon as Gilchrist hung up the phone, an attendant would knock on the door and demand immediate payment in cash for the overseas call: there was no thought of putting the phone charges on the hotel bill. That was just the way business was done in China. Gilchrist had to pay cash for his laundry as soon as it was delivered, too.

Back at headquarters, AMC's China contingent became a small clique with its own bonds, its own grumbles, its own jokes that no one else could possibly understand. One of the jokes—not as funny or trivial as they made out, Clare thought—was about the "mystical experience." What was your top mystical experience in China on *this* trip? one AMC China hand would ask another. For during those first, early trips to China in 1979 and 1980, each AMC official would at some point find himself completely detached from any link to America and the corporate culture they all knew so well.

For Clare, the moment came one morning when he woke up in Beijing jet-lagged, at five o'clock, on a cold winter day when the grimy coal smoke and the dust blowing in from the Gobi desert created a thick gray fog over the city. Looking out from his hotel room window, Clare could see nothing but a gray mist and bicycles on their way to work. There were no cars, no other sound at all, just people silently pedaling from one gray cloud bank into another. It was as if they weren't real. Clare thought to himself, Oh, Christ, where am I?

Years later, when China seemed much more Westernized and he felt much more at home there, Clare would recall those early trips, how there were few or no other white faces on the street. Those days back then knocked you out, he said. Back then China was so overwhelming, so encompassing, that it just sucked you in. It was as though you had been there all your life. You lost any connection with where you had come from and where you were going.

5

Bargaining Around the World

Finally, in 1981, as Clare and his American Motors team were beginning to despair of ever making any progress in China, the climate changed. China's economic situation was beginning to improve. The Chinese leadership began to push the cumbersome bureaucracy to seek out deals that could bring in technology from abroad. Beijing Auto Works, the Chinese enterprise, succeeded in getting high-level clearance for a new five-person group with decision-making and negotiating authority to supervise the talks.[1]

The AMC officials noticed that the pace of the talks began to accelerate. The Chinese seemed interested in reaching an agreement. The Americans saw new faces across the table at the bargaining sessions, among them Chen Zutao, a trained engineer and plant designer who was one of the most knowledgeable people in China's auto industry. Once Chen was involved, the atmosphere changed. The negotiations were still slow and difficult, but at least the AMC executives felt they could get some sort of response to their offers, even if it was negative. For those first two years they hadn't been able to get anything specific at all.

Clare supervised the negotiations, but Gilchrist, working under Clare as head of AMC's Far East Operations, took the lead role for the American side at the bargaining sessions. It was all new territory for both sides. At that point there were no manufacturing joint ventures of any kind in China.

The talks took place in a spartan conference room at the Chinese jeep factory. AMC brought only a handful of officials at a time and no lawyers. Preparing or distributing any kind of written material proved difficult, because the Chinese factory had no photocopying machine. By then Unison, Sung's consulting firm, had a small office at the Beijing Hotel with a single copying machine in it. But Unison's office was halfway across Beijing, and Gilchrist had to lug in copy paper for the Unison photocopier on the plane from Detroit. Sometimes Gilchrist would watch while Chinese negotiators asked their aides to make several copies of a document. Laboriously Chinese assistants would each prepare a single handwritten copy. There wasn't even any carbon paper.

The AMC officials had no idea what to expect from their Chinese counterparts. Points they thought would be tough turned out to be extremely easy, and those they considered trivial produced astonishing reactions from the Chinese side. In trying to calculate how much equity each side would put into the new venture, it was necessary to come up with some valuation of the assets —that is, the dollar value of the Chinese factory in South Beijing and the technology the Americans would be bringing to China. The AMC officials expected these questions to be extremely troublesome and time-consuming. They suggested bringing in an international auditing company, expecting that the Chinese would reject the idea outright or treat the auditors from abroad with great suspicion. Instead the Chinese auto officials quickly went along; the auditors came in and submitted their estimates of the assets, and their report was quickly accepted. The AMC officials were astonished. But then, on another occasion, AMC suggested setting up an escrow account for some disputed money, thinking this would be a simple solution. "What is escrow?" a Chinese official asked. It was five days before the negotiations could move on to the next paragraph of the proposed contract.

Clare thought you could never tell where the obstacles were going to be. You could roll up your sleeves and plan for a long haul and then problems would evaporate. Then, just when you believed you would wrap things up in a day, something would come up and you'd be there for another month.

Sometimes the AMC officials found themselves giving the Chinese negotiators lessons in what they considered fundamental capitalist principles, the Economics 1 of their college days. Some of the Chinese officials didn't seem to understand the first thing about economic realities. They had operated under a centrally planned economy for so long that they didn't understand how any other kind of economy would work. Though the AMC executives were prepared for the fact that the Chinese didn't care about profits, they were surprised to find that the cadres also didn't seem to care about efficiency—about the relative costs of production and the sales price of the final product. The Chinese cadres in charge of the Jeep factory got their raw materials from the state allocation system, and they distributed the Jeeps they made through the state allocation system. What mattered to them was production, the level of output.

Some of the Chinese cadres were hopeless, Clare thought. They seemed to be beyond the point where they would be able to learn anything new. The Chinese were pressing AMC to build a four-door vehicle in China. AMC officials said they couldn't do it, meaning that it would not be economically feasible. One day, one of the cadres came into the talks with a picture of a Hovercraft. "How come you can't build a four-door vehicle when we can build a Hovercraft?" he asked.

"How many of these have you built?" Clare asked. Actually none had been built, but China knew how to do it, the official said.

"Well, I can build a four-door vehicle, too," said Clare in exasperation. "But you've got to pay $50 million for the first one, $25 million for the second, $10 million for the third, $5 million for the fourth, and if you ever bought five million cars from me, you know, you'd probably have it down to $1.75 apiece." Anybody can build a car that costs more than you sell it for, Clare told the Chinese. AMC had come to build a car that cost less than its sales price. But sometimes he thought it was like yelling at a stone wall.

In at least a few instances, the Chinese officials feigned ignorance as a negotiating ploy. The stratagem worked. At one point AMC was introducing a provision in the contract permitting the prices that AMC would charge the Chinese joint venture for parts to be adjusted in the event of inflation. "What is inflation?" asked the Chinese negotiators, reacting as though AMC were trying to steal money from them.

The AMC executives found themselves slowly and patiently explaining how, although prices in China remained stable, they sometimes tended to rise in the rest of the world. AMC finally succeeded in winning approval for the inflation clause, but it was a tough fight, one that diverted time and energy from other issues. After the contract was finally signed, AMC Chairman W. Paul Tippett, echoing earlier remarks by his negotiators, would marvel to the *Detroit Free Press:* "They [the Chinese] weren't used to inflation. They don't know what inflation is." The newspaper ran the story under the headline "TOUGH NEGOTIATORS" UNAWARE OF IN-FLATION.

In fact, the Chinese knew well what inflation was. To believe that they were ignorant about inflation betrayed an ignorance of Chinese history and current life. In 1947 and 1948, under the Nationalist government of Chiang Kai-shek, China had suffered from one of the worst episodes of hyperinflation in the history of the world, one that was rivaled in this century only by the inflation of Germany's Weimar Republic. Its currency, the Chinese dollar, was pegged at 3.33 to the U.S. dollar in 1936 and 20 during World War II; in 1947 the rate went up to 12,000, in early 1948 to 324,000, and in late 1948 to more than 1 million. That was the official exchange rate, and the black market rates were higher. The inflation had been one of the principal factors underlying the victory of Mao and the Communists in the civil war.

Any Chinese who lived through that hyperinflation, even a child of ten, would have remembered those days. And a Chinese child who was ten years old in 1948 would have been only forty-four in 1982, when the negotiations with AMC were moving toward their final stages. Was it really possible that no Chinese official involved in the talks with AMC was old enough to recall what inflation was? (Chen Zutao, for example, was fifty-four years old at the end of 1982. He had been twenty years old in 1948.) Apart from the memories of the civil war era, China's Communist regime had for years spoken with pride of the stability of prices under its leadership. One common economic tract published by China in the 1970s was called, "Why There Is No Inflation in China." Even in its absence, inflation was a concept commonly understood by the Chinese.

The AMC team came to be able to spot some Chinese negotiating ploys. The Americans learned to expect that the Chinese would heap scorn upon the AMC proposals on the first day or two of a negotiating session, so that the Americans would walk out of the room at the end of the day in low spirits. The AMC team also began to realize that the people with whom they were talking were often just lower-level cadres, and that the unidentified, unnamed officials sitting silently in the back of the room were the decision makers. It was frustrating, because you wanted to talk directly with the most senior people, but if this was the Chinese way, so be it. Clare came to feel that the Iranians, whom he had once called the world's toughest negotiators, were second-rate compared with the Chinese.

Among the toughest sticking points in the negotiations were the questions of exports and price. China wanted AMC to guarantee that many of the Jeeps produced by the new joint venture would be exported. AMC wasn't eager to make promises about exports, because the company wasn't sure the Chinese-made Jeeps would be of world quality, and it didn't want to undermine the name and reputation of the AMC Jeep. Exports were linked to the question of price, because the Chinese were arguing that a low-priced, Chinese-made vehicle would sell well overseas. Chinese officials thought the new joint venture could price its Jeeps well below the competition to get into the world market, just as the Japanese had done in the late 1960s and early 1970s. AMC argued that if the sales price was too low, people wouldn't buy the vehicle, because they would assume it was of poor quality. Moreover, they said, the more local content (that is, Chinese content) in the vehicle, the less chance there would be of producing an internationally recognized, world-class Jeep.

With remarkable speed, AMC began getting reports of Chinese-made jeeps for sale in Europe, just one or two of them, for prices like $2,995. The surprised AMC officials realized the Chinese were testing the market, checking out the truth of what the AMC negotiators were saying. Then they began hearing reports of commercial attachés at Chinese embassies in places like Venezuela and Mexico doing surveys on the prices for various parts and commodities or obtaining price lists; the Chinese were double-checking the prices the AMC negotiators had quoted to them. The Chinese negotiators would bring back the results of their investigation to the negotiating table and throw them across to the Americans.

It became evident that the Chinese liked to travel. Most of the negotiating sessions took place in Beijing. But at one point, midway through the talks, the Chinese team came to Detroit for a month. AMC set aside a room for the Chinese downstairs from the executive offices and had food shipped into the room each day.

From the Chinese perspective, walking into AMC's headquarters outside Detroit was like entering a world of fable. AMC operates from its own modern, high-rise glass-enclosed office building, the American Center, in the Detroit suburb of Southfield. The building is surrounded by grass, carefully landscaped trees, and so many parking lots that they have to be lettered. Although on an average day several hundred cars are parked outside, there is so much open space that the concrete of the parking area is barely noticeable. To a Chinese visitor, the amount of unused, vacant land in this still-urban setting is overwhelming; one would have to look hard to find so much space and so few people in an entire province along China's most heavily populated eastern coast.

To drive from Detroit's Metropolitan Airport to the AMC's Southfield headquarters, the visitor takes one expressway, Interstate 94, and then another, I-275, and then another, I-696, each one permitting cars to travel at speeds faster than one can drive anywhere in China. Once inside the American Center, a visitor finds an eerie, air-conditioned tranquillity, the dream of a modern-day Confucius, the lost hope of a resident of Beijing or Shanghai. In the ground-floor lobby of the building, the visitor finds only a lone receptionist and a few models of old cars, celebrating AMC's old triumphs.

Clare thought the month the Chinese delegation spent in Detroit was awful. The toughest part was that the Chinese (who, at home, were accustomed to six-day work weeks) didn't want to take Saturday or Sunday off. Moreover, the Chinese officials had been used to dealing with AMC in China, where they had been led to believe that the entire American company lived for its China project. In China, no one from AMC said too much about domestic American sales of Jeeps, or about Pacers, Gremlins, Renault Alliances, and the other auto products and ventures that occupied the time of the company's chief executives.

In Southfield, at the month-long negotiating sessions, the Chinese seemed a little hurt, disappointed that they were not attracting more attention. AMC could muster only five or six people a day to spend up to ten hours with the Chinese, and these Americans weren't always the board chairman or president of the company. Clare felt that the Chinese had a bit of the attitude that everyone at American Motors should stop doing everything else and devote his or her entire attention to the Chinese. He thought this attitude reflected the visitors' belief that China was the center of the world.

At first the AMC executives enjoyed socializing with the Chinese team, but after two weeks Clare thought that became tiring, too. The AMC executives were used to going home to see their families in the evening. Banquets night after night were something the Americans did in China, not in Southfield.

It was another, more extensive round of travel that seemed to clinch the deal.

At the beginning of 1983 Chen Zutao and other Chinese officials came to Detroit for another series of negotiations. Once again they seemed coy and noncommittal. Clare tried out what he thought would be just a new sales pitch. I'm tired of having to tell you how great we are as partners, he said. You don't have to listen to me. We've got partners in joint ventures all over the world. Why don't you go talk to them? Go talk to our partners in Egypt or Venezuela and see what they say about AMC. Ask them whether our company is any good. We'll leave you alone to talk to them, out of our presence.

Clare thought it was a throwaway line. But the next thing Clare knew, the Chinese delegation embraced the idea, and AMC officials found themselves arranging for Chen Zutao and his whole delegation to travel to Cairo. Chinese officials then told AMC that since they were headed in that direction, they also wanted to stop by and take a look at the operations of Renault, AMC's parent company. AMC hurriedly added Paris as in intermediate stop on the itinerary.

None of the Chinese delegation had ever been to Cairo before. Holy Christ, thought Clare, I'm not going to let them wander all over Egypt getting lost or sick. So he went to Cairo with the Chinese delegation, which looked at every millimeter of the Jeep plant in the Egyptian desert. The Egyptian officials gave the Chinese a big welcome and heaped praise upon AMC. The Chinese were delighted with the trip. So was Clare.

Chen and his associates were scheduled to leave Egypt on an Ethiopian Airlines flight to Athens, where they were to catch flight connections to Moscow and Beijing. The flight was canceled at the last minute. At the Cairo airport, the Chinese had to endure a mob scene and a four-hour ordeal as passengers vied to get seats on other airlines. Finally AMC officials straightened out the plane tickets for the Chinese delegation and arranged new flights back to Beijing.

At three o'clock in the morning, Clare went out to the Cairo airport to say bon voyage to the Chinese delegation. That was the sort of personal gesture that Chinese hosts routinely make for foreign guests departing from China itself. It seemed to have an impact. For the next two years, every time Chen Zutao gave a toast or banquet speech with Clare in the room, Chen would say, "At three o'clock that morning in Egypt when Mr. Clare said good-bye to us at the airport, I knew we had a deal."

The tour of Egypt ended in February 1983. After seeing that it had gone so well, Clare told Chen Zutao that AMC would like to have the contract signed in May. Chen told him the timing was extremely tight, but that it could be done.

By early 1983 the two sides seemed to be nearing agreement on the general outlines of a deal. At that point the AMC negotiating team came back with a draft of a written contract. After reading it, the Chinese became frosty and angry. Mystified, the AMC team turned to their consultant, Sung, for help. It turned out that Chinese officials didn't like the legal language in the contract. They said it was insulting to be confronted with clauses spelling out the penalties or remedies if the Chinese partner couldn't make good on its commitments. Sung brought their objections back to AMC. "That's boilerplate," AMC officials said. "It's standard language for our contracts in developing countries."

For Sung, that touched a patriotic nerve. "You should not deal with China as just another developing country," he lectured the AMC team, "because a couple of thousand years ago, some of your ancestors were living in caves, but China was already developed. China is a developed country that's now developing and will be a developed country once again." Some of the standard language was thrown aside.

In April 1983 negotiators settled on the details and the language of the deal and won approval for them both in Beijing and in Detroit. The two sides—AMC and the Beijing Auto Works (BAW), the Chinese enterprise—would form a new joint venture called the Beijing Jeep Company, Ltd., with equity of $51 million. The company would remain in operation for twenty years.

The Chinese side, Beijing Automotive Works, agreed to contribute $35 million in assets, or 69 percent of the new company. Of this sum, $28.4 million was the value of the buildings, workshops, and equipment at the existing Beijing factory, and the remaining $6.6 million was cash in the form of Chinese renminbi, the Chinese currency. American Motors agreed to put up equity worth $16 million, or 31 percent of the company; half of the American contribution was to be in cash, and the other half was American technology valued at $8 million. The board of directors of the new company would include seven Chinese representatives and four Americans. The two sides agreed that a Chinese official would serve as chairman of the board. For the first three years an American would hold the title of president and chief executive officer. After that time the job would rotate between the Chinese and American sides.

The agreement envisioned that at the outset the new joint venture would simply modernize the old Chinese jeep, the BJ212. But it also specified that Beijing Jeep would soon begin to develop what was called "a new, second-generation vehicle," to be produced in China for sale both in China and on the international market. The exports of these new jeeps were expected to produce the foreign exchange necessary to obtain parts from abroad until that time when the new jeeps could be made entirely with Chinese parts.

These new products to be built in China were described in the contract as "light-duty, cross-country vehicles"—in effect, a new form of jeep. The written language also mentioned the use of some components from one of American Motors' Jeeps, the CJ series. However, the agreement did not spell out exactly what this new jeep would look like, how "new" the second-generation Chinese jeep would be, or whether it would be new to AMC as well as to China. In this vague language were contained the seeds of future conflict between the Chinese and the Americans.

One of the provisions in the contract called for what were, in effect, little more than cash payments from AMC to China. The Chinese negotiators won approval for a clause calling for Beijing Jeep to pay the equivalent of salaries for at least five top Chinese managers at rates of $40,000 a year—nearly as much as the managers from AMC would be paid. The Chinese managers themselves would not take home this money; they would continue to take home wages based on local standards of no more than $1,200 a year. Instead, the contract said, the $40,000 "salaries" would go into a special Chinese bank account, and the Chinese government would later decide how it was to be used. AMC officials were annoyed but later explained away the provision to reporters as simply a roundabout means of taxing them.[2]

The most important Chinese negotiating victory was what the contract didn't say. China's currency, the renminbi, is useless overseas; it is not convertible into dollars or other foreign exchange. There was no clause guaranteeing AMC the right to take Chinese currency earned in China and convert it into dollars to bring back to Detroit. Nor was there any provision specifying how the new company would find dollars or other foreign exchange to buy parts from AMC or from other companies overseas except through export earnings.

If Beijing Jeep made money by producing Chinese Jeeps in China, it would be paid in renminbi. And if the company wanted to make purchases overseas, it would have to find some way to earn that foreign exchange, presumably by exporting motor vehicles or parts. "To assure the success of the Beijing Jeep Corp., export sales will be given high priority," the contract said. China clearly wanted AMC to have a strong financial incentive to export. AMC officials rationalized away the problem, explaining that they would at first use whatever Chinese currency they earned to increase their equity in the new company; under the contract, AMC had the right to raise its share in Beijing Jeep to 49 percent. Anyway, AMC's top executives said, they hadn't come into China for short-term profits.

Clare thought the negotiations came out well. To be sure, the written agreement, which was the result of constant negotiations over a period of years, didn't read very well. Nevertheless, Clare felt, the contract laid out the general blueprint under which AMC could do business in China. When he presented the deal to AMC's board of directors, he told them that the price of playing poker in China was so reasonable that they had no reason not to get into the game. "If we can get into China for eight million cash, let's go," Clare told them. The board gave its approval.

For China, the AMC agreement was a landmark. There had been other deals with foreign companies, setting up joint ventures for oil and coal exploration, for hotels, restaurants, and tourism. But in 1983 Beijing Jeep was the largest single manufacturing joint venture any foreign company had agreed to enter into in China. It was exactly the sort of deal China had envisioned when it first opened its doors to the West in the late 1970s. Until AMC, no foreign company had been willing to make such a large commit-ment to manufacturing in China.

Both AMC and China had reasons to want to boast about the new contract. Both wanted to attract as much publicity as possible. Both sides thought it was a big deal, and both intended to say so.

6

Hoopla

The story of AMC's landmark deal in China was page-one news in the United States. JEEP MAKER PLANS FACTORY IN PEKING, announced *The New York Times* on its front page of May 2, 1983, three days before the contract was officially signed. The AMC deal made the networks' nightly news shows and was mentioned in William Safire's column. JEEP IN PEKING: AN 18-COURSE DEAL, read *Newsweek*'s headline. *Time* suggested that the China deal marked a turning point for the fortunes of American Motors. "The AMC train is finally leaving the station," AMC Chairman and Chief Executive Officer W. Paul Tippett told *Time;* the newsmagazine observed, "After the agreement in China, the AMC train might be called the Orient Express."

Why was the China deal thought to be so important? The news stories emphasized three different themes: first, that China represented a huge market for cars and trucks, one that AMC's deal would put it in excellent position to capture; second, that Chinese labor costs were so low that manufacturing motor vehicles in China would bring about important cost savings to AMC; and third, that China offered AMC a strategic location from which to ship exports to the rest of Asia.

The press coverage contained a number of false assumptions and misunderstandings. Some of the press coverage suggested that the Jeep deal was a turning point for American business, showing a way through which U.S. companies could compete successfully with the Japanese. At least as far as trade was concerned, it was going to be the United States and China teaming up against Japan. *The New York Times* said AMC would export Jeeps from China "in competition with four-wheel-drive Japanese vehicles that now dominate the Asian market."

The *Detroit Free Press* even gave its readers the outdated and dangerous myth that Japanese auto manufacturers were outselling their U.S. competitors primarily because of lower labor costs—overlooking other competitive factors such as the reliability of Japanese cars and the efficiency of Japanese manufacturing. "American Motors' plan to join with the Chinese in auto manufacture could well turn out to be one of the shrewdest industrial strokes of the decade," said the *Free Press* on May 7, 1983. "The success of the Japanese auto industry is so mesmerizing that the possibility it could be challenged by other Far Eastern nations is not often considered. AMC is considering it seriously. . . . The gap between labor costs in Japan and the United States is narrowing, but the Japanese still have a competitive advantage. In competition with the Chinese, however, they would have a problem, and that is what seems to be coming at them."

In a few instances, the newspapers themselves were responsible for errors. *The Washington Post*'s story, for example, said that the AMC deal was "expected to create 4,000 jobs in China." That was a bizarre prediction, since it was AMC's intention from the outset to cut back drastically on overstaffing at the Beijing auto factory. The joint venture would have a staff of four thousand, but these employees would be taken from the existing work force.

Generally, however, the press coverage accurately reflected the rosy, upbeat views that American Motors executives themselves had put forth in their public statements. No one was more extravagant in his rhetoric than Tippett, AMC's chairman and chief executive officer. "Everyone salivates when they think of the China market," he told *The Wall Street Journal*. "This is a major, long-term opportunity for us," he told *Time*. The China deal gives AMC "a low-cost manufacturing base from which to compete with the Japanese in Southeast Asia," he told the *Los Angeles Times*.

Tippett reminded reporters that China represented the largest single potential market in the world for four-wheel-drive vehicles. He expected AMC to raise output at the Beijing auto plant from 20,000 vehicles a year to 40,000, of which a quarter or more would be exported to other Asian countries. This doubling of production, he said, could hopefully be accomplished in "a couple of years." The output would at first consist of the existing, antiquated Chinese jeeps but would quickly be shifted to a new vehicle, one that would be based on AMC's own basic model, the CJ7 Jeep. Tippett glossed over the uncertainties about how different from a CJ7 the new Chinese vehicle should be.

Although the contract called for AMC to have less than one-third ownership in the Chinese venture and for the Chinese partners to have seven of the eleven board members, including the chairman, Tippett told reporters, "We will essentially run it [the new company]." He boasted that AMC "will be making a profit from day one"—ignoring the problem that any such profits would be in Chinese currency and could not be converted into dollars or brought home to the United States.

AMC had launched an extensive public relations campaign to attract this press coverage. Once the details of the contract had been settled, the company decided there should be a well-publicized signing ceremony in Beijing to commemorate the deal, attended by a delegation of five AMC executives, including Tippett and Clare.

The week before the ceremony, during the final week of April 1983, Jerry L. Sloan, AMC's vice president for public relations, called journalists for fourteen national news and automotive publications, offering them a session with the AMC chairman. Sloan informed the reporters about the impending China deal and said Tippett would discuss it with them, if their publications would all agree not to publish anything until after the deal was signed—the sort of embargo arrangement that is not uncommon in the United States.

The reporters agreed and met with the AMC chairman in two separate groups of seven each. When *The Washington Post* couldn't come to one of these sessions in Southfield, Tippett took the occasion of a scheduled trip to Washington to stop by the *Post* and give the newspaper's automotive writer, Warren Brown, a one-on-one background briefing. Sloan insisted that the primary reason for these briefings was that AMC's top executives were the only ones who knew anything about the China project, and that all of them would be in China, out of reach of the American reporters, at the time the contract was to be signed.

The signing ceremonies were scheduled for Thursday, May 5, 1983. The AMC delegation, including the five executives and their wives, flew to Beijing the Sunday beforehand, planning on a relatively quiet week of meetings, sight-seeing, and nightly banquets.

Within a day after they landed in China, news organizations in the
United States began falling over one another to publish stories in
advance of the signing, based on the embargoed background briefing.

This competitive rush apparently began with a weekly trade
publication, *Ward's Auto World*. On Monday *Ward's* began promoting on a public relations newswire a story it planned to publish
later in the week about AMC's contract with the Chinese. Other
news outlets felt that *Ward's* was breaking the embargo. *Ward's*
insisted that its own story had come not from Tippett's briefing,
but from a separate interview with Clare a few weeks earlier. Nonetheless, within the next twenty-four hours virtually all major
newspapers and TV networks in the United States published stories
about American Motors' deal in China, on grounds that the news
embargo had already been broken.

Sloan was amused and delighted. He hadn't planned it this
way, yet it was a lucky break. If he or Tippett had stood up on their
own to announce officially some major new AMC development
like this one, they would probably have made only the business
pages. But the way things worked out, the AMC deal was being
treated as unauthorized and unofficial news, as a scoop—and consequently the story jumped up a notch to the front pages. Not only
that, but if news of the China deal had broken only at the time of
the Thursday signing ceremony, it would have been a one-day affair
in the American press. When the story broke three days before the
official signing, Sloan decided he would try to see if he could get
stories into the press every day of the trip in China. At forty-six
Sloan had already been in the PR business for a long time, coming
to AMC after a stint at Ford. He was experienced enough to know
what to do. I'm going to make a week-long story out of this sucker,
Sloan said to himself.

On Tuesday Sloan got special permission from Chinese authorities to let photographers come into the factory and shoot Tippett
on the Chinese assembly line. Then he called the Associated Press
wire service, whose photographer wasn't particularly excited with
Sloan's offer. United Press International will be there, Sloan
bluffed, and the AP photographer decided to come. Next Sloan
called UPI and played the same game in reverse. Later in the week
Tippett posed alongside an AMC Jeep and a Chinese BJ212 jeep at
the Temple of Heaven, one of Beijing's leading historical sites.

AMC had had the foresight to ship one of its Jeeps to China in time for this photo opportunity.

As the final act in its public relations effort, AMC had scheduled a press conference for foreign correspondents in Beijing on Thursday morning, an hour after the contract was to be signed. On Wednesday Chinese officials shifted the time of the signing to late Thursday afternoon, explaining that French President François Mitterrand would be in the Great Hall of the People Thursday morning.

Despite all the briefings and news stories in the United States, Tippett was still afraid to make any official announcement of the contract with China before it was signed. He told Sloan to postpone the press conference, but Sloan had already done battle with the erratic Beijing telephones for one round of calls that week and doubted he would be able to reach everyone again. AMC went ahead with the press on Thursday morning, nervous that the company would be embarrassed if its Chinese partner backed out or demanded changes in the final hours.

To the relief of the AMC officials, there were no last-minute hitches. Shortly before four o'clock in the afternoon on May 5, 1983, the AMC delegation filed into the Great Hall of the People. Inside, the Americans found red carpets; exotic sweet, flowery scents; hostesses silently motioning directions; and, incongruously, a set of small wooden bleachers, placed in such a way that the visiting American delegation could have its picture taken with smiling Chinese hosts. Tippett thought the bleachers made the event seem like an American choir rehearsal.

The American Motors executives stood together on the bleachers while Tippett and Wu Zhongliang, manager of the Beijing Automobile Industry Corporation (BAIC), the official who was to become chairman of the new Beijing Jeep Corporation, sat at a table in front of them and put their names onto the contract.

Afterward the celebrants sipped champagne in a reception room inside the Great Hall. At one point Wu Zhongliang tugged at Tippett's elbow and took him aside to ask a question that was troubling him. "I've never been a chairman before," Wu said. "Can you tell me what a chairman does?" Tippett did his best to describe to Wu how, in the West, a chairman of the board helps to supervise a company's management. He thought Wu seemed like a typical Chinese bureaucrat, but a very nice man.

Some AMC officials had suggested that China's paramount leader, Deng Xiaoping, might be at the reception; instead the Chinese leadership was represented by a midlevel figure, Chen Muhua, minister of foreign economic relations and trade, the leading woman politician in China. Back in the United States there were signs of government interest and approval. Both U.S. Commerce Secretary Malcolm Baldrige and Chinese Ambassador to the United States Zhang Wenjin issued statements praising the new agreement.

On the way out from the Great Hall, Tippett, relieved that the contract had actually been signed, turned to Sloan and said, "You know, Jerry, you're really a lucky guy. If things hadn't worked out so well, you'd be responsible for one of the great Edsels of public relations history."

Others in the press corps later accused Sloan of orchestrating the entire week's worth of press coverage, including the leak by *Ward's Auto World*. "You played us like a Stradivarius," one reporter told him. Sloan insisted it had been an accident, and when he returned home to Detroit, he acted as though he were angry at the reporter for *Ward's*. Privately Sloan thought he should have given the guy a bottle of Scotch.

In a private memo to other AMC executives after his return home, Sloan summed up the benefits that these stories about China had provided to the company. "The press, radio, and television coverage of the American Motors joint agreement in China was phenomenal," he said. "It placed [the name] JEEP in headlines, news stories, and photographs to set the stage for the important introduction of the new generation of Jeep SportWagons, portrayed AMC as having an innovative international presence, gave credit to AMC for pulling off a business coup, and added a new dimension to American Motors." Sloan's boss, Tippett, was pleased. The China deal helped foster the image Tippett wanted for American Motors—that of a company with a pioneering spirit.

The most important and dramatic impact of Sloan's PR blitz had been on Wall Street. For several years American Motors had been perceived as a company in deep trouble. It had lost $66.1 million in the first quarter of 1983. Over the previous three years, from 1980 to 1983, it had reported twelve quarters in the red in a row, losing a total of $491 million. The company was in such severe financial trouble that it didn't even have the customary briefings for stock analysts; Sloan wanted to do so, but AMC's financial executives told him they shouldn't do it, at least not until the company had turned the corner. Now, the press coverage about China accomplished more than AMC could have done with the stock analysts, even if it had brought them a shipload of opium.

Within a period of twelve days, AMC's stock jumped 40 percent, from $7.50 a share to $10.50. For those with a financial stake in AMC, the Jeep deal had produced a huge short-term windfall.

Clare had been required to fly on from China to other business in Tokyo. Several years later—in 1986, when AMC stock was trading at levels ranging from $2 a share to $5—Clare said ruefully that he was a little sorry about that Tokyo stop. As vice president Clare had stock options at AMC, and if he had been back in the United States and exercised them right after the China deal, they would have been worth a lot of money.

But no matter. AMC and Clare were enjoying the glory as well as the money. The following year the trade magazine *Automotive News* included Clare as one of the seventeen Detroit executives on its annual "1984 Model Year Automotive All-Star Team." Clare was selected as Detroit's top executive for international operations. His picture appeared on the publication's cover, together with men like General Motors Chairman Roger B. Smith, Chrysler Vice Chairman Gerald Greenwald, and United Auto Workers President Owen Bieber. The only other AMC executive chosen for the all-star team was Sloan, who was named Detroit's leading public relations man.

"AMC's China venture was the main factor in Clare's election," reported *Automotive News*. Clare and AMC "are setting the pace among U.S. auto companies in digging up business in China," noted one of the magazine's selectors. Another of the *Automotive News* judges said of Clare: "If he can sell Jeeps in China, he could have sold Kelvinators in Alaska."[1]

7

Ceremonial Occasions

The Great Hall of the People is the largest building in Beijing. It takes up most of the west flank of Tiananmen Square, the huge, usually vacant open space in the center of the Chinese capital just south of the Forbidden City. Inside the Great Hall, Chinese leaders such as Mao, Deng, and Chou En-lai have entertained foreign leaders from around the world. The massive building has a banquet hall for five thousand people, an auditorium for ten thousand, and numerous smaller reception rooms. It has six different formal entrances, allowing Chinese foreign ministry officials, for example, to greet one delegation from Kuwait at a southern gate, while at the same time on the other side of the building, their colleagues throw their arms out to a North Korean delegation entering from the north. Chinese officials boast that in 1958–59, during Mao Tse-tung's Great Leap Forward, the Great Hall of the People was constructed within ten months—or less than a quarter of the time it took China and American Motors to negotiate their contract.

Foreign dignitaries are usually driven to the Great Hall of the People for welcoming ceremonies immediately after they first set foot in Beijing. They return to the Great Hall for some or all of their meetings with Chinese leaders. The Great Hall thus serves as a familiar backdrop for political events of great moment. During a visit by British Prime Minister Margaret Thatcher to Beijing in 1982, Chinese officials broke the news that China wanted to recover Hong Kong, the British Crown colony. Inside the Great Hall, Thatcher, apparently shaken, slipped on the red-carpeted stairs and fell to her knees. Thatcher came back to the Great Hall on December 19, 1984, to sign the agreement relinquishing British sovereignty over Hong Kong in 1997. On that day Thatcher and Deng stood in front of the wooden bleachers posing for photographs. Behind them stood smiling Chinese officials and British officials with expressions of sadness.

Visiting businessmen, on the other hand, rarely see the inside of the Great Hall so quickly. For foreign business leaders, entertainment there is saved as a reward, a symbol of official acceptance. After three or four years of negotiations in dingy hotels and conference rooms, the foreign company that signs a contract and is at last admitted into the Great Hall of the People has moved nearer to the center of Chinese power. What could be more impressive to business associates back home in the United States or Europe than to say you have just returned from a reception in your company's honor at the Great Hall of the People?

The 1983 ceremonies commemorating American Motors' contract in China were not unique. Through the early 1980s many of the world's most illustrious executives were ushered into the Great Hall of the People to sign or celebrate contracts for new business ventures in China. From the United States, so many board chairmen and chief executive officers made the trek to Beijing that their journeys became known as "the Westchester County syndrome." In the country clubs of the American suburbs, business leaders swapped stories about their trips to China, about their deals and their hopes for the future. It was not much different in London, Paris, Frankfurt, or Milan.

The parade of board chairmen included Carl H. Hahn of Volkswagenwerk AG, the West German car company, who signed a deal to produce passenger cars in Shanghai. The VW contract was concluded in October 1984, the year after the American Motors contract, at ceremonies attended by West German Chancellor Helmut Kohl. Hahn told the press that Volkswagen wanted "to establish a presence at an early stage in a promising market with evident long-term potential and sales prospects." The move into China was intended to be VW's "competitive bridgehead into Southeast Asia," Hahn said. Robert O. Anderson, the chairman of the board of the Atlantic Richfield Company (ARCO), made the journey to Beijing in 1985 to sign a deal for the development of natural gas reserves off China's coast in the South China Sea. "We anticipate this to be the start of an ongoing relationship in China," Anderson told reporters. "We expect to have further investments." As was so often the case, the deals that the Volkswagen and ARCO chairmen signed were soon to be beset by serious problems.

In the business leaders' rush to sign pieces of paper in China, no other Western executive could top Armand Hammer, the venerable chairman of Occidental Petroleum, the U.S. oil and coal conglomerate. In trying to negotiate a deal to develop a coal mine project in China, Hammer acted as though he were in a competition to see how often he could get his signature onto a piece of paper. In the early 1980s Hammer staged five different signing ceremonies in Beijing for the same coal project. Each of the first four marked what was a new, but still preliminary, stage of the process.

On each occasion Hammer acted as though the signing were a landmark event. His company churned out press releases and offered interviews with Hammer, who would quickly launch without invitation into reminiscences about his brief meeting with Lenin in 1921. Part of the motivation was simply Hammer's own ego and desire for publicity. (One Occidental staffer in China begged a reporter not to use his name in a news story, even though representatives of all rival companies were willing to be named. "There's only one person in my company who's allowed to be quoted by name about China in the press, and that's Hammer," he said. "We may not like it, but that's the rules.") Yet Hammer's showmanship also served a business purpose: he was trying to line up financing for the coal mine project and hoped that each series of news stories about a signing ceremony would help validate his deal in the banking community. By the time Hammer signed the final contract in the Great Hall of the People in June 1985, his credibility was so low that he felt obliged to tell reporters, "I guess you are wondering whether this is just another signing ceremony and there will be another. There will be no other signing. This is it."

The ceremonies to launch business contracts in China have a ritual quality to them. In early 1985, for example, Robert M. Schaeberle, chairman of the board of Nabisco Brands, Inc., flew into Beijing with several of the vice presidents from his corporate headquarters in Parsippany, New Jersey, to help launch a new venture to sell American-style crackers in China. Nabisco had been working on a deal in China for more than four years.

To a visitor from Nabisco, China must have seemed like a nation crying out for a good cracker: the only crackers sold in the Chinese stores were bland and had the consistency of sand. With the help of Chase Manhattan Bank representatives, who jokingly call themselves "marriage brokers," Nabisco had located a Chinese state-owned enterprise called Yili Products, with which to begin to talk about the possibilities of a joint venture. Nabisco executives then began an exotic form of product testing to see what sorts of crackers and snacks might sell in China. "We brought over five thousand pounds of stuff and let the Chinese taste it," explained Gerardo Rodriguez, Nabisco's vice president for operations. "I took everything, including Milk Bone dog biscuits. It was an amazing process. Once, one of the Chinese tasters told me there must be something wrong with one of the products, because it had turned into a dark color. It turned out he had an Oreo cookie."

After all the market testing, Nabisco settled on Ritz Crackers and Premium Saltines as the products most likely to be popular in China. They then signed their contract with Yili in ceremonies at the Great Hall of the People in a third-floor banquet hall called the Shandong Room, named in honor of one of China's twenty-nine provinces and regions. The room is notable for its astonishingly ugly decor. The wallpaper and rugs are a faded light green. Over a large banquet table, on a red banner of the type that once carried quotations from Mao, the Chinese had printed the words:

Yili-Nabisco Biscuit and Food Co. Ltd.
To Celebrate Establishment Reception

Schaeberle, standing at a microphone in front of a large banquet table, told the seventy assembled American and Chinese guests that Yili-Nabisco "looks forward to bringing nutritious food to the people. We look forward to doing it soon, and doing it prosperously for both of us." He went on to emphasize the importance of China to Nabisco. For years, Schaeberle said, Nabisco had been considered a large international business. Nevertheless, he went on, "No organization could claim to be worldwide today without an association with your country of China. Starting today, Nabisco can really say it is worldwide."

From the Chinese perspective, the presence of the chairman of the board of the foreign company, either at the beginning of negotiations or at the signing of a contract, served a number of important purposes. When they chose to be, the Chinese could be the world's best and most experienced hosts. They knew how to make sure that the world's top business leaders got warm, friendly, extravagant receptions in China, and that they left the country with favorable impressions.

Discussions of business were kept on a very lofty, abstract plane: board chairmen were flatteringly told that they need only agree to a few general principles, and that the details and fine print could be ironed out by their underlings. The result was that the chief executive left with the idea that his company was on the right track in China, that doing business in China was relatively easy. Other company officials—either lower-ranking executives from abroad or representatives stationed in China itself—thereafter found themselves on the defensive when problems arose.

The board chairmen who visited China in the early 1980s returned home believing they understood China well and got along splendidly with its top leadership. If a company had difficulty after the contract was signed, then the chairman felt it was the fault of his subordinates: they must be seeing the wrong people or approaching the Chinese in the wrong way. Why were his people in China always so negative and cynical about the place? Creating divisions between the representative on the spot in China and the boss back home is a skill in which Chinese leaders have long excelled. Dealing with China's Communist regime in the 1980s, the chairmen of the boards of Western companies reacted in much the same way that President Franklin Roosevelt did with the Nationalist regime during World War II. Why was General Joseph Stilwell, his commander in the China-Burma-India theater, always so negative about China? Roosevelt wanted to know. Why did Stilwell have such trouble with Chiang Kai-shek? He, Roosevelt, had met Chiang Kai-shek and knew how to deal with him.

In the view of Chinese officials, having the board chairmen attend the signing ceremonies underscored the importance of the relationship between the foreign company and China—and thus made it easier for the Chinese partner to make new demands or ask new favors of the foreign company as soon as the contract was signed. Western and Japanese businessmen learned to their surprise and chagrin that the signing of a contract often marked not the end of business negotiations, but the beginning of them. Once the signatures were on paper, the Chinese partner often began seeking new concessions. Sometimes these requests involved issues that were not covered in the contract; sometimes they sought to change provisions in the contract before the ink was dry.

Here, Western businessmen (particularly Americans) found themselves in conflict with Chinese traditions, concerning both the idea of "friendship" and the meaning of a "contract."

In modern-day America, a friend is someone with whom one has a close relationship that is based on compatibility and intangible qualities—and not, necessarily, on the favors or benefits the person might be able to bestow. If a person wants something from you, then his motives for friendship are impure and he isn't a *true* friend. In China, whether in personal or organizational relationships, a friend is by definition someone who does extraordinary favors for you, and someone who refuses to do these favors is by definition *not* your friend.

Moreover, in the West, and particularly the United States, with its traditions of law, a contract is an entity of fundamental importance, the final word in defining a relationship. But in China, with its traditions of rule by personal authority and not written constitution, a contract means far less; the contract is important not for its own sake, but as a symbol of harmonious relations between two parties. The signing of a contract shows that a foreign business and a Chinese enterprise get along well and want to do business with each other. Now that they are "friends," each side can begin to ask favors from the other side.

"The Chinese seem to have less feeling for the drama of agreement and little expectation that any formalized contract will end the process of negotiations," wrote Lucian Pye in his study of Chinese negotiating style.[1] "For the Chinese, the very achievement of a formalized agreement, like the initial agreement on principles, means that the two parties understand each other well enough that each can expect further favors from the other."

On some occasions China exploited the visiting board chairmen and chief executive officers for other purposes. The timing of signing ceremonies could be important; after a period of retrenchment, or when China wanted to attract more foreign investment, it could create the impression of change. It could also send the message to foreign companies that their competitors were moving into China, and that they should hurry to strike deals, too. Anderson's 1985 visit to sign the ARCO deal, for example, was timed by Chinese officials in such a way that news stories of the contract were published just as China was about to open up a series of new offshore oil tracts for bidding by foreign oil companies. The idea was to convey the message, at a time when the price of oil was low and multinational oil companies were beginning to lose their enthusiasm for China, that there was money to be made in drilling for oil off China's coastline.

None of these considerations deterred the board chairmen and CEOs. They had their own reasons for wanting to be personally identified with their new China ventures. China was associated in the West with change and the future. If China could ever reorganize itself properly, why, with its population and talent, it might dominate the world in a hundred years or so. Signing a deal in China showed that a chairman of the board was thinking ahead, planning his company's future. For a chairman of the board, a deal in China could mean publicity, visibility, and prestige.

When Anderson, the ARCO chairman, sat in his Beijing hotel room with three other high-ranking ARCO executives preparing to sign the natural-gas contract, he voiced one regret. "If we'd had any sense, we'd have brought a public relations guy along," he said. That was a sentiment shared by many of the executives visiting China. It wasn't long before two of the world's leading public relations companies, Hill & Knowlton and Burson-Marsteller, started up operations in China.

"We're probably in every other market already," said Robert S. Leaf, the president of Burson-Marsteller International in London, echoing the sentiments of Western executives in other industries. "We're the world's largest public relations firm, and we've got to be on the cutting edge of this business." Burson-Marsteller didn't open up an office in China; instead, it entered into a deal under which a subsidiary of the New China News Service, China's government-owned wire service, was to handle the international firm's business in China.

Hill & Knowlton, by contrast, opened its own office in Beijing, churning out press releases, inviting Chinese and foreign correspondents to signing ceremonies and news conferences, and helping out board chairmen and chief executive officers on their trips to Beijing. Like many of the international corporations it would later help, Hill & Knowlton launched its new venture in Beijing with elaborate ceremonies and lots of hoopla.

8

Presents and Megabucks

It was April 6, 1984, and President Reagan was about to make his first and only trip to China. In room 450 of the Old Executive Office Building in Washington, Deputy Assistant Secretary of Commerce Eugene Lawson was briefing the White House press corps on the bright prospects for American business in China. Reagan administration officials were going to great lengths to get reporters informed and excited about the trip, and one of the themes they kept emphasizing was the role the president could play in landing new contracts for American business.

"We're talking about megabucks," said Lawson. "It's my own view that we are on the eve of a whole new phase in our economic, commercial, and trade relations with China. And the reason for this can be summed up in four words: oil, hydropower, coal, and nuclear power." Lawson said he could predict safely that within five to seven years U.S. investment in China's oil industry would be between $10 billion and $15 billion. Within two years, he went on, Armand Hammer's mammoth coal mine project would be producing fifteen million tons of coal. In hydropower there would be enormous prospects for high-arch dams; in nuclear power China intended to build twelve plants within the next few years, each one worth $1 billion in reactors and equipment and another $1 billion or so in consultants' fees.

Robert McFarlane, Reagan's national security advisor, took things a step further. At another pretrip press briefing McFarlane predicted that along with billions of dollars in new business for U.S. companies in China, there would be "tens of thousands of Americans" living in the country. A few weeks later McFarlane upped his prediction by a power of ten, suggesting on nationwide television that "perhaps hundreds of thousands of Americans and other Westerners" would be going to China to work on oil, coal, and nuclear power projects.

Such rosy projections were in vogue. At the time of Reagan's trip, the China gold rush was on in earnest, and the United States, like other nations, was eager to participate. From around the world, presidents and prime ministers, Politburo members and cardinals, kings, queens, and princes traveled to China, bearing gifts and prospecting for deals.

In early 1984 China's economy seemed extraordinarily healthy. China had money to spend. The clampdown on expenditures of the 1979–82 period (including the delay or cancellations of contracts with foreign companies) had been successful, at least from China's point of view. China reported now that its reserves of gold and foreign currency had reached $19 billion. At the current levels of China's trade, the country had enough in reserve to cover eight months of imports (three months' reserves is generally considered sufficient).

China's domestic economy was also flourishing. By 1984, after five years of steadily increasing harvests, China no longer needed to import food and was turning into a grain-exporting nation. It was a year of glorious weather. There was so much rice, wheat, and corn in the fields that the main agricultural problem was finding a means to store it all. The harvest for 1984 was the largest in Chinese history. Satisfied that it had mastered the millennia-old problem of feeding its population, the Chinese Communist Party had shifted its focus to urban economic reforms.

Foreign governments were excited by China's increasing affluence. Reagan was not the only head of state eager to impress upon the Chinese leaders how much his country's businesses could do for China. Some heads of state were behaving in a way that must have confirmed the views of the old-line Chinese Marxists who believed that bourgeois governments were ruled by monopoly capital.

When West Germany's Prime Minister Helmut Kohl traveled to China in 1984, he brought with him representatives of Siemens, the West German nuclear manufacturer. When Queen Elizabeth and her husband, Prince Philip, visited Shanghai, they invited 120 British businessmen and their Chinese counterparts onto the royal yacht *Britannia* to take part in a floating "seminar" on the wonders of buying British.

Under Deng's leadership, China became adept at dangling the bait of future trade in front of foreign leaders. The British were probably the most susceptible. During their 1982–84 negotiations over the future of Hong Kong, Chinese officials repeatedly told the British that once the agreement transferring Hong Kong to Chinese sovereignty was finally signed, all "impediments" in relations between China and Britain would be resolved, and the British would then be in position to land Chinese trade and contracts. The zeal with which the British pursued commercial ties with China thus became an important factor in the negotiations. In 1984, after British Prime Minister Margaret Thatcher finally signed the Hong Kong agreement, Chinese Premier Zhao Ziyang promised Thatcher she could send a high-level British trade mission to China. The mission landed only a single contract for the upgrading of the Beijing Dump Truck Plant.

Some American businessmen and officials felt that, in comparison with the West Europeans and Japanese, the U.S. government wasn't doing enough for its private companies. It was helpful, they argued, to have your president or a prime minister talk directly to the Chinese prime minister about the importance of landing a particular contract for a specific company. Kohl, Thatcher, French President François Mitterrand, and other European leaders seemed willing to do that, but U.S. presidents wouldn't.

In 1984 Westinghouse was urging the Reagan administration to help the company win contracts for nuclear power plants in China. Its nuclear business in the United States had collapsed, and it needed to make sales in China in order to keep its factories running.

The international competition to sell nuclear reactors to China was fierce. Siemens had flown a delegation of Chinese officials to Europe and Brazil to inspect the company's nuclear plants. It galled Westinghouse that the French firm Framatome, which had obtained Westinghouse nuclear technology under license, seemed to have the inside track on the contract for the nuclear plant that the Chinese were planning to build at Daya Bay near Hong Kong. France's top political leadership had been lobbying the Chinese since 1979. Winning the Daya Bay nuclear contract had been the top item on the agenda when French President Giscard d'Estaing visited China in September 1980. When President François Mitterrand made his own trip in May 1983, Daya Bay once again figured

prominently. The French hoped that once China selected Framatome for the Daya Bay reactors, China would then stick with the
French company for other Chinese nuclear plants.

"Maggie Thatcher and Mitterrand are the leading salesmen in
their countries," grumbled Dwight Porter of Westinghouse. "No
one in this country gives a goddamn about exports." (When asked
about complaints such as Porter's, Arthur W. Hummel, Jr., the U.S.
ambassador to China, pointed out that U.S. officials were inhibited
by antitrust laws. If Reagan had put in a good word for Westinghouse nuclear plants, competitors such as General Electric could
have charged official favoritism.)

Begging for specific private contracts just wasn't the American
style. Lawson cautioned, "The president is not going out [to China]
as a trader. He's not going out to push individual projects [or to]
present some sort of project list to the Chinese." Rather, he said,
"The president is going out there to inform the Chinese that we
intend to be helpful in their economic modernization program, in
general, broad-brush strokes."

For Western Europe, China was important primarily because
of its commercial potential. The United States placed a higher premium on China's geopolitical importance in tying down Soviet
military forces in Asia. Still, commercial relations between the two
countries were significant, both for their own sake and as a means
of keeping China aligned with the West.

For the Chinese, Reagan's visit had important political implications. This was the most conservative and fervently anti-Communist American president in a half century. During his 1980
campaign, Reagan had suggested upgrading relations with Taiwan;
Peter Hannaford, Reagan's former aide from his days as governor of
California, was Taiwan's public relations agent in the United
States. A visit by Reagan to Beijing would eliminate any lingering
hope Taiwan ever had of galvanizing American conservatives to
attempt to overturn the 1979 U.S. recognition of the Communist
regime. Reagan's trip would also further undermine any resistance
on the right wing of American politics toward supplying American
technology to a Communist country. In exchange, China would
welcome Reagan warmly and boost his 1984 reelection campaign,
just as China had helped Richard Nixon's reelection twelve years
earlier.

. . .

To show that Reagan's trip to China was more than just public relations, the two sides needed some agreements to sign. In the months before Reagan's trip, there was talk of having the president sign a treaty with China spelling out rules and providing detailed legal safeguards for private American companies investing in China. But negotiations broke down a month before Reagan's trip. The United States wanted language guaranteeing that American companies could transfer any profits they earned inside China back to the United States. The Chinese regime refused, arguing that the disposition of profits should be resolved on a case-by-case basis.

U.S. negotiators also sought language guaranteeing that any American joint venture in China would be treated as a Chinese enterprise. This was standard language in American investment treaties with other nations, but it made no sense to the Chinese. In China, foreigners—both individuals and businesses—are almost always treated differently from Chinese. Foreigners usually pay higher prices than Chinese; on the other hand, they are shielded from the crowds, the long waits, and other unpleasant realities of ordinary Chinese life. Chinese officials argued that American companies or their joint ventures could not possibly be treated like Chinese enterprises under China's socialist system. For example, they pointed out, the Chinese government was legally obligated to subsidize Chinese enterprises in order to prevent them from going bankrupt.[1] China certainly didn't want to have to subsidize a failing American joint venture. On the other hand, foreign companies had greater leeway to punish or dismiss Chinese workers than did Chinese enterprises. Chinese officials argued that an American company wouldn't want to operate under Chinese rules, which virtually guaranteed lifetime employment.

With the investment treaty stalled, Chinese and U.S. officials looking for a deal to sign during the Reagan trip turned their attention to the field of nuclear power. A nuclear agreement with China was being pushed upon the Reagan administration by the American nuclear industry. Westinghouse and several other influential companies, including General Electric and Bechtel, were hoping to sell nuclear equipment, technology, and designs to China. In addition, American utility companies—some of which had built nuclear plants inside the United States and had then been forced to close them because of the antinuclear movement—were privately offering to sell their unused American plants to China for 10 percent of their original cost. Without a government-to-government nuclear agreement, none of these companies could do business in China.

Under U.S. law, American companies are permitted to sell nuclear technology only to countries that agree to a series of safeguards aimed at limiting the spread of nuclear weapons. In China these requirements were a touchy subject. China had possessed nuclear weapons for two decades and thus could hardly be accused of using nuclear power as a covert means of developing nuclear weapons. Furthermore, since the 1960s China had been arguing that U.S. and Soviet efforts at preventing the spread of nuclear weapons amounted to a conspiracy through which the two superpowers intended to dominate the rest of the world.

The turning point in the nuclear negotiations came in January 1984, three months before Reagan's trip to Beijing, when Chinese Premier Zhao Ziyang visited Washington. At a state dinner, Zhao offered a banquet toast in which he pledged that "we do not engage in nuclear proliferation ourselves, nor do we help other countries develop nuclear weapons." On the eve of Reagan's departure for China, U.S. negotiators accepted this language as the formal guarantee necessary for a nuclear agreement between the two countries.

At every stop on the presidential trip to China, Reagan administration officials pressed the twin themes that there were fabulous prospects for American businesses in China and that the White House was doing all it could for U.S. companies. Commerce became the principal justification for the trip.

In Honolulu, Reagan's first stopover, McFarlane leaked news of the impending nuclear agreement to reporters traveling with the president. The stories, which made front-page news in the United States, were coupled with suggestions of billions of dollars of new business for the American nuclear industry.

Soon after arriving in China, the president gave a speech on Chinese television emphasizing the importance of Sino-American trade and economic relations. (Reagan also threw in some anti-Soviet remarks, telling the Chinese that "America's troops are not massed on China's borders," but the Chinese regime censored these lines from the broadcast.) Later in the trip Reagan toured a new American joint venture, one in which the Foxboro Company of Massachusetts was beginning to manufacture industrial-control instruments in China. "Business partnerships between Chinese and American companies are bound to succeed," declared the president.

While in Beijing, the White House entourage and press corps stayed at the Great Wall Hotel, the twenty-two-story, glass-enclosed tourist facility that C. B. Sung had struggled for years to build. There had been long delays while American and Chinese engineers argued over the hotel's construction. Even when the Great Wall opened its doors in December 1983, only forty rooms were ready for use. By the time of Reagan's trip, 800 of the 1,007 rooms had been finished, and some of them were being slept in for the first time. The hotel epitomized the image of sleek modernity China aimed to present to the world. Yet its construction defects, its bashful new workers, and its silent, eerie detachment from the surrounding city demonstrated how far China had to go in achieving that modernity.

The Reagans were lodged in the blue-tiled presidential villa at China's Diaoyutai State Guest House, rather than at the new hotel. But they chose the Great Wall Hotel's Grand Ballroom as the setting for the plush dinner they hosted in honor of Premier Zhao and other Chinese officials.

For weeks officials of the U.S. embassy in Beijing had been sending "immediate" cables back to the White House, seeking "first family approval" of menus, table settings, dinner music, and seating arrangements. American officials working on the dinner cabled the White House that the Great Wall's tableware was "not . . . of the quality we think necessary," and urged that White House china be brought to China on the presidential plane.[2] Under Nancy Reagan's direction, U.S. officials also arranged to fly 150 turkeys to the hotel for what a White House press release said would be a "thoroughly American" dinner.

So elaborate were Nancy Reagan's preparations for the China trip that she won an odd compliment from Deng Xiaoping. As the Reagans sat down for their first meeting with Deng, he turned to Nancy Reagan and joked, "Your first visit [to China] is really too short. I hope you'll come the next time and leave the president home. You come just by yourself, independently. You can bring your grandchildren along. We won't maltreat you." Deng laughed. Reagan, assuming the smile of the genial, tolerant husband, broke in, "It sounds like I'm the one being maltreated."

On the night of the Reagans' state banquet, Sung's wife, Beulah, waited inside the Great Wall Hotel with red "First Lady" roses she had imported to Beijing for Nancy Reagan. Just before the presidential motorcade arrived, U.S. Secret Service agents rushed into the hotel, took the roses from Beulah Sung's hands, and examined them carefully. The roses passed inspection.

Approximately three hundred Chinese officials and three hundred Americans were invited to the banquet. The guest list concentrated on leaders of business and industry in the two nations.[3] The Americans included the Beijing representatives of U.S. corporations such as Boeing, American Motors, IBM, Pennzoil, Kodak, Exxon, the Fluor Corporation, Wang Laboratories, ARCO, Honeywell, Hewlett-Packard, Chemical Bank, Chase Manhattan, and American Express.

At one table, Sung and the redoubtable Armand Hammer sat with representatives of the Chinese coal and machine-building ministries. (Hammer—who at that point hadn't concluded the final deal for his coal mine—attempted to have Reagan attend yet another signing ceremony for Occidental Petroleum while in Beijing, but White House officials rebuffed the request.) Nearby, Dr. Daniel Ruge, the president's physician, was seated with Dr. George Hatem, the famed Lebanese-American who had been living in China ever since the Communist takeover and was widely credited with having wiped out syphilis in the country.

In his banquet toast, Reagan said the United States and China "have begun economic exchanges that are growing in importance every day. . . . Already, some of the many joint Chinese-American business ventures have begun to bear fruit. This magnificent hotel is the outcome of just such a joint venture."

On April 30, 1984, just before leaving Beijing, Reagan stood as witness in the Great Hall of the People while his negotiators signed the nuclear agreement. "It brings a new dimension of peaceful cooperation to our relationship," he said. "This agreement will permit American firms and experts to help China meet the ambitious energy goals of its modernization program."

Reagan also signed an income tax agreement negotiated before the trip that set the ground rules for the taxation of American companies investing in China. The tax agreement "will make it easier for Chinese and American firms to engage in trade and cooperate in joint ventures," announced the president.

It was a far different Reagan from the anti-Communist candidate who had asked in 1979, at the time the Carter administration reestablished diplomatic relations with Beijing, "Haven't we . . . betrayed millions and millions of Chinese on the mainland who lived with a dream of one day regaining freedom?" At that time, only five years earlier, Reagan branded the People's Republic of China "a statist monopoly founded on violence and propaganda, and destructive of the humane tradition of the Chinese people themselves."

Now, in 1984, even the most obvious symbols of ideology were being either ignored or translated into the terms and ideas of American commerce and advertising. As Reagan headed for the Beijing airport, his motorcade drove through Tiananmen Square, which was decorated for the following day's May Day parade with huge portraits of Karl Marx, Friedrich Engels, Vladimir Lenin, and Josef Stalin. (Stalin has remained an official hero in China even as his legacy is being attacked in the Soviet Union.) White House Press Secretary Larry Speakes acknowledged Reagan had seen the pantheon of Communist heroes in the Chinese capital but made light of their significance. "He [Reagan] thought they were the Smith Brothers [the bearded figures on the boxes of American cough drops]," Speakes joked.

Later, flying back to the United States on Air Force One, Reagan referred to China as "this so-called Communist country."

"They [Chinese leaders] are opening up now that American concerns can create branches of their own in China, in this so-called Communist China," the president observed. "And they [American companies] don't have to be in partnership with anyone, and capitalism will be there in these plants."

At the end of the trip, Secretary of State George Shultz depicted the nuclear accord as the most important tangible accomplishment of Reagan's six-day stay in China. Yet Reagan's agreement turned out to be virtually meaningless.

Congress did not know that China's promises to prevent the spread of nuclear weapons were based exclusively on Zhao's banquet toast rather than written guarantees. When this fact was made public shortly after Reagan returned home from China, the agreement ran into trouble. Meanwhile, U.S. intelligence agencies reported that Chinese nuclear scientists had been secretly helping Pakistan to develop nuclear weapons. The nuclear agreement with

China ran into strong opposition in Congress from three separate constituencies: those seeking strict controls on the spread of nuclear technology; supporters of Taiwan; and supporters of Israel, who feared that Pakistan might help other Islamic countries build nuclear weapons.

In the face of this opposition, the Reagan administration postponed asking for congressional approval of the agreement. Two months after Reagan's trip, U.S. officials began seeking new assurances from Chinese officials that were firmer than Zhao's banquet toast. Infuriated, Chinese officials denied giving help to Pakistan and said no new commitments were required. Over the following year, China's National People's Congress passed a new law promising to protect nuclear technology, and U.S. intelligence agencies reported that there was no longer any evidence of Chinese nuclear scientists in Pakistan. At the end of 1985 the Sino-American nuclear deal was finally approved.

But the long delay was deadly for Westinghouse. China awarded Framatome the Daya Bay contract. British firms won contracts to supply turbines and other equipment to Daya Bay. Whether this amounted to a victory for the French was questionable, because in the end China negotiated such a low price that distraught French officials said it would be difficult to make any money from Daya Bay. Meanwhile, in 1985 China announced that it would use its own Chinese-made reactors at a second nuclear plant in Jiangsu Province, near Shanghai, forsaking the help of Siemens, Framatome, Westinghouse, and other foreign companies. Plans for other nuclear power plants in China were held up, and Chinese officials began to talk instead about the value of small, thermal-fired power plants.

Westinghouse had hoped to sell China as many as six nuclear reactors. It wound up selling none.

A few years later it turned out that all of the predictions of Reagan administration officials such as McFarlane and Lawson about the great prospects for American business in China were wildly optimistic.

China's offshore oil reserves were not as great as had been believed in 1984. The low price of coal slowed down Hammer's mine project. China scaled back its plans for nuclear power and decided to do some of the work on its own. McFarlane's idea that

China was willing and ready to open up its doors to hundreds of thousands of Westerners showed a profound misunderstanding, at the highest levels of the Reagan administration, of the realities of China's history, leadership, politics, and public opinion.

Nevertheless, the overall effect of Reagan's trip was to legitimize the idea that Americans could do business in China—and that in fact companies might be missing the boat if they didn't try to get into the China market.

Living in China: The Lost Boys

If the president or others on his trip were looking carefully, they could have seen some signs that the reality of Western businessmen in China was not quite as attractive as the grand rhetoric of the banquet toasts. Now that Western companies were signing deals, a few of their employees were beginning to move to China. These foreign residents of China became a new element in the equation.

In Beijing, members of the presidential party met Lauren Giglio, one of the first American Motors officials assigned to AMC's China venture. Newly arrived in Beijing with his wife and small children, he looked lost and overwhelmed. While Giglio waited for permanent housing for himself and his family, they found themselves confined to tiny hotel rooms at the Great Wall that cost more than $100 per night. For the moment there didn't seem to be any space for his children in Beijing's small international school.

When Reagan visited the Foxboro plant, its general manager, Donald N. Sorterup, made little effort to disguise the frustrations he and his company had experienced since starting operations in Shanghai the previous year. The first year in China "has not been a totally calm journey," Sorterup admitted. He told Reagan, "As your trip is nearing an end, ours is just beginning."

Those who came to work in China had an entirely different perspective on the country from their company presidents or board chairmen. They were not thinking of the China of the twenty-first century, but of how to get through the day. They were impressed less by the huge potential of the China market than by the colossal inefficiencies they confronted at the factories or offices where they were working. Their personal ties to China were colored not by the expansive warmth of a Chinese vice premier or state minister, but by the malice of the Customs Bureau, the awful condition of the state airlines, the rapacity of the government agency that supplied them with office staff.

For foreign businessmen or workers, China worked in reverse fashion from other Third World countries. In most developing countries, the foreign business representative would often become convinced that the place to which he was assigned had tremendous potential. But whenever such an enthusiastic businessman cabled home about the great prospects he foresaw in this remote location, his bosses at company headquarters would think their man had lost all perspective, had gone native, lost his mind.

China was the opposite. In China the enthusiasts were the bosses in the executive suite back home, and the skeptics were the men and women trying to work inside China.

Ed Schulze had lived half his life without thinking much about China. He had been working as maintenance manager at the American Motors plant in Kenosha, Wisconsin, and when a job opened up to help set up a new assembly line at the factory in Beijing, Schulze, then forty-two years old, grabbed it. He went without his family: his wife stayed behind in her own job at Stamp-On Tools in Kenosha. His two daughters were grown, one of them in the U.S. Air Force.

Schulze was attracted primarily by the money AMC was offering. If you went to China, you got a big promotion, up two pay scales within the company. Furthermore, there was a 25 percent addition to your salary for hardship pay. With the promotion and the hardship pay, most of AMC's staffers in China earned $7,000 to $8,000 a month. Schulze had been earning about $5,000 a month in the United States. Under a company-sponsored tax equalization program, AMC paid Schulze's taxes, so that the China earnings were virtually tax free. Because there was little in China to spend money on, Schulze found that he could easily put away $6,000 a month in savings. In addition to the salary, AMC gave each of its employees in China coupons for gas and another $15 per day in spending money, which Schulze figured just about paid for his beer. From China, each AMC staffer got three trips a year back home to the United States, with first-class air tickets, and another $1,500 a year for a week of rest and recreation in Hong Kong, Bangkok, or Manila.

Schulze couldn't speak any Chinese and hadn't had time to learn. In China he found that communication was a problem even in English, which some of the Chinese dealing with foreigners had not quite mastered. When he arrived in China, he stayed at the Yanxiang Hotel, a small, sparse, poorly constructed building near the road to the Beijing airport. The first day, he picked up the phone and asked for a luggage cart to bring up his cartons of books. "You want to make a long-distance call?" said the hotel operator. They went on like that, over and over again, Schulze shouting, "Luggage cart!" and the operator replying, "Long-distance call?"[1]

In his early months in China, Schulze did a lot of sight-seeing and shopping for Chinese artifacts. But he was working a grueling twelve to sixteen hours a day at the factory, and after a while the novelty of exploration wore off. On his days off he would simply sleep, go off to the hills, or stay in his room listening to music and reading.

"You want to get away from the people," he explained. Real relaxation came from the trips out to Hong Kong or the United States.

The foreigners working in China generally fell into three categories. The first were the China hands: those who had studied Chinese history and language and then gravitated to jobs in business that would take them to China. The second were the overseas Chinese: Hong Kong Chinese or Chinese-Americans who were employed by Western companies to help make contact in China. And the third were the careerists who had no particular background in China but had gone for money or career advancement.

A handful were there simply because their companies needed someone in China quickly.

Ted Welatoc, a thin, blond young chemist for an American company that tested the quality of offshore oil, was working in Dallas in 1985 when his boss called him into his office. "Ted, we've got a proposition for you," his boss said. "We want you to go overseas." The company was offering him a choice, either China or Bangladesh. Welatoc knew enough to realize that Bangladesh was one of the poorest countries in the world, a real basket case. "That's easy. I'll choose China," he replied.

Welatoc was dispatched to Canton, the city where most of the foreign oil companies drilling in the South China Sea were based. There was no one to greet him at the airport when he arrived in China, and when he asked for the Dongfang Hotel in his Arkansas twang, it took ten Cantonese taxi drivers before one of them recognized what he was saying. For the first week, Welatoc was sick and nearly quit. His predecessor had bailed out of the China job within three months, but Welatoc was determined to hang on.

Soon after his arrival, Welatoc discovered that his company didn't have an operation in Bangladesh. "Giving me a choice of countries was just to make me feel better when I got over here," he explained.

However they had happened to come to China, whatever their circumstances, the foreign businessmen usually found themselves facing the same obstacles. The most important problem was housing and office space. When China opened its doors in the late 1970s, the country had no space at all to accommodate the waves of foreign businessmen who began flooding into the country.

For the first wave of businessmen, the focus of life became China's cavernous old hotels, many of them built by the Russians in the 1950s: the Beijing and Qianmen hotels in Beijing; the Jinjiang Hotel in Shanghai; the Dongfang in Canton. These old hotels weren't the Ritz, yet they began to cost as much.

At the beginning of 1981, Hervé Pauze, the Beijing representative of Rhône-Poulenc, the giant French pharmaceutical firm, moved into a two-room suite at the Beijing Hotel, where he paid 3,600 yuan (about $1,300) a month in rent. After four years he was paying 8,400 yuan ($3,000). There was no comparable increase in service or other benefits. "We still have the same good-looking cockroaches, the same rats in the corridor," Pauze said. "It's still overheated in the winter and overcooled in the summer."

Tokyo prices for Chinese quality: it represented a significant change, Pauze said. "When I got here [in 1981], we paid what seemed like a high price for a dirty little hotel room, but it was much less expensive than Tokyo. Today, the room is still small and dirty, but the price is the same as you would pay in Tokyo."

And yet, Pauze acknowledged, his company would stay on and

continue to pay. His company was already making some money in China and hoped to make more. "You cannot pack up and leave China, because the market is here," he admitted. "They [Chinese officials] know that when you take the world economy, there are very few countries with anything near the potential of China. There are four billion people in the world, and one billion of them are in China. You can't really say, 'I don't care.' We are like sheep here, ready to be sheared."

By 1984 the focus of the business community began to shift to newly completed joint-venture hotels such as the Jianguo, the Great Wall, and the Lido-Holiday Inn in Beijing and the White Swan, the Garden, and the China in Canton. These were elaborate complexes with coffee shops, bars, delicatessens, discotheques, swimming pools, and even bowling alleys. Their staffs were Chinese, their management generally foreign, and their clientele exclusively foreign.

The hotels in Beijing stationed Chinese security guards at the front door to make sure no ordinary Chinese walked inside. The glitzy, strobe-lit Juliana's discotheque at the Lido-Holiday Inn was notorious for its strict segregation. Chinese officials would stand outside guarding the discotheque from native Chinese. When in doubt, the gatekeepers would stare at the entrants' clothes and shoes: a Hong Kong Chinese would be dressed more expensively than a Beijing local.

In Canton the hotels were more permissive. Hotel workers there found it more difficult to distinguish a local resident from a Hong Kong Chinese. Residents of Canton were often better dressed than residents of northern China; they spoke the same Cantonese dialect as Hong Kong Chinese (who, in some instances, were their own relatives). On Sunday afternoons Cantonese families made sight-seeing tours through the lobbies of the strange new hotels where the foreigners lived.

Throughout northern China, the foreigners-only hotels produced tremendous resentment among ordinary Chinese—resentment not only of the foreigners, but also of the Chinese leadership that allowed this segregation. "Some high-level cadres, they are all for opening up China, but only for themselves," said one young Chinese moments after he was forced to leave Beijing's Lido-Holiday Inn. In one city, Chengdu, municipal authorities sought to ease local resentment over foreigners-only hotels by establishing a disco exclusively for Chinese—no foreigners allowed—on the top floor of the foreigners' Jinjiang Hotel.

By the last half of the 1980s, the foreign businessmen and women didn't have to live in hotels, because a few apartment complexes and office buildings began to open up in the leading Chinese cities. In some cases the apartments were attached or next door to the foreigners-only hotels. The plumbing didn't always work, and the fixtures didn't always fit. With fewer Chinese working inside the apartment complexes, the units were even more insulated from the ordinary run of Chinese life than the hotels had been. But the apartments were spacious and reasonably comfortable. They were also astonishingly expensive.

In 1985 Stephen E. W. Mulder found a way to save his firm, the Cummins Engine Company, some money in China. He rented an apartment in Beijing for $72,000 a year. The rent was payable one year in advance and didn't include utilities or a $300-a-month management fee.

This didn't sound like much of a bargain. Mulder doubted there was a single apartment that expensive in the state of Indiana, where Cummins had its corporate headquarters. But Mulder had learned to operate by different standards. At the time he rented the apartment, he and his wife, Linda, and their three children were living in a three-room suite at the Great Wall Hotel, where the rent was more than $125,000 a year and where the monthly laundry bills ran $400. "My personnel director back home asked me if I had thought of a Laundromat," said Mulder, laughing at the thought of trying to find a Laundromat in China.

The Mulders had tried to cook in their hotel suite, but it took three hours to find the right food and another couple of hours to prepare it. They gave up and paid the expense of room service. Meanwhile, Mulder's office rent had been raised 40 percent, and the government-run Foreign Enterprise Service Corporation (FESCO) was trying to require his company to hire a full-time driver.

When I wrote a story about Mulder and his $72,000-a-year rent for the *Los Angeles Times*, his own company was displeased. Cummins dispatched one of its executives from the United States to Beijing to make sure Mulder didn't discuss such things in the press

again. At the time, Cummins was in the midst of a series of cutbacks in Indiana. Mulder was told Cummins's workers and labor
unions might cause trouble if they saw how much money the company was spending in China.

The Chinese, of course, had simply calculated what foreign companies were willing to pay to do business in China and raised the
prices accordingly.

The increases began in 1980. Within a matter of weeks businessmen discovered that the cost of installing a telephone went
from $20 to $1,400 and the price of a telex machine from $100 to
$2,800. Restaurants started charging foreigners as much as $120
per person. The government-run agencies that provided personnel
to Western businesses demanded $700 a month for a translator,
even though the translator himself was given no more than $70 a
month in take-home pay.

The Chinese government didn't hesitate to make foreigners
pay two, three, or ten times as much as their own citizens, even for
public services like airplane and train tickets. In 1982 flying from
Beijing to Shanghai cost $37 for Chinese and $87 for foreigners.
That was simply part of the system; foreigners and Chinese were
different. Starting in 1980, China imposed a new income tax on
foreign businessmen of up to 45 percent of their salaries. The customs duties for office equipment was raised between 100 and 200
percent. At the end of 1984, the duty on imported cars was raised
from 80 percent to 120 percent and then, in the spring of 1985, to
260 percent. A new Toyota that cost $8,000 without duty thus shot
up to $28,800.[2]

In 1985 the Beijing representatives of the European Economic
Community presented a detailed report to the Chinese government
complaining about the price increases. The living conditions and
prices encountered by businessmen in China "are now so serious
as to act as a deterrent to some companies setting up offices here,"
the report said. Individual governments and businesses made similar complaints.

But the complaints had little effect. China remained a country
where prices of raw materials, labor, even the most minute objects,
were generally fixed by the government—and where, in those instances when prices were allowed to float, vendors often made use
of monopoly power to charge whatever the market would bear.

Chinese officials argued that the high prices they imposed were merely in line with what foreign businessmen were paying in Tokyo, Hong Kong, New York, and Paris.

However, the EEC report found that in some instances the Chinese prices were even higher than in these other world capitals. Beijing's first office complex for foreign companies, the China International Trust and Investment Corporation (CITIC) building, demanded rents that were twice the going rate in Hong Kong and four times the rates in Paris. Yet the quality of the offices was well below the standards of other cities. The twenty-nine-floor CITIC building was constructed without parking space; its expensive offices had no private toilets; and its four elevators were so inadequate that there was usually at least a five-minute wait on the crowded ground floor.

In effect, the price increases amounted to a sort of license fee —China's way of imposing a tax, or charge, for the privilege of doing business in the country. As long as the businesses were willing to pay these sums, China was not going to pass up the opportunity.

Particularly in the major Chinese cities, the foreigners lived an isolated life. They dined together, shopped together, drank together, and dated each other. In Beijing, Charlie's Bar at the Jianguo Hotel, a small, darkly lit room overlooking an interior courtyard, became the setting where businessmen recounted to one another the agonizing stories of stymied negotiations, broken contracts, and doubled rent. Businessmen also gravitated to the Bell, the pub at the British embassy where beer and darts offered a change of pace.

To be sure, there were exceptions. Everyone had a couple of Chinese friends, and some of those businessmen whose Chinese was good had more than a few. But social mixing was strictly channeled and limited. Either the foreigners and Chinese met at banquets, from which the Chinese would depart, punctually, at 8:30 P.M., or the businessmen could entertain informally, meeting select friends at restaurants or, sometimes, in each other's homes. But these informal meetings were usually awkward. There was no neutral turf, and there was little or no privacy. If the foreign businessman invited a Chinese friend to his hotel room or apartment, both of them would have to prepare themselves for the stares, or questions, of Chinese guards, floor attendants, and elevator operators, who reported to China's security apparatus. If they went to the apartment of a Chinese friend, they often had the sense that the neighbors upstairs, downstairs, across the hall, and at the front gate were watching. For the Chinese, the rules were unclear: no one knew whether you had to register at the front desk of the foreigners' hotel this month or not, whether you had to inform the neighborhood committee or the police that you were having a foreigner over to your place.

Sex was, of course, even riskier. It wasn't completely out of the question: some foreign businessmen and women managed to carry on relationships with Chinese. But the consequences of getting caught, for both sides, could be severe.

One of the Beijing residents for American Motors was accused by Chinese officials of sleeping with a Chinese telex operator working for the joint venture. Chinese officials asked AMC to send the man home, and AMC did so, figuring that if the company didn't go along, China would have expelled him anyway. In several other instances, foreign businessmen were thrown in jail, at least overnight, and forced to pay heavy fines for having Chinese women in their hotel rooms.

In the late 1980s China's traditional suspicion of foreigners was compounded by its efforts to keep AIDS out of the country. China was the only major country in the world where contacts between citizens and foreigners were so limited that it was feasible for health officials to hope to stop the spread of AIDS by limiting sex with foreigners. In September 1987 officials in Beijing approved a series of anti-AIDS measures that forbid sexual contact with foreigners.[3]

Surrounded by scarcity, foreigners swapped stories about what few things were available to buy. It was big news in 1984 when imported bananas became so abundant that they were available on the streets of Beijing at virtually any time of year. It was even bigger news in 1986 when a Western "supermarket"—actually a small package store—opened up inside the Lido-Holiday Inn Hotel. The prices were outrageous, but it meant that businessmen with small children no longer had to lug a three-month supply of Pampers on the flight from Hong Kong.

Families sent their children to special schools for foreigners.

The foreign business community in Beijing helped support the International School, which was run by five English-speaking embassies (the United States, Britain, Canada, Australia, and New Zealand); and there were separate schools for French, German, Japanese, Indian, and Pakistani children. The International School grew so large and admission became so difficult that some applicants wound up going to the Indian school instead.

Even the workday lunch usually became a separate affair. Western businessmen might eat in a Chinese dining room for a few weeks, but after a while they found that they couldn't take the food anymore. It was not like the Chinese restaurants at home; there were strange ingredients, low-grade cooking oils, and peculiar smells, and after a while it all began to taste the same.

In Canton, Ted Welatoc quickly gave up on eating in the Chinese cafeteria of the Nanhai East building; instead, he asked the White Swan Hotel to pack him a sandwich for work. In Beijing, Schulze, like other AMC employees, drove from the jeep factory to the Jianguo Hotel, where he ate with other Westerners at the buffet of Charlie's Bar. There was an artificiality and a lack of variety in the food at the Western hotels: the hamburgers didn't taste right, most of the food seemed like plastic, and you could get awfully tired of Qingdao beer and canned Sunkist Orange soda. But at least they were vaguely familiar.

When businessmen traveled outside the major cities, they faced different obstacles. Rail travel was pleasant, but too slow for long distances. Air travel in China was unpredictable and hazardous. Virtually everyone in the small business community knew someone from Boeing or McDonnell Douglas or the British-French Airbus consortium with harrowing stories about inattention to maintenance and safety. Some of the foreign aviation experts simply refused to travel on CAAC, the national airline, which was such a symbol of inefficiency that it became the one institution that even the most careful Chinese felt free to criticize openly in the presence of foreigners.

The greatest hazard on the road was to become embroiled in some dispute with local officials. One of the enduring slogans of Chinese political life maintained, "The mountain is high and the emperor is far away." No matter what the current policies were in

Beijing, local officials wielded tremendous power. Acting on behalf of local enterprises, they could limit a businessman's travel—or his freedom.

In November 1981 Danuta Hocker, director of a Hong Kong picture frame company called Artpost International, was held in Canton and barred from leaving China for more than three weeks because of a contract dispute. She was allowed to leave her hotel and travel around Canton, but her exit visa was canceled, and Chinese security officials took her British passport. Mrs. Hocker had refused to accept or pay for approximately $15,000 worth of timber she had ordered from the Number Two Machinery Factory of Taishan, because she felt it was defective and below specifications. Chinese officials argued that regardless of her complaints, she was required to pay the agreed-upon price. After six court hearings, the two sides reached a compromise on a reduced price and Mrs. Hocker was free to depart from China.[4]

The most ill-fated of all foreign business trips in China was the one that Richard S. Ondrik of Kokomo, Indiana, made to the Manchurian city of Harbin on April 18, 1985.

Ondrik, thirty-four, an alumnus of Middlebury College's special intensive Chinese language program and a former employee of the National Council for U.S.-China Trade, was working for a Hong Kong firm called Energy Products Southeast Asia Ltd. He and a Chinese-American business partner, Alan Eng, went to Harbin to try to sell oil equipment to a Chinese refinery. They checked into the Swan Hotel, a new, cheaply built eleven-story hotel on the edge of town, and then went off for the customary six o'clock banquet with refinery officials. It was the usual routine on the road, an endless series of new dishes and refilling of glasses. Ondrik later testified that he had between eight and ten glasses of Chinese *mao tai*, as well as perhaps four glasses of wine and a few beers. He insisted he became "happy, but not drunk."

The refinery officials ended the banquet at eight o'clock. Like so many other foreign businessmen in China, Ondrik, with little else to do, returned to his hotel early and checked for telexes from the home office. He found a message and wanted to send a reply, but the telex office was too crowded. So he returned to his room, room 1116 on the eleventh floor.

What happened next is a matter of dispute. Chinese prosecutors later said Ondrik sat down on his bed, lit a cigarette, and then fell asleep. Ondrik testified that he didn't recall smoking in bed but conceded he may well have done so. There is no dispute that on that night, the eleventh floor of the Swan Hotel erupted in flames. Ondrik fled to safety, but Eng, his business partner in a room down the hall, choked to death from smoke inhalation, and nine other people—four Chinese hotel employees and five hotel guests in a delegation from nearby North Korea—died trying to leap to safety.

It turned out that the hotel had purchased smoke detectors and exit lights but failed to install them. There were no fire-rated doors or sprinkler systems. A fire extinguisher didn't work. Because the telephone lines didn't work, either, it took thirty minutes to notify the Harbin fire department and another five minutes for them to reach the hotel. Gu Su, the Chinese attendant assigned to the eleventh floor, admitted that he had left his post and was off taking a bath in room 816 when the fire broke out. The hotel's nighttime security chief, Zhang Guoyun, had gone to a dance in the hotel ballroom and had at least three drinks; it was Zhang's responsibility to have the emergency exits opened and the water taps turned on, but he admitted he had neglected to do so.

In the United States, the Swan Hotel would have been deluged with negligence and liability suits. But the Chinese legal system is not geared to American notions of negligence and is far more accustomed to prosecuting individuals on criminal charges. While a Chinese prosecutor, Zhang Weixiao, admitted that the Swan Hotel "had some serious problems in fire protection," he and other law-enforcement officials in Harbin held the fire to be mainly Ondrik's responsibility. After the fire, Ondrik was first questioned for several days, then officially prohibited from leaving Harbin and put under house arrest. Two months after the fire, he was jailed on charges of negligently causing the hotel fire—charges that carried penalties of a seven-year jail term and a $90,000 fine.

At a public trial in July 1985, Ondrik, brought to court from a local prison, made an extraordinary plea, a plea that was a testament to both the tenacity and the desperation of foreign businessmen in China.

While Ondrik said he could not remember smoking in bed and said the evidence of the hotel's negligence had made him "very angry," he did not directly challenge the prosecution's case. Instead, he begged the three-judge panel to let him continue working in China. "If I am to go to prison, let me start my sentence so that it may end soon," he said. "It has taken me more than ten years to prepare for my career in China. . . . I am a friend of China and a guest in your country. If this court decides that vengeance and punishment are necessary according to your law, I would accept that. I only ask that you do not destroy the work that I have done in the past in China, or prevent me from continuing my work after I complete my punishment."

Ondrik was sentenced to eighteen months in prison and a fine of $52,000, a sum that represented about 60 percent of the estimated damage to the hotel. After five months, on Thanksgiving Day 1985, he was released from prison and allowed to leave China after paying the fine. Within two years he was back in China, doing business for a moving company, Crown Pacific.

The jokes the foreigners told each other in China were also revealing of the business community's despair.

Each year at Christmastime, the British embassy in Beijing would put on a skit for the foreign community. Businessmen, foreign news correspondents, British intelligence agents, and other assorted characters gave their own amateur Monty Python routines, with burly men playing women's roles and singing in falsetto. It was a hot ticket.

In 1986 the show was an updated version of *Peter Pan*, in which Wendy, Michael, and John Darling were brought to a Never-Never Land that seemed a lot like China. There, they found the "Lost Boys," businessmen who sat around drinking endless cups of tea and waiting for contracts that never appeared, or who, occasionally, engaged in "joint misadventures."

"I suppose we could count the carpet tiles again," said one of the Lost Boys. "That's usually quite fun."

"We could get drunk again, I suppose," said another.

"We did that last night," said a third.

Wendy started to tell the Lost Boys about doing business in the real world, where there were honest-to-God deals, mergers, contracts, free remittance of profits, loans at commercial rates.

But Captain Hook, who seemed to be a British embassy official, sought to cut Wendy off. "If the Lost Boys were ever to discover the real situation here in Never-Never Land, they would realize they couldn't possibly do any trade here, and they'd return home," he explained. "The embassy would close."

It was an especially popular show.

One February, the American Club, the social organization for the American business community in Beijing, sponsored a Valentine's Day "Sweetheart Supper Buffet" at the Great Wall Hotel. The dinner guests were serenaded by a Filipino band. Near the end of the evening, the businessmen had a contest to see who could write the best "Roses Are Red" verse to his or her spouse.

The winning entry was the simplest and most direct. It came from the wife of an American businessman:

> *Roses are red*
> *Violets are blue*
> *You brought me to China*
> *But I still love you.*

10

Arriving at the Plant

On a typical weekday morning, a visitor to the jeep factory in the southern section of Beijing finds the usual scenes of Chinese factory life. Primitive clattering carts driven by horses and donkeys carry supplies into the plant. A group of old women practice t'ai chi. Young men and women on bicycles pedal their single child to the factory kindergarten. Office workers trudge along, carrying Thermoses of hot water for their morning tea.

For a moment, the visitor might think he has returned to the China of the 1950s. But the placards posted around the plant serve as a quick reminder that this is China of the 1980s, the era of Deng Xiaoping. Just inside the front gate, a red Chinese banner of the sort that once denounced American imperialism and Soviet hegemony proclaims the slogan of the new era: "Time Is Money, Efficiency Is Life."

In the last half of 1983, Americans began to move into this traditional Chinese factory. Now that AMC's contract had been signed, the jeep plant was no longer just a place to visit and study, but a place to work. AMC had to begin to learn how to run the jeep factory and make new cars there.

Increasingly, the Americans on the front lines in dealing with the Chinese were no longer Clare and his aides at corporate headquarters, but the AMC employees in Beijing. The joint venture, Beijing Jeep, wasn't scheduled to begin operations until January 1984, but an interim team from American Motors began commuting to China in the summer and fall of 1983 to get everything ready. The members of the team would work in Beijing for a month or so and then return home for a month. The team included two young AMC employees, Lauren Giglio and Richard Swando, who were preparing to live with their families in Beijing as permanent employees of the joint venture. Meanwhile AMC selected a competent plant manager who had headed one of its domestic operations, Angus MacGregor, to become the head of its China venture, the first president of Beijing Jeep.

From Detroit, Clare continued to supervise the China venture. He flew to Beijing several times a year. Ron Gilchrist, who worked for Clare as AMC's head of Far East operations, crossed the Pacific even more often. But inevitably the day-to-day affairs were in the hands of the new people they assigned to launch Beijing Jeep.

When the new AMC employees arrived at the jeep factory, they quickly noticed the beds.

Near the assembly line, inside the office building that housed the factory's management team, virtually every Chinese office had a bed inside it. Many of the Chinese offices had a curtain or some paper placed carefully over the window of the door. The office doors were usually locked, so that the visitor had to knock before entering.

These beds weren't double beds or fancy pull-out couches, just simple, functional, old-fashioned single beds, of the sort you might find in an American summer camp. Except for the occupant's own desk and chair, a bed was sometimes the only piece of furniture in an office. One of the new AMC arrivals went in to meet Chinese finance director Li Bolin and found Li sitting on the only chair in the room. The American uncomfortably plumped down on Li's bed.

There was nothing unusual about the jeep factory. Other Chinese offices had beds in them, too. In early visits to the headquarters branch of the Bank of China, Giglio, AMC's finance director, wound up sitting on beds in the offices of senior bank officials. Giglio soon realized he had stumbled across one of the reasons Chinese officials entertained foreigners in formal reception rooms and rarely allowed the foreigners into their offices or internal working areas. The Chinese didn't want the foreigners to see the modest offices—or, in particular, the beds.

The Americans quickly saw that the beds were being used for afternoon naps, or what the Chinese call *xiuxi.* Chinese officials at the jeep factory awoke, with the rest of the country, at daybreak; after lunch many of them moved off to their beds and slept for an hour or so. It was a national custom. During one brief period in the mid-1980s when the Chinese leadership was urging the nation to abandon many old Chinese traditions and clothing styles in the drive to Westernize, official Communist Party newspapers launched a brief campaign against the *xiuxi*. The campaign petered out within months, surviving only a trifle longer than Communist Party Secretary Hu Yaobang's ill-fated move to goad his country-men away from using chopsticks. Some Chinese writers rushed to the defense of the *xiuxi*, arguing that the Chinese metabolism was different from that of Americans or Europeans, that China's early waking hours and low-protein rice diet made a *xiuxi* more neces-sary than it would be in the West.

To the Chinese office workers at the jeep factory, the beds were merely a convenience and, indeed, a symbol of prestige. Out on the assembly line, workers who wanted to take a *xiuxi* had to impro-vise and find a bench or some space on the floor. To the newly arrived Americans, however, the beds, locked doors, and covered windows were symbols of indolent management.

Soon after his arrival at the factory, MacGregor, the ranking AMC staffer in Beijing, ordered that all the beds be removed. Noth-ing happened. Finally MacGregor took matters into his own hands. He ran into one Chinese office and began hauling out the bed. Chinese officials held him back but over the next few days relented and removed all the beds on their own.

The AMC team also ordered that the office windows be kept uncovered, so that they could see what was happening inside each room. Despite these measures, the Americans still sometimes found that an office window would be covered up with newspaper and a Chinese official would be inside, asleep on his desk.

Four years earlier, as a visitor on a quick tour, Clare had thought the Chinese factory was in passable condition. But when Giglio arrived at the plant and began working there every day, he saw that the Chinese factory was filthy. He had worked overseas before, in Costa Rica, had traveled around the world and had seen several other AMC plants. He had never seen conditions as bad as in Bei-jing. In the winter there was virtually no heat. After the end of one frigid all-day meeting at the plant the first winter, the Americans went to pick up their overcoats. One of them looked down on the floor and saw a mouse, frozen to death.

The office building the Americans and their Chinese partners were working in was only three years old, yet any visitor would have guessed it had been around for as long as the plant itself. The walls were whitewashed, the floors an uncovered dirty concrete. MacGregor and the AMC team had the walls painted for the first time. The Americans spent much of their time and energy in their early months there just making the plant livable.

By the time the Americans arrived, the Beijing Jeep factory was thirty years old. Built in 1953, four years after the Communist takeover, it was initially used only to make auto parts. At the time, China didn't have a single automobile plant within its borders. In 1956, with the help of the Soviets, the first car factory was built in the Manchurian city of Changchun. Two years later, during the Great Leap Forward, Mao Tse-tung's unsuccessful effort to galvanize the nation into stepping up industrial production, the Beijing factory was rebuilt as a complete auto factory. Its first products were passenger cars, but soon the plant began making BJ212's, the Chinese jeeps. The factory's most important customer was the gargantuan People's Liberation Army. By the early 1960s, the relationship between China and the Soviet Union had changed from an alliance to a bitter enmity, and the PLA found itself preparing to defend China against a Soviet invasion.

Originally the jeep factory was called Beijing Auto Works. After the outbreak of the Cultural Revolution in 1966, it was given its more revolutionary title: the Dong Fang Hong, or "East Is Red." The havoc of Mao Tse-tung's zealous Red Guards quickly found its way into the East Is Red, as it did throughout all of China. Red Guards and young workers at the plant demanded the abolition of existing rules, including those concerning workers' health and safety, arguing that these were representative of old ways of thinking. Production plummeted to the point where the army, which couldn't defend the country without an adequate supply of jeeps, intervened. The PLA dispatched Qing Ping, fifty-four, a veteran of the elite Eighth Route Army, to the plant to calm things down.

Officially Qing served as head of the factory's Revolutionary Committee, and like many other skilled Chinese leaders, he knew how to borrow the Red Guards' rhetoric when it suited his purposes. When American reporters visited the plant during Nixon's 1972 trip and asked whether workers were ever given bonuses for hard work or new ideas, Qing replied: "In the days before the Cultural Revolution, there was such a system. But in our view, it is revisionist. In the course of the Cultural Revolution, the workers' consciousness was raised. Now, we rely mainly on their political awareness, not on a bonus system."

Like others at the Jeep factory, Qing maintained that many innovations and new equipment had been inspired by the precepts of Chairman Mao. When author James Michener asked Qing to show him some of these, Qing brought him to a crude assembly line. "In the old days, the chassis of a Jeep stood in one place, and each workman had to walk to it," Qing explained. "In 1965, a workman, inspired by Mao, had the idea of placing the chassis on a moving belt, so that it came to the men." Qing scornfully dismissed the idea that Henry Ford, and not Chairman Mao, had thought of the assembly line.

Under the colonel's leadership, the Dong Fang Hong managed to get production up to ten thousand jeeps a year. By 1975 Qing's presence was no longer necessary, and he returned to army work. After the 1976 death of Mao and the arrest of his wife, Jiang Qing, and other leftist leaders, the plant was renamed Beijing Automotive Works. And by 1978, as Deng Xiaoping consolidated his hold over China, bulletin boards at the factory were offering special incentives and bonuses to workers for harder work and greater output.[1]

Despite the incentives, when the AMC employees arrived the jeep plant still seemed, by American standards, an extremely sleepy, slow-moving place. On an ordinary afternoon, activity along the assembly line slowed to a crawl well before the five P.M. closing hour. In late afternoon small groups of workers lounged around, smoking cigarettes and drinking tea. Some of them left the assembly line early to take an afternoon shower before bicycling home.

By the time the contract had been signed, the American Motors team had met with Beijing Automotive Works and other Chinese officials for more than four years. Now that the joint venture was preparing to start operations, AMC's people were supposed to start working alongside the same people who had been their adversaries in the endless rounds of bargaining.

Chinese cadres, loyal members of the Communist Party, were supposed to adapt to an American corporate culture that emphasized profits, markets, and labor-saving techniques. American executives were supposed to adapt to a Chinese work unit whose raw materials and supplies were provided by the government, whose output was taken by the government, and whose leaders decided where workers lived, what doctors the workers saw, and how workers were educated. It was a strange experience for both sides.

Even in little ways, the first American Motors staffers in China began to sense what Chinese life felt like from the inside. There was, for example, the surprise discovery of the furniture in the factory's reception room.

During the years of negotiations, the Americans and Chinese had held many meetings in a large reception room at the Beijing factory. The Americans, who had always sat on opposite sides of the table from the Chinese, had noticed that the Chinese didn't sit up straight. The Chinese negotiators always seemed to be slouching to one side or another. The Americans figured that they were just inattentive or sleepy.

Now, the Americans from AMC and the Chinese from Beijing Automotive Works were increasingly required to join together, to form a management team for the new joint venture. When visitors came to the plant to talk business, the Americans joined their Chinese colleagues on what had previously been the all-Chinese side of the negotiating table. When the Americans sat down, they learned why their Chinese counterparts had been slouching. The chairs and couches on the Chinese side of the room had broken springs. The Chinese had placed their only comfortable furniture on the foreigners' side of the room. On the broken chairs, the Americans found themselves slouching, too.

Slouching alongside his Chinese counterparts, Giglio realized that he and his fellow Americans really didn't know their Chinese partners. The Americans had negotiated with the Chinese for years. They had gone to banquets together over and over again. But none of that was the same as working together.

It was impossible for the AMC people to blend into daily life at the factory. The Americans were a curiosity; there were only a handful of foreigners among four thousand Chinese.

The Chinese workers protected their own turf from any intrusions. At lunch hour the workers went to the factory canteen, a small, busy, crowded place where they stood in long lines holding metal bowls to be filled with rice. An American who intruded on

the workers' canteen, even to the extent of standing in the door-
way, was greeted with mocking taunts.

A few yards away was a special dining room. It was meant for
high-level Chinese cadres at the factory and their guests. The
newly arrived AMC staffers began eating their lunches in this dining room. Scores of workers lined up outside, staring at the foreigners.

In the Chinese cadres' dining room, waiters served delicacies
like shrimp, special buns, mushrooms, and watery orange soda. As
a regular diet, the Americans found it hard to take. After a while
many of them grew accustomed to driving off from the factory for
lunch and heading for the accustomed food and isolated comfort of
Western hotels such as the Jianguo. As a result, the guest dining
room at the factory was often only half-full, patronized mostly by
the Chinese cadres.

The worst problem was that the old adversarial relationship
remained. All too often the Chinese and the Americans found
themselves back on opposite sides of the negotiating table, just as
they had been for the four years before the contract had been
signed. As was true for so many other foreign companies in China,
AMC learned to its consternation that the signing of the contract
had marked the start, not the end, of the hard bargaining.

Throughout the last half of 1983 and the early months of 1984,
the American and Chinese sides at Beijing Jeep wrangled over several different issues. The Chinese team surprised the Americans by
seeking changes in the original deal. None of these disputes was
crucial to the fate of the joint venture, but the way they were
handled was important. In each case the controversy was resolved
when the Americans gave way. The effect was to create a climate
in which the Chinese side believed the Americans were so committed to the success of the joint venture that they would be willing to make no end of concessions.

The first dispute was over where the eight Americans from AMC
should live.[2] Under the contract, the new joint venture was to pay
for the foreigners' housing, and the Chinese side of the venture was
supposed to make arrangements for this housing. AMC executives
argued that it would be hard to recruit good American automotive
experts for China if there weren't decent apartments for them and
their families.

At the outset, Chinese officials told American Motors that Beijing Automotive Works, the Chinese partner in the joint venture, would build a completely new apartment building for the AMC employees. The apartments would be up to Western standards. Since it might take time to build such a complex, Chinese officials proposed a "short-term plan," an interim solution. The Americans might have to stay for a brief period at the Friendship Hotel, the old, walled, Soviet-built complex on the western outskirts of Beijing that had served as home for three decades to foreign teachers, advisers, and other foreigners working in China.

The Americans didn't like it, not even as a short-term solution. The Friendship Hotel was on the other side of Beijing from their factory. It wasn't near the International School or the Friendship Store, where foreigners bought groceries. Furthermore, the living conditions were austere. It was like a college dormitory, with small apartments, many of which didn't have kitchens, and a communal dining room where the residents ate. The Friendship Hotel might be fine for Third World nationals, or for those Westerners willing to endure hardship because of their eagerness to live in China. But it was not the sort of place that would attract an engineer or a mechanic from Detroit.

At first Clare told Chinese officials the Friendship Hotel was simply unacceptable, even for the short term.[3] He urged the Chinese partners to arrange for diplomatic housing for AMC. But he soon relented and agreed that the Americans would live briefly at the Friendship Hotel while new housing was being built for them.

Chinese officials began arranging for some Friendship Hotel apartments to be renovated. In the meantime AMC's people found themselves in Western hotels such as the Great Wall. Although Beijing Jeep was supposed to pay all the foreigners' housing costs, American Motors agreed to pay the difference in costs between the Friendship Hotel and the Western hotels (where rooms were over $100 per night) while the Americans were waiting for their new apartments.

At a board of directors meeting in December 1983, seven months after the contract was signed, Chairman Wu dropped a new bombshell on the Americans. Work on the new apartment building for the Americans had not yet begun. Arranging it was proving extremely difficult, Wu said. He proposed that the Friendship Hotel should serve as the long-term solution to the Americans' housing difficulties.[4]

The Americans were furious. They had been promised their own apartment building. They hadn't even wanted the Friendship Hotel as a temporary expedient. The Chinese had even gone so far as to show them a site in Beijing where the new housing was to be built. AMC objected vehemently to the change in plans. But in the end, after Chinese officials explained that it would be virtually impossible to build the new apartment building they had once promised, the Americans acquiesced. The two sides agreed that eight special new Western-style apartments would be renovated at the Friendship Hotel. The Chinese would install wall-to-wall carpeting and wallpaper, redo the plumbing, buy new beds, and knock down walls to enlarge the apartments.

These special apartments were supposed to be ready in March 1984 but weren't completed until July. When the apartments were finally finished, the Americans didn't like them. The new toilets ran, the bathrooms weren't caulked, and the construction crews had set up an outhouse outside the front door. Even if the apartments had been comfortable, they were far away from the factory, shopping, schools, and life downtown. One by one, the AMC employees assigned to Beijing rebelled against living in these apartments and began moving out, back into Western hotels.

Two of the mainstays of the first AMC team in China, Swando and Giglio, remained with their families at the Friendship Hotel. In 1986, after their tours in China ended, there was no one from American Motors left in the renovated wing of the Friendship Hotel. The apartments were rented out to other businessmen with jobs nearby. By that time, American Motors and its Chinese partners were arguing once again, this time over the costs of the housing into which the Americans moved after they fled the Friendship Hotel.

There was another dispute over what to do with the $40,000 "salaries" for Chinese managers.

In negotiating the contract, the Chinese had argued that their top managers should be paid roughly as much as the Americans. Since the Americans were sending managers and experts at salaries of $40,000 a year or more, Chinese officials said, the top Chinese managers should be paid equivalent sums. It was, the Chinese contended, a question of equal pay for equal work. Moreover, they said, there were Chinese regulations requiring the payment of American-style salaries. When the Americans asked to see these rules, they were told that, unfortunately, the regulations themselves were *neibu* (internal)—that is, classified, for Chinese eyes only.

The Americans realized that the very highest take-home pay in China, even for high-level cadres, was less than $100 a month. They had asked Chinese negotiators where the extra money would be going but got no answers. So the Americans added a provision setting up a special escrow account into which $40,000-a-year salaries for eight senior Chinese staff members would be paid "until such time as the pertinent law is published in the PRC" explaining who would get this money.[5] The Americans didn't want to be governed by the supposedly classified law they couldn't see.

The following year China made public a new law that left it up to the board of directors of each individual joint venture to decide what should happen to the "salaries" foreign companies like American Motors were paying for their Chinese managers. Giglio, who was in charge of AMC's finances in China, urged the company to insist that the money be paid out only if it went directly into the pockets of the eight Chinese managers.

Giglio didn't care whether it was $20,000 a year or $60,000 a year. If the Chinese staffers were actually going to get the money and be able to spend it like a genuine salary, he was willing to go along. If the money was going to go into some slush fund, he didn't want any part of it. But Chairman Wu and other Chinese officials told Giglio he didn't understand. It would be a distortion of the Chinese system to have individual Chinese get American-style salaries. And besides, Chinese officials had many costs, such as expenses while traveling abroad, which were paid by the state. Why, they asked, shouldn't a major portion of their American salaries go to the state?

Eventually the Americans gave in again. One day Chairman Wu told Giglio he had talked to Clare and that the matter had been decided. At a board of directors meeting soon afterward, the Americans and Chinese agreed that the $40,000-a-year Chinese salaries might be paid from the funds of the joint venture to the Chinese partner. "The Chinese side can decide how to distribute it," the two partners concluded, according to the confidential minutes of that board meeting.

The Americans thus acquiesced in the payment of hundreds of thousands of dollars each year in phony salaries, without having any idea how this money would be used. In the United States it would have been scandalous for any corporation to be so careless with its money. But American Motors persuaded itself that China was different, and that it had to play by Chinese rules.

By the end of 1983, at a board of directors meeting in Beijing, American and Chinese officials agreed that there had been enough preparations. Beijing Jeep was ready to start operations. The two sides set a date of January 15, 1984, for the formal establishment of the joint venture. But in the final weeks before Beijing Jeep came into existence, a new, particularly nasty financial dispute erupted. It was precisely the sort of last-minute hitch that the Americans had feared the previous year when they had come to Beijing to sign their contract.

At issue was what property and equipment should be included in the assets that China was contributing to the joint venture. The value of the Chinese plant and equipment had been calculated in 1980 by the Hong Kong office of the accounting firm of Deloitte, Haskins & Sells. Their appraisal had served as the basis for the contract the two sides had signed in May 1983.

But a few weeks before the date for the start-up of Beijing Jeep, Chinese officials suddenly announced that there was a problem. They said Beijing Automotive Works, the Chinese partner, had installed some new machinery and equipment into the jeep factory in the three years since the appraisal, and the Chinese unit would have to be paid additional money for these assets. The Americans said they thought that under the contract the joint venture would get *all* of the Chinese equipment used to produce the BJ212. But Chinese officials insisted that Beijing Automotive Works should be paid an additional $6 million for the "new" assets. Otherwise, they argued, the equipment in question should be given back to BAW, the Chinese partner, which was going to continue operating as a separate automotive unit at a separate location in Beijing.

Years later the Americans realized they should have asked for a complete reevaluation of all the assets and financial arrangements. Much of the Chinese equipment they were obtaining was antiquated and obsolete, and a new appraisal might have found it to be worthless.

Underneath all the complexities of assets and appraisals, the

Americans felt that what the Chinese wanted was more money. In the final days before the opening of the joint venture, the Chinese were testing whether American Motors would pay more cash to Beijing Automotive Works. In effect they were seeking a change in the deal setting up the joint venture.

The Americans resisted. It was a major confrontation, one that lasted until past midnight on the night before the joint venture was supposed to open. Gilchrist took the lead for AMC. Things got so tense that at one point the AMC officials waved their bank check for nearly $8 million—representing the cash equity AMC was scheduled to contribute the following day to the new joint venture —and asked whether the Chinese wanted to go ahead with the deal or not.

In the early-morning hours, the Americans caved in and agreed to a compromise. Over a period of several years, BAW, the Chinese unit, would be paid 70 percent of the value of the assets in dispute. The money would come from the joint venture; Chairman Wu would have considerable discretion in settling the dispute. It took more than a year to straighten out exactly which assets should be covered by this last-minute negotiation and how much they were worth.

During these and other negotiations, the AMC staffers in China learned that whenever they took tough positions, someone from headquarters would arrive in Beijing on a five-day visit and, in the end, make new concessions to the Chinese negotiators. Giglio felt that the Americans working in the trenches in China weren't getting the support they needed from Detroit.

Back in Detroit, Clare saw it differently. His job was to get the joint venture in China up and running and not to get stuck on the details. China was an essential part of his global strategy. It was important to American Motors' future. He wanted his company to have a presence there. If the Chinese wanted to haggle a little bit over a few million dollars' worth of assets, if they wanted to set up a little slush fund of $40,000 "salaries," if they couldn't follow through on their promises for housing Americans, well, none of this was as important to Clare as the big picture. He didn't think the dispute over the assets was such a big deal. The problem eventually went away, didn't it?

. . .

Gilchrist felt that the financial dispute sounded a sour note for the formal launch of Beijing Jeep. There were other nuisances as well.

Some of the Americans believed that Chinese officials at BAW had stripped some equipment from the factory in the last weeks before the start of the joint venture. BAW, the Chinese unit, also continued to occupy one of the buildings on the grounds of Beijing Jeep, acting in effect as squatters within the factory they had once owned. Beijing Jeep was being required to pay rent of more than $5 per square meter for its land and more than $2 per square meter for its buildings, and the Chinese unit wasn't paying any rent to Beijing Jeep. Each time the Chinese were asked to leave the building, they promised to do so soon. It took roughly two years for the joint venture to get possession.

None of these disputes was allowed to disturb the outward appearance of harmony that the two sides wanted to convey.

On January 15, 1984, a frigid winter Sunday, Chinese workers at the factory beat drums and cymbals and set off firecrackers in ceremonies marking the start-up of operations for Beijing Jeep. After eight months of preparations, the Americans and Chinese officially launched China's first joint venture for automobile production.

Chen Muhua, minister of foreign economic relations and trade, the same Chinese official who had attended the previous year's contract signing, unveiled a plaque inaugurating the joint venture. The American delegation to the ceremonies was headed by Clare, who told reporters that American Motors hoped to produce a "totally new and fresh" export-model jeep within two to four years. The new Chinese jeep would cut into Japan's share of the Asian market for four-wheel-drive vehicles, Clare predicted.[6]

But at the very moment when the Americans were boasting about outflanking Japan in Asia, the Japanese were in the process of outmaneuvering the Americans within China itself.

11

Chinese Consumers and Japan

BEIJING (UPI). A successful chicken farmer has become the first Chinese peasant to buy a private car, the newspaper *Beijing Daily* reported Tuesday.

The farmer, Sun Guiying, paid $4,650 for her new Japanese Toyota.

Sun, a member of a suburban Beijing commune, sold 70,400 pounds of eggs last year and made a net profit of $18,400—a fortune for China, where the average worker earns less than $50 per month.

Peasants like Sun, who only a few years ago would have been denounced as greedy capitalists, are now portrayed as models of success through private enterprise and other capitalistic reforms launched by China's new leaders.

Beijing Daily carried a front-page picture of the smiling farmer and her family standing in front of their new silver-colored Toyota, which the newspaper said they would use to "help make business contacts and promote egg sales."

—United Press International, April 3, 1984

It was a typically tantalizing news story from China—short, skimpy on details, puzzling, yet hinting at startling change. The story, accompanied by a picture of a smiling peasant family around its truck, was put out by China's state-controlled New China News Service and distributed by foreign news agencies. *The Washington Post* ran the picture in its front news section. Needless to say, it was the sort of picture that attracted the attention of auto industry executives around the world.

The story was essentially a fraud. At the time of the article, there wasn't a store or office in all of China where one could buy a car or truck, even if one had the money. Foreign reporters in Beijing who sought to see Mrs. Sun and her new Toyota truck found themselves unable to do so. There was no proof that she or her Toyota truck ever existed.

This was a common occurrence when foreign correspondents tried to verify slice-of-life stories in the government-controlled press. In the fall of 1984 I tried to check out an account of turmoil at the Jiaodaokou Clothing Factory in northern Beijing, which had been featured in a story in the magazine *Chinese Youth*. The story said that a series of protests by factory workers to the neighborhood committee, a local Communist Party organization, had forced the clothing factory to suspend a series of reforms, such as bonuses for increased output and cutbacks in fringe benefits for those who took time off from work. According to the story, these reforms had produced thousands of dollars in monthly profits, but when the recalcitrant workers forced a postponement of the changes, the factory began losing several thousands of dollars a month. Finally, the story said, other, more farsighted workers came to the defense of the reforms, and they were reinstituted.

The story about the factory appeared to have a moral lesson: Chinese workers should support the leadership's reform program. When I visited the neighborhood committee, officials told me they wouldn't answer any of my questions until I applied to the municipal government for an interview. There wasn't time, I said, but I wanted to know whether the magazine account had been accurate. "Generally, yes," one official replied, "except for the parts about profits and losses."

The feature story about the peasant woman buying a truck, like others of its genre in the Chinese press, was intended primarily as a parable. It was meant to convey a message both to domestic and foreign audiences. To the Chinese people and the rank and file of the Communist Party, the message was that the Party leadership now permitted, indeed encouraged, the nation to buy consumer goods. To foreigners, the message was that China was a huge market waiting to be tapped and willing and able to buy foreign goods. What if China's eight hundred million peasants someday were able to buy cars and trucks?

Still, like some other fraudulent accounts, the story about Mrs.

Sun the truck owner contained a couple of kernels of truth. Many Chinese peasants—not in remote areas, but in the suburbs of major cities—were indeed becoming wealthier than they had been for decades. Though individual peasants were not purchasing trucks (in fact, even a television set was a major acquisition), rural cooperatives, enterprises, or townships were beginning to do so. It was also true, as the story suggested, that when the Chinese people were given the green light to buy foreign goods, they rushed for Japanese products.

In 1984, as the Chinese leadership made a deliberate effort to stimulate personal consumption and spending, the regime gave both individuals and enterprises unprecedented latitude to buy goods from overseas. At the time, American and West European companies such as American Motors were just beginning to start up their manufacturing operations inside the country. Meanwhile, the Japanese, who had held back from investing money in China and instead concentrated on sales and trading operations, reaped the benefits of the consumer boom. Japanese goods were available in China, in abundance, at just the right time.

China's decision to stimulate consumerism had both political and economic components. By the beginning of 1984, Chinese economic planners found a situation in which consumer demand was far exceeding the ability of Chinese industry to satisfy it. State enterprises producing television sets, washing machines, radios, refrigerators, and bicycles all raised output between 10 and 90 percent in 1983; and yet, with the rural economy booming, Chinese consumers put $11 billion into bank accounts and kept countless billions more in cash in their homes. This relative prosperity raised for the first time the prospect that China might stimulate economic growth through consumption, in the fashion of Western countries. China's own light industries could be pushed to keep on increasing their output. At the same time imported consumer goods could help satisfy the nation's increased demand and could stimulate domestic industries to increase efficiency and the quality of their products.[1]

The official tolerance of consumer goods was also, in a sense, a political payoff. In the countryside peasants were being given new, tangible rewards for the rapid increases in grain output. In the cities the regime was planning in 1984 to launch a series of urban reforms that included the use of wage incentives, bonuses, and other income differentials to try to increase output and efficiency. The Party wanted to show both ordinary workers and loyal cadres in the factories that the reforms would improve the standard of living.

On October 20, 1984, following a week-long series of meetings, the Central Committee of the Chinese Communist Party approved a series of radical changes in the nation's urban economy, including a gradual lifting of price controls and a drastic reduction in the role of centralized state planning. A crucial part of the thirty-nine-page document was a shift to a consumer economy. For a Communist Party nurtured in the traditions of thrift and struggle, it was a stunning ideological change. "The essential task of socialism is . . . to create ever more social wealth and meet the people's growing material and cultural needs," the Party said. "Socialism does not mean pauperism, for it aims at the elimination of poverty." Traditional Marxist theory was revised and reinterpreted to take account of the importance of consumer goods. "According to the basic tenets of Marxism, production is the starting point and the predominant factor of all economic activities and determines consumption," the Party said. "But consumption also determines production in that the growth of consumption gives a strong impetus to creation of new social demands, opens up vast markets, and encourages production. We must gradually bring about substantial increases in the pay of workers and staff members and in the people's level of consumption."

When Communist Party newspapers and magazines translated this theory into a propaganda campaign for ordinary Chinese, the result was, from a Western perspective, downright amusing. The Communist Party, using the same media techniques it had once employed to wage revolutionary struggle, now daily urged the masses to go out and devoutly spend money for the good of the nation. On October 12, 1984, *People's Daily* suggested that China was on the verge of an epochal change in life-style. After the 1911 revolution overthrowing the Qing dynasty, the newspaper pointed out, progressive Chinese men cut their pigtails and replaced their old, traditional long robes with *Zhongshan zhuang* (Sun Yat-sen suits, later called Mao suits). Now, loyal Chinese cadres were urged to abandon their Mao suits for Western clothes.

The New China News Service, one of the nation's most tradi-
tion-minded bureaucracies, ushered in 1985 with this feature story,
which echoes an old American rock-and-roll song:

BEIJING, Jan. 4. She walks down the street in her fashionable
boots, styled pants, and light down jacket, her shoulder-length
hair hugged by a rose-pink knitted cloche hat. She may even sport
a touch of makeup.

She is a perfectly ordinary Beijing worker, and others like her
are a common sight in any Chinese city this winter as fashion
takes off.

Her young husband probably sports a natty suit with a collar
and tie, and they will go home to well-decorated and furnished
rooms in apartments where houseplants and goldfish soften the
brash modernity of fridges, color televisions, and radio cassette
recorders.

A few years ago, they would have interested the neighbors.
Nobody pretends they are the norm today, but they are admired
and they are the trend-setters.

Gone are the days when drab blue clothes were worn "new
for three years, old for three years, and threadbare for three years,"
and food was for filling the belly. A poll of 2,000 young factory
workers in the Hubei provincial capital of Wuhan showed 70 percent preferred fashionable clothes, whereas the rule used to be
"the shabbier, the more revolutionary. . . ."

Ordinary Chinese, of course, hardly needed much encouragement to buy the things they had been wanting for years. Once they
had official authorization, they were ready to respond.

A couple of other factors helped stimulate the buying spree.
One was the fear of inflation. The new urban reform program was
supposed to lift some state-controlled prices, and the word quickly
spread across China to buy as much as possible before prices went
up. The second factor was what might be called the Chinese rush:
it was standard wisdom in China that once any opportunity opened
up, you had to seize it immediately, because it wouldn't be there
for long. In political terms, the Communist Party often altered
course after a few months; in economic terms, China was a nation
of scarcity, and what was in the stores one week might not be there
the next.

And so, beginning in the fall of 1984, China went on a consumer binge unprecedented since the Revolution of 1949. Individual Chinese bought television sets, washing machines, refrigerators, tape recorders. Chinese work units, state enterprises, local governments, and townships bought cars, trucks, videocassettes, and large color TVs.

On the streets of Beijing, even horse carts and bicycles were carrying boxes of television sets. On the eve of the Chinese new year in early 1985, passengers traveling on the Shanghai–Beijing Express to visit their families lugged television sets, radios, and tape recorders along with the traditional lunar New Year cakes.

It was a kind of frenzy. Early one cold, gray Saturday morning in November 1984, I watched a young woman named Zhang Jizhang as she stood outside Xidan Department Store in western Beijing waiting for the doors to open. As soon as they did, she rushed with a crowd of about fifty other men and women to the store's appliance section. A clerk at the counter told them there would be no washing machines for sale that day and only two refrigerators. Unfortunately, the clerk said, both refrigerators were slightly damaged. Zhang, a newly married schoolteacher, pushed past the others and immediately bought one of the two refrigerators. Because it was scratched and dented on the side, the state-owned store had cut the price by less than one percent, from 890 yuan (about $342 at the time) to 885 yuan (about $340). Zhang didn't care about the dents and scratches. "I've been trying to get one for about a week," she told me. "You have to spend the money you have. There's no point in saving it."

Individuals like Zhang represented one part of China's consumer boom. The other part—the major part, at least in the volume of goods purchased—came from organizations. In 1984, as China launched its new urban economic reforms and sought to decentralize its economy, Chinese provinces, municipalities, and individual work units were granted new freedom to make their own decisions. To a greater extent than ever before, they could buy and sell goods and spend foreign exchange without getting approval from the ministries and the central-planning apparatus in Beijing.

These work units represented a much more important element in the consumer economy of socialist China than did private companies in the capitalist economies of the West. In the United States,

Western Europe, or Japan, a few executives might drive company cars, but for the most part, of course, individuals owned their own private automobiles. In China, private car ownership was virtually unknown, and most of the cars on the road were owned by work units, which bought cars, or fleets of cars, for their leading cadres. Similarly, the Chinese *danwei*, or work unit, might buy other consumer goods, such as video recorders, which would be privately owned in the West; and if a video recorder found its way to the home of the Communist Party secretary for the work unit and stayed there for a while, who from the outside would know the difference? Meanwhile, in true Confucian tradition, the leaders, the factory managers and party secretaries, often took care of their own workers and made sure that they got their share of consumer goods as well. Particularly at the end of 1984, during the earliest phase of the urban reform program, it was commonplace for factories and other work units to distribute food, clothes, even radios and black-and-white TVs for their workers as special in-kind bonuses. After all, the factories were owned by the state, and their profits would be either remitted directly or at least heavily taxed by the state. There were no private stockholders to complain if factory leaders used their profits to buy blue jeans, boots, sugar, and soap for their workers.

In a nation newly obsessed with consumer goods, shrewd and savvy hustlers began migrating to China's special economic zones (SEZs), the areas in southern China where goods from abroad could be imported duty-free. The special zones included Shenzhen, a town just across the border from Hong Kong's New Territories; Zhuhai, just across from Macao; the old towns of Shantou and Xiamen on the South China coastline; and, starting in 1983, the entire island of Hainan in the South China Sea. In the early 1980s, under Deng's leadership, these special zones had been established as enclaves that might serve as models for the reform program. The idea was to attract Western businesses, especially manufacturers, by offering the companies lower tax rates and greater freedom to hire and fire workers than they would find elsewhere in China.

But what counted the most was the waiver from Chinese customs regulations. Inside the special economic zones, both Western companies and Chinese work units could import goods from abroad without paying duty on them. In theory the goods were supposed to be used inside the zones themselves; Chinese enterprises were supposed to be importing supplies and raw materials from abroad and using these imports for manufacturing. In practice the system was set up in a way that led to rampant smuggling and speculation. An imported car that cost the equivalent of $8,000 duty-free, on the island of Hainan would be worth as much as $20,000 to $30,000 in Beijing or Shanghai. A television set that cost $400 in the shops of Shenzhen would cost $700 or more in the rest of China. Generally the buyers needed foreign currency, although occasionally, for a huge premium, the seller might accept Chinese renminbi.

Any Chinese who could find an excuse to travel to the special economic zones made the pilgrimage. Work units sent representatives there on official business, with a kitty of foreign exchange and instructions to buy as much as they could. To help those who couldn't travel south, middlemen soon began riding the rails, buying duty-free goods in the special economic zones and then reselling them for profit in Shanghai and Beijing. The demand for foreign currency to purchase these imported goods soared, and so in the fall of 1984, money changers began appearing on the downtown streets of Chinese cities. At first they disguised themselves as banana sellers, offering foreigners imported bananas (which until then had been unavailable in China) for foreign exchange. After a while the money changers operated in the open, aggressively approaching foreigners outside their hotels with offers to buy foreign exchange at prices that often ran as much as 70 to 80 percent above the official rates of change.

These black market transactions were illegal. However, the money changers became so numerous and flagrant that it was widely assumed by both Chinese and foreigners alike that the authorities had decided to look the other way; indeed, there were reports that some powerful government agencies and work units were profiting from the transactions. The money changers, too, became regular passengers on China's north-south rail route, buying foreign exchange from the tourists and the foreign communities in Beijing and Shanghai and carrying it south to the special zones, where the money could be used to buy a new haul of imported goods.

The smuggling of duty-free goods outside the zones—and the eagerness of Chinese to get into the zones—was so pervasive that the government erected a fifty-mile-long electrified barbed-wire fence around Shenzhen, isolating the zone from the rest of the country. Inside the special zones, a hustling, anything-goes atmosphere prevailed. Even government offices in the zones began setting up special units to buy duty-free cars and then resell them elsewhere in China.

For an ordinary Chinese cadre on a salary of perhaps $30 to $40 per month, the chance to buy a television set in Shenzhen at $300 below its Beijing prices represented a once-in-a-lifetime opportunity. During one trip I made to Shenzhen, a Chinese cadre I had met—a dutiful, loyal bureaucrat from a northern city, the sort of person who obeyed the rules and kept his distance from foreigners —called me in my hotel room late one night, talking fast and with a furtive air that seemed out of character. He was searching in desperation for someone who would trade him foreign exchange for Chinese currency, so that he could buy a new television set for his family. I had to politely decline the request.

The old Chinese port of Dalian is located across the water from North Korea at the point where the old rail lines from Manchuria reach the sea. Dalian is one of the largest cities in China, and the overall tonnage of imports and exports passing through it exceeds that of any other port in the nation. Yet in the center of Dalian, the only foreign community in evidence is Japanese; Americans and Europeans are rare. At the stately old Dalian Guest House, the choice rooms are occupied by the branch offices of leading Japanese companies such as Sumitomo Corporation, Mitsui & Company, and Mitsubishi Bank. In the hotel's restaurant, where earlier in this century Japanese naval officers dined, Chinese cooks now serve tempura at lunch. A Japanese firm built a golf course for Japanese businessmen, and there is air cargo service from Dalian to Osaka, Yokohama, and Kobe.

Though the Japanese influence was strong in Dalian—the Japanese occupied the city from the Russo-Japanese War until the end of World War II—what was happening there was also taking place in most other Chinese cities. Outside the major business centers of Beijing, Shanghai, and Canton, the Japanese presence was greater than that of any other country.

Japanese businessmen had a number of natural advantages over their American and European competitors. China was not far away from headquarters. Shipping and transportation costs were much cheaper than from Western Europe or the West Coast of the United States. For personal hardships or emergency business meetings, a plane ride back to Japan took roughly four hours, less than a third the time of a trip home from Beijing to the United States or Western Europe. Because the Japanese language was based on Chinese written characters, it was relatively easy for a Japanese businessman to read Chinese or for a Chinese cadre to read Japanese. The two countries had a long history of trading relations with one another. In the years immediately preceding the outbreak of the Sino-Japanese War and World War II, China ranked first in the world as a market for Japanese exports and third in the world, behind the United States and Korea, as a source for Japanese imports. Even during the 1950s, while the United States maintained an embargo on trade with China's new Communist regime, Japan carried on hundreds of millions of dollars a year in trade with China, more than the combined total of China's trade with Britain and France. By 1978, when China began opening its doors to the West, trade between the two countries had already reached $5 billion.[2]

Japan also had some special advantages in China during the period stretching from, roughly, 1978 through 1985. China's currency was tied to the U.S. dollar, and the Japanese yen was trading at levels well over 200 to the dollar, making Japanese goods much cheaper then than they became in the last part of the decade.

At the time, there was minimal economic competition from other Asian countries. South Korea and Taiwan had not yet fully developed their export industries; furthermore, their businesses confronted serious diplomatic problems in trying to do business with China. In Taiwan, the Nationalist government officially prohibited any travel to or direct trade with China. Similarly, South Korea had no diplomatic relations with China, which, through the first half of the 1980s, sought to maintain its close ties to the North Korean regime of Kim Il Sung. As a result, South Korean and Taiwanese businessmen were obliged to arrange transshipment to China through Hong Kong. Sometimes the deals were merely papered through Hong Kong, and the goods themselves were shipped directly to the Chinese mainland. But the unapproved, often clandestine nature of these transactions made them more expensive than they would otherwise have been.

Most important of all, from 1978 to 1985 Japanese political and cultural influence in postrevolutionary China was at its apogee.

In 1978, when Deng Xiaoping became the first leader of the People's Republic of China to visit Japan, he said he had come to "learn from . . . the great, industrious, heroic, and wise Japanese people."

For a time Chinese economists and political leaders viewed Japan as a blueprint for showing China how to modernize and obtain technology from the West without losing political control.[3] Deng's second in command, Communist Party General Secretary Hu Yaobang, who saw an industrial democracy for the first time in his life during his 1983 visit to Tokyo, was thought to particularly admire Japan. In Beijing in the mid-1980s the Japanese ambassador to China, Yosuke Nakae, saw Hu so often that they once had dinner together three times in a single week. By contrast Hummel, the U.S. ambassador to China from 1981 to 1985, was able to obtain one single, stiff meeting with the Communist Party general secretary in four years.

Deng, too, seemed for a time to give special consideration to the Japanese. In early 1985, when the ten-member British trade mission arrived in Beijing after the Hong Kong agreement was signed, its members found that their trip coincided with a visit by one hundred members of the Japanese Chamber of Commerce. The Japanese delegation had an audience with Deng; the British trade mission did not.

When China went on its buying binge, the cadres looking for new motor vehicles for their work units bought Japanese. Toyota cars, commuter vans, and pickup trucks were the special favorites. When Chinese owners went looking for electronics goods for their homes, they turned to the Japanese, too: to brands such as Hitachi, Toshiba, Sanyo, Sony, and National.

The statistics were startling. In a single year Japan's car and truck exports to China increased sevenfold, from 10,800 vehicles in 1983 to 85,000 in 1984. (Before 1984, Chinese motor vehicle imports had been at such low levels that the largest single overseas supplier was the Soviet Union.)[4] In the first half of 1985 sales shot up even more. From January through June of that year, Japanese companies collected $249 million from sales of passenger cars to China and another $601 million from the sales of buses and trucks. By mid-1985 China had become the second-largest export market for the Japanese car industry, after the United States.

For color television sets, China became Japan's biggest single export market in the world. In 1984 Japan exported 2.3 million color TV sets to China, seven times more than the previous year and nearly twice as many as Japan sold to the United States. In 1985 the Chinese bought another 3.5 million Japanese TV sets, spending close to $1 billion on them. Of all Japan's TV exports to the entire world in 1985, 40 percent went to China. For Japanese electronics companies, China represented the last untapped color TV market—a final chance to make big money before they abandoned TV exports to the cheaper competition from Taiwan and South Korea and moved on to video recorders and other higher-technology products. In February 1985, for the first time in several years, the growth in output of color TVs in Japan was larger than the increase for video recorders.

"Sales executives from Matsushita, Sanyo, Hitachi, Toshiba, and other major [electrical appliance] makers are busily shuttling between Japan and China, making the trip so often that some people have jokingly said they should buy commuter passes. But for them, the stakes could be very great. . . . Never in history has there been a national market of this magnitude, untapped," said the Japanese External Trade Organization (JETRO) in its *China Newsletter*.[5] In 1984–5 sales of Japanese refrigerators, washing machines, and video recorders all increased severalfold from previous years. China became Japan's second leading export market for refrigerators.

Needless to say, China's unprecedented spending on imported consumer goods had a quick and drastic impact upon the economy—in particular, its balance of trade and its foreign reserves. In 1983, before the consumer boom started, Japan was already China's leading trading partner, with $10 billion in business between the two countries. At that time the trade was in balance, with Japan's purchases of oil and coal making up for Chinese purchases of Japanese equipment. But in 1984 Japan's overall exports to China increased by 47 percent, and the following year they went up another 71 percent from the record 1984 levels. In 1984 Sino-Japanese trade jumped to $13.2 million, with China running a deficit of $2 billion. In 1985 the total trade figure was $18.9 billion, and China's deficit with Japan alone was $5.9 billion.

From a nation with regular trade surpluses, China turned into a country facing mounting deficits. Its foreign exchange reserves were dropping month by month. Starting from levels close to $19 billion in early 1984, the reserves dropped to approximately $11 billion a year later.

China's consumer spending was getting out of control. From both an economic and a political standpoint, the situation was unsustainable. The Chinese leadership was getting itself into trouble. At first the regime had been caught unaware of the scope of the spending spree, but within a few months it realized what a mistake it had made. By the first few months of 1985 Chinese leaders began taking steps to rein in the consumerism.

Their first target was the "spend money" propaganda campaign. The stories about revolutionary changes in clothing and lifestyle vanished from the Chinese press. In late March 1985 Chinese Premier Zhao Ziyang appeared on nationwide television wearing a Mao jacket instead of the Western business suit that he, like Communist Party General Secretary Hu Yaobang, ordinarily wore in public. In his annual report to the National People's Congress, China's analog to America's State of the Union address, Zhao, looking chastened, ruefully admitted that he and his government had made errors in the first few months of the new program of urban reforms. He admonished the nation to adhere to the values of modesty, prudence, and thrift. It was a stunning reversal. "Our country has a population of one billion, organized in more than two hundred million households," Zhao said. "The domestic market, consequently, has an enormous capacity. If everyone rushed to buy the same commodities at the same time, no state reserve, however rich, could cope with the situation." He announced that the regime would keep the economy under tighter control. Local officials soon found that they needed approval from Beijing again before spending large sums of money and particularly before spending foreign exchange.

The regime gradually began to take steps to curb imports. Local officials were told they should stop rushing to buy foreign products. Even those provinces and municipalities that still had foreign exchange were ordered by Beijing to use it on major projects for China's infrastructure and not to waste the money on imported consumer goods. In March 1985 China increased its customs duties on imports, and a few months later it added on a new "regulatory tax" on imports in addition to the high customs levies. A few months later Beijing ordered that Chinese factories manufacturing consumer goods should stop importing components from abroad. By the fall of 1985 the regime adopted a two-year moratorium on the importation of most motor vehicles from abroad.

The next group of targets were the special economic zones. In June 1985 Deng announced that Shenzhen, the most advanced of the special zones, was merely an experiment. "If it fails, we can draw lessons from it," he remarked one day, raising the possibility that Shenzhen might someday be closed down. (On such words of less-than-complete support from China's top leader, the course of the nation can change.)

A few weeks later the Party leadership made public the details of an unprecedented, multimillion-dollar scandal on Hainan and dismissed the two top government officials on the island. The Hainan scandal demonstrated that the scope of profiteering and corruption in the special economic zones had been staggering. Communist Party and government officials and the People's Liberation Army were all involved. According to the Party's Central Commission for Discipline Inspection, during a fourteen-month period in 1984 and early 1985, officials on Hainan approved the importation of 89,000 foreign cars, 2.9 million television sets, 250,000 video recorders, and 122,000 motorcycles, virtually all of them for resale inland.

In order to obtain the foreign exchange to buy the goods, local bank branches on Hainan charged illegal fees for the issuance of 4.2 billion yuan (about $1.5 billion) in loans. They also solicited money from other governments across China: according to the authorities, Hainan bought $570 million in foreign exchange from twenty-one different provinces and municipalities. At least two billion yuan ($700 million) of the loans had not yet been repaid. On this tropical island virtually every public institution, even a kindergarten and the *Hainan Daily* newspaper, set up its own private trading corporation to buy and resell foreign goods. The *Liberation Army Daily*, the official newspaper for the armed forces, later reported that the Chinese navy had used military aircraft to transport 6,000 video cassettes, 1,000 video recorders, nearly 400 television sets, and a minibus from Hainan to the inland province of Sichuan, where the goods were resold for profit.

While the emphasis was on Japanese cars and electronics, the importers of Hainan bought other foreign goods as well. Hainan was so undeveloped that there were not many paved roads or indoor toilets. Yet visitors to the island in 1985 found Cadbury chocolates in the stores, a luxury to be found virtually nowhere on the Chinese mainland. The chocolates had probably been brought in from Hong Kong.

Soon after making public the details of the Hainan scandal, the Chinese leadership urged the nation to turn away from foreign products. "Do not blindly worship Western goods," said one press commentary.[6] Needless to say, that commentary and others like it did little to dampen the desires of the Chinese people for Western consumer products. But such warnings by the Chinese leadership demonstrated the growing political sensitivity of China's open-door policy. They showed how tempting, and threatening, foreign goods and ideas were becoming inside the People's Republic.

The final target was Japan itself. In May 1985 Wei Xiaorong, an official of China's Ministry of Foreign Economic Relations and Trade, told Japanese reporters that because of its trade deficit, China was hoping to limit imports from Japan for the remainder of the year. That month Japanese companies noticed that new purchase contracts for televisions and for household appliances virtually dried up.

Those steps were only the beginning of a concerted campaign against Japanese goods. Chinese news organs denounced what they called the poor quality of Japanese products. In early September 1985 *People's Daily* wrote that Chinese buyers of "inferior imported Japanese Mitsubishi trucks" were demanding their money back. "There are quality problems in all the 31 Japanese trucks bought by the Xinjiang Cereals and Oils Transport Company," the newspaper said. Mitsubishi said it would replace the trucks and compensate the Chinese purchasers for any financial losses.

On September 18, 1985, as officials of the Communist Party from around China gathered inside the Great Hall of the People for the first day of a special Party conference to select a new Central Committee, several hundred students from local universities staged a protest outside in Tiananmen Square to denounce "Japanese militarism." It was a relatively small demonstration, at least by the standards of 1989, when hundreds of thousands of Chinese jammed Tiananmen Square. But at the time, in 1985, it was daring and significant: There had been no political demonstrations of any kind in Tiananmen Square since the beginning of the decade.

Over the next few weeks there were anti-Japanese protests in several other Chinese cities. Students protested Japan's modern-day "economic invasion" of China. In one city, Chengdu, American officials planning a visit by Vice President George Bush hurriedly switched the cars for his motorcade from Japanese Toyotas to Chinese-made Shanghai sedans in order to avoid getting caught up in the anti-Japanese turmoil.

To a certain extent the wave of anti-Japanese protests served the purposes of the Chinese regime, both demonstrating that there was strong public support for restricting imports and strengthening the position of the Chinese leadership in economic negotiations with Japan. On the other hand, from the point of view of China's top leaders, Deng, Hu, and Zhao, the demonstrations were at best a mixed blessing. The three of them, and particularly Hu, had fostered the economic policies that had led to the student protests. At the time, some foreign observers believed that the anti-Japanese protests were encouraged by conservative forces within the Chinese Communist Party to embarrass the leadership. (Such speculations were given credence by subsequent events. In early 1987, under intensified criticism by hard-liners in the Communist Party leadership, Hu Yaobang was forced to step down as Communist Party general secretary. The Party's official criticism of Hu included charges that he had mishandled China's relations with Japan—in other words, that he had become too close to the Japanese. Moreover, one Party circular concerning Hu's ouster said he "went too far in calling for greater consumption and was not well disposed toward slogans that called for caution and economy.")

The period where China looked upon Japan as its model came to an end. Japan's transgression had been merely to sell its goods to China, but by doing this so rapidly and in such large quantities, the Japanese revived old memories of Japan seeking economic domination of China. The 1984–85 period rekindled popular Chinese hostility to Japan and made Chinese leaders much more wary in their dealings with the Japanese. By the end of the 1980s, when its trade was in balance once again, China began reaching out for new trade and economic links with its Asian neighbors—this time, however, with Taiwan and South Korea.

When China clamped down on Japanese imports, a number of Japanese manufacturers and middlemen got caught in the squeeze. By September 1985 more than a million Japanese television sets and video recorders were being held up in Chinese ports because of Chinese import restrictions. Another 300,000 TV sets and 100,000 video recorders and an estimated 5,000 to 10,000 cars were stranded in Hong Kong.[7]

Some of Japan's largest manufacturers had run up profits so large in China that they couldn't be matched elsewhere in the world. For the first half of 1986 Hitachi reported that its after-tax earnings declined by 47 percent from the previous year. One of the principal factors, the company said, was a slowdown in the sales of color television sets to China.

When American Motors officials saw how many cars the Japanese were selling to China, AMC hurriedly tried to get in on the action.

The Americans told their Chinese partners that they would be happy to ship AMC Jeeps quickly from the United States to China for immediate sales. At one point AMC Vice President Joseph E. Cappy came to Beijing and promised the joint venture's board of directors that Beijing Jeep would get a commission of $500 for every AMC Jeep that was imported from the United States.[8]

But it was no use. China wanted American Motors for a different purpose. It needed AMC to give China the sort of technology and expertise necessary for China to develop a modern automobile industry of its own. That was, after all, what the two sides had been talking about for the previous five years. AMC had happily accepted the idea, believing it would gain, in exchange for its technology, not only an entrée into the Chinese market, but also a low-cost labor base from which to export to the rest of Asia.

It was too late for the Americans to try to ship built-up AMC Jeeps from the United States to China. Officials in Beijing reminded the Americans that they had their own, different sort of deal. The Americans were supposed to teach China how to manufacture jeeps.

12

Launching the Cherokee

Oddly enough, at the time Beijing Jeep opened for business in 1984, American Motors and its new Chinese partners had still not decided what sort of jeep the new joint venture was going to produce. While Japanese businessmen were fanning out through the cities and provinces of China, selling millions of dollars' worth of Toyotas and Nissans, American Motors and its Chinese partners were still groping for the right product.

The factory was manufacturing the old Chinese jeeps, the BJ212s. In 1984 it turned out 16,412 of these old jeeps, considerably more than in the previous year—even though the number of workers had been reduced from more than ten thousand, under Beijing Automotive Works, the Chinese state enterprise, to only four thousand in the new joint venture. Under the 1983 contract the BJ212 was supposed to go out of production after five years. Using some of the basic technology of the AMC Jeep, such as the drive train, American Motors was supposed to help China to design and manufacture a completely new Chinese jeep.

But despite this general agreement, there were fundamental differences between the Americans and the Chinese about the nature of the new Chinese jeep and the method by which it would be made. At best American Motors had been merely stringing the Chinese along. At worst it was deliberately misleading China with a sales technique that is commonly known to American consumers as bait-and-switch.

The Americans didn't really want to design a completely new Chinese jeep. At the time they negotiated the contract, they thought this idea might at least be feasible. But the Americans wanted the new Chinese jeep to be as close as possible to the Jeeps they were selling in the United States and the rest of the world, so that the parts in the new Chinese jeep would be interchangeable with those used elsewhere. China's primitive auto industry could hardly be expected to begin producing parts for American Jeeps that were up to world standards, so naturally the Americans hoped to export American-made Jeep parts to China.

There is a common term for the technique of shipping all the parts for a motor vehicle abroad and having these parts assembled in an overseas factory. It is called CKD ("complete knock-down"). During the negotiations leading up to the 1983 contract, Chinese auto officials had angrily rejected the idea of CKD production. "What do you take us for?" some Chinese officials asked C.B. Sung, AMC's consultant. "You just want us to put things together? You don't want us to be able to manufacture? You really consider us to be a colony." Sung realized there was no way China would accept CKD production at the outset. You had to pussyfoot around the idea, Sung thought. Another AMC official working on the China project later put it more simply: AMC executives realized that if, while negotiating the contract, they had rejected outright the idea of designing a completely new Chinese jeep, they wouldn't have concluded any deal in the first place. There would have been no contract.

Officials at Beijing Jeep such as Chairman Wu made clear that China's desire for a new jeep was influenced largely by the People's Liberation Army. Although it was a part of the deal that was little advertised in the United States, American Motors was indirectly helping to modernize China's army, which had been badly embarrassed in 1979 by its unsuccessful invasion of Vietnam. For military reasons the PLA wanted a jeep that was radically different from the ones being made in America. The PLA wanted a four-door jeep, so that Chinese soldiers could quickly get into and out of both front and back seats. And it wanted a jeep with a soft top, a convertible. With the top down, it would be easy for Chinese soldiers to open fire from inside the car. Ordinarily the PLA took only 10 percent of the output of the Beijing Jeep factory, and the rest were sold to civilian work units. But in wartime or other emergencies, the Americans learned, the PLA was entitled to take every jeep that came off the assembly line.

The sort of vehicle Chinese officials wanted couldn't be made from any of AMC's existing Jeeps. But in signing the contract, the two sides had glossed over this point. The Chinese intended to persuade the Americans to invest the effort and money necessary to build a completely new jeep in China. The Americans hoped to persuade the Chinese to abandon the idea of having its own unique new jeep and accept one based largely or, better yet, entirely on the American model.

Throughout the year after the contract was signed, the two sides held meeting after meeting to discuss the new product Beijing Jeep would manufacture. At first Chairman Wu and other Chinese officials startled the AMC team by urging that the timetable for production be speeded up. Instead of trying to launch a newly designed jeep within five years, the Chinese said, perhaps it could be done in three. AMC officials, meanwhile, suggested that the joint venture could start by producing an American Jeep, the CJ, from imported kits, while working to design some new Chinese jeep based upon the CJ.

American and Chinese engineers began working up clay models, plans, and detailed specifications for the new Chinese jeep. A small AMC design team began doing the drawings, and financial specialists calculated what the Chinese jeep would cost. But the more AMC looked at the idea, the less feasible it seemed. Even Clare, the strongest supporter of the China project, later conceded that the costs were extraordinarily high. Designing a new vehicle from scratch would cost more than $200 million and another $200 to $300 million if it had to be tooled. A new factory would probably have to be built. When added up, a really high-class new vehicle would cost around $1 billion; even a simple, truck-like jeep, with not much ride or sophistication, would cost around $700 million. It was out of the question. Where was Beijing Jeep going to get that kind of money? China didn't have it, and American Motors didn't, either.

During this period, AMC's corporate headquarters in Southfield was in political turmoil. Five years earlier the company had been bought by Renault, France's state-owned automobile company. Within AMC's top management there were tensions between the French and the Americans. In September 1984 these tensions boiled over when Paul Tippett, AMC's chief executive officer, who had signed the China deal, was replaced by Jose J. Dedeurwaerder, a Renault official who had been working in Detroit for the previous three years.

Dedeurwaerder, who is Belgian, had never been enthusiastic about AMC's move into China. He was famous around American Motors for saying that the China project was crazy, that the Communists were just going to steal American Motors' technology. Dedeurwaerder wouldn't even go to China and see Beijing Jeep. To make matters worse, Dedeurwaerder had an especially frosty relationship with Clare. The China venture had made Clare famous in Detroit, and Clare felt Dedeurwaerder resented it. After *Automotive News* named Clare the industry's best international executive the year after the China deal was signed, Clare noticed that Dedeurwaerder stopped taking him to their twice-a-month lunches. Years later Clare would look back and reflect that the *Automotive News* article had probably marked the beginning of the end of his career at American Motors. Dedeurwaerder wasn't going to kill the China project, but he didn't intend to help it much, either.

At the same time there were also tensions between AMC's international division, headed by Clare, and AMC's domestic manufacturing people. These were the usual prejudices, ones that can be found in virtually any American company with both domestic and overseas operations. AMC's international division thought the domestic people were a bunch of provincial hicks who didn't know much about the world outside Toledo and Detroit. The domestic divisions thought the international people were better at ordering wine than at making cars. In 1984 Clare's international division was in trouble: The high value of the dollar was making it increasingly difficult to sell Jeeps overseas. The China deal got swept up in these tensions, too. On the one hand, Beijing Jeep was an international operation, but on the other hand, the problem immediately confronting it was how to design and build a new motor vehicle, and that was a problem the manufacturing people thought was their bailiwick.

Gradually, in mid-1984, authority over the China venture shifted from Clare's international division to the manufacturing executives back home. And the manufacturing people said that the China deal made no sense. You just can't design and build a completely new car in China, they said. Dedeurwaerder supported the manufacturing people.

The biggest problem was convincing the Chinese. At a Beijing Jeep board of directors meeting in June 1984, Chinese officials again pressed for a newly designed jeep. Suggestions by the Americans that the joint venture start by assembling AMC Jeeps in China from American parts were rebuffed. The Chinese board members argued that AMC was unwilling to cooperate with China and was simply trying to find a way to control the Chinese market.[1]

Finally AMC's management team decided to overwhelm the Chinese. In September 1984 AMC organized what later became known as "the vice presidents' visit" to China. Ordinarily the highest-ranking AMC official to visit China was Clare. But this time AMC dispatched to Beijing a high-powered delegation that included the heads of four different international and domestic units: the vice presidents in charge of manufacturing, product development, finance, and purchasing. The vice presidents' mission was to persuade China to accept the idea of assembling AMC's newest product, the Cherokee Jeep—which had been introduced on the American market in 1983—from parts kits imported from the United States.

Over a period of several days, the AMC vice presidents met with senior Chinese officials at the Beijing Jeep factory. First each of the Americans sat down individually with a Chinese counterpart, and later they all assembled for large meetings. Clare, by now AMC's version of an old China hand, found himself holding back, letting the other vice presidents do the talking. They were the ones who were supposed to be delivering the message from AMC headquarters.

Again and again the vice presidents told their Chinese counterparts that designing a new Chinese jeep would be absolutely impossible. It was just not economical, and it was a waste of time. If China wanted to get the joint venture moving, then CKD production, assembling from American parts, would be the way to go. The new jeep China wanted was really pretty close to AMC's Cherokee, the vice presidents said: why, AMC's manufacturing division had even managed to fit a Cherokee drive train into one of the old Chinese jeeps in some tests in Kenosha.

If China accepted the idea of making Cherokees, the vice presidents continued, Beijing Jeep could even begin producing cars in China within a year or so, two or three years faster than even the best projections for making a new Chinese jeep. Furthermore, the vice presidents contended, starting with a CKD assembly operation would be the best possible way for China to learn how to manufacture automobiles with modern techniques and equipment. China could begin with imported parts kits for the Cherokees and then gradually move toward "localization"—that is, gradually replace the imported American components with parts that were made inside China. That way, the Americans argued, China could slowly build up an infrastructure for its auto industry.

Chinese officials listened but said little. They nodded occasionally, indicating that they understood the Americans' message but didn't necessarily agree. The Cherokee wasn't exactly what they wanted. No matter what the Americans said, the car didn't have the soft top or the four doors and easily accessible rear seats that the PLA was seeking. Still, as the meetings with the vice presidents ended, the Chinese agreed to consider AMC's new ideas.

The Chinese officials at Beijing Jeep were under pressure themselves. They were eager to get production started. It was clear that the Americans wouldn't immediately go along with the idea of designing a new Chinese jeep. If the joint venture fell apart, the Chinese would have been seriously embarrassed.

Furthermore, Beijing Jeep faced competition from within the Chinese automobile industry. It is difficult to overestimate the rivalries among Chinese enterprises, even when they are all state-owned. And it is equally difficult to overestimate the rivalries among Chinese cities, particularly between Beijing and Shanghai. The Shanghai Automobile Factory was on the verge of signing a major deal with Volkswagen to assemble VW Santanas in Shanghai. The Volkswagen deal, which would be signed in Beijing in the presence of Chinese Premier Zhao Ziyang and West German Chancellor Helmut Kohl, would compete for attention within China. At Beijing Jeep, Chairman Wu was seen driving around in a Volkswagen Santana, testing it out, thinking about it.

Gradually the Chinese auto officials decided to accept the idea of having Beijing Jeep produce AMC's Cherokees. There were some advantages to the idea. At the time, the Cherokee was virtually brand-new technology; it had just been introduced onto the American market. During the early 1980s, as China began doing business with the rest of the world, its leaders became extremely fearful of spending lots of money on old technology that would soon be outdated. The Cherokee was the cutting edge of the jeep business.

Moreover, Beijing Jeep could start producing the Cherokees, watch the Americans introduce the new technology to China, and still continue to make the old Chinese BJ212s.

The final decision was made on October 10, 1984, during a special board of directors meeting in Detroit. Some of the AMC officials were distracted: At the time, the Tigers were playing the San Diego Padres in the World Series, and the Americans wanted to sneak off and see some baseball. But at the board meetings, Chinese officials from Beijing Jeep for the first time agreed to CKD production. Starting in the fall of 1985, Beijing Jeep would assemble Cherokees from American parts. The Americans promised that the joint venture would aim to gradually replace the American parts with ones of Chinese manufacture. Clare thought that in going along with the Cherokee, the Chinese seemed fatalistic. There wasn't really anything else they could do, short of scrapping the entire joint venture. The Americans had made it plain that there was no way they were going to agree to build an entirely new Chinese jeep.

It was a fundamental change of plans. Yet after all the endless meetings, it was not clear that either the Americans or the Chinese participants in the joint venture foresaw all the implications of what they were deciding.

Chinese officials seemed to believe they were going along with a short-term expedient. They didn't think of themselves as abandoning the idea of eventually producing a new, Chinese-made jeep. In fact, over the next few years they would continue to raise the idea on a number of occasions, suggesting that perhaps a Chinese jeep of the sort the PLA wanted could be produced from the American Cherokee. Nor did the Chinese realize that once they gave the go-ahead for the Cherokee, that decision would shape AMC's commitment in China. AMC would be making money by selling kits of Cherokee parts to Beijing Jeep, and inevitably it would want to sell as many of those kits as possible.

The Americans, meanwhile, made even more fundamental mistakes. They didn't yet understand the nature of Chinese socialism or the workings of China's socialist economy.

When officials at Beijing Jeep gave their blessing for the switch to the Cherokees, AMC went forward without getting written approval from any higher-level Chinese authorities, even though the change to CKD production had significant economic implications for China. Importing Cherokee kits from the United States required large amounts of foreign exchange. Spending that foreign exchange required government approval. Bringing in the kits meant asking the government for import licenses. Yet the CKD production of the Cherokees was not formally cleared with China's State Planning Commission and the State Economic Commission—the two agencies responsible for running the Chinese economy, allocating supplies and raw materials to state enterprises, setting levels of output, and deciding how much foreign exchange state enterprises can spend. While Chairman Wu and the other Chinese officials at Beijing Jeep had approved production of the Cherokee, AMC had no guarantee that the central government would spend the money necessary to import the American parts. The Americans were taking a big risk.

In the fall of 1984 China seemed to be decentralizing its economy, giving increased decision-making power to individual provinces, municipalities, and state enterprises. Yet anyone who believed that an individual Chinese enterprise could approve important economic decisions on its own was putting too much stock in romanticized and exaggerated Western notions of a China that had "gone capitalist." Centralized state planning was not dead in China. It was far from certain that the decentralization measures of 1984 would last—and, as things turned out, they didn't.

After many months of wrangling over what sort of jeep to make, the two sides now finally turned their attention to the job of production. The launch of the Cherokee in China was set for October 1, 1985. There was only a year to prepare the factory for the launch. Time was short. In Beijing, the Americans and Chinese rushed to make the changes necessary to assemble the new jeep.

One of the most important jobs was to set up a new assembly line for the Cherokees. American Motors was sending over the equipment for the new line from the United States. The Americans at Beijing Jeep needed a large open space in which the boxes of machinery could be unpacked and then delivered to the assembly line. The area they needed was in the factory's body shop. But Bob Steinseifer, the American in charge of industrial management at Beijing Jeep, couldn't get Chinese officials to clear away the space. Within the factory, two different Chinese departments were at loggerheads. Chinese officials in the body shop refused to do the work, because the material was destined for the assembly line. It was not their responsibility, they said. Yet officials in charge of the assembly line also refused, because the work that needed to be done was inside the body shop. Furthermore, the assembly-line people pointed out that handling materials wasn't their responsibility.

In utter exasperation, Steinseifer and Ed Schulze, the AMC official in charge of production, decided to do the work on their own. One day they wore their usual dress clothes, shirts and ties, to the factory to take care of their regular management tasks. That night, after dinner, they changed into overalls, returned to the plant, and, without telling the Chinese, started to clear away the space. The two Americans—Steinseifer, big and overweight; Schulze, thin and wiry—looked like Jackie Gleason and Art Carney transported to China. They spent several hours that night hauling away old boxes and sweeping the floor.

Until that time, none of the Americans working at Beijing Jeep had really gotten their hands dirty. Most of their efforts had been devoted to planning and paperwork. Word that the foreigners were doing manual labor at the plant, on their own, at night, spread quickly through Beijing Jeep. The following night, when Steinseifer and Schulze returned in their overalls to continue the job, the Chinese vice president for manufacturing and his entire team of associates came in to greet them. As the Americans kept on clearing away boxes and sweeping the floors, Chinese cadres grabbed the brooms out of their hands to do the sweeping on their own. After a couple of days, others in the factory joined in. When Steinseifer and Schulze began delivering new equipment to workstations on the existing Chinese assembly line, workers began clearing spaces on their own areas to get ready for the Americans. During breaks from the work, Chinese factory officials brought in beer, watermelons, and ice cream. It seemed to Steinseifer that once the bureaucratic hassles were overcome, everyone seemed to have a good time. It was a hot summer week, Steinseifer was sweating a lot, and the work was leaving him blackened with soot. Chinese officials were continually telling him, "You've got to rest, you've got to *xiuxi* [rest] for a while." He wasn't even tired. Still, he thought to himself, this must be the first time anyone here had ever seen foreigners work with their hands. In China, it was rare enough for even Chinese managers to do manual labor, much less Americans.

The American team in Beijing had serious management problems of its own. Angus MacGregor, the first president of Beijing Jeep, the man AMC had sent to run the joint venture and who was known mostly for his campaign against the office beds, stayed only a half year before leaving in mid-1984. The Americans, Chinese, and MacGregor himself apparently agreed that he wasn't the right man for the job. Chairman Wu felt MacGregor wasn't accustomed to Chinese management or, in general, to the Chinese way of doing things. As time went on, Chairman Wu thought, MacGregor became less confident and less involved in the joint venture.

AMC's next choice for president of Beijing Jeep, Richard Chatterton, lasted roughly a year before he, too, was replaced. Chatterton's arrival and departure were partially the result of AMC's internal turmoil. He was a veteran of AMC's plant in Kenosha. AMC's China staff considered him an old-style manufacturing man, the sort of authoritarian plant manager one AMC colleague called a "dinosaur." Chatterton had been pushed for China by AMC's domestic manufacturing people, but once there, he couldn't get along either with the AMC team in China or with Clare and the international division. To make matters worse, in the view of the AMC people, when the Chinese and Americans had disputes within the joint venture, Chatterton increasingly sided with the Chinese. He began firing off telexes to Detroit, urging AMC to take on big new projects in China.

At AMC headquarters, Clare won the support he needed to replace Chatterton. Without telling Chatterton or any of the other Americans working in China, Clare then made a secret trip to Beijing to break the news to AMC's Chinese partners. The Chinese rushed to Chatterton's support. Chairman Wu even flew off to Detroit to try to persuade AMC to keep Chatterton on the job. The mission failed. In the final months before the Cherokee was launched, the job of the American president of Beijing Jeep was vacant.[2]

Still, these unpleasantries affected only top management. Through the summer of 1985, in the final months before production of the Cherokee was to begin, morale at Beijing Jeep was high and relations between the Americans and Chinese unusually good. AMC sent a huge task force of nearly forty Americans on short-term assignments to China to do all the work that was necessary to launch the Cherokee. These were some of AMC's best people, the company's old-timers, the Jeep professionals. There were too many of them to house in any one or even two hotels, so they wound up in small groups all over Beijing. Every morning buses would make the rounds of the hotels to pick them up and bring them to the plant. Some members of the launch team worked as many as forty to fifty days without a day off.

It was a remarkable achievement in such a short period of time. The Chinese could see the progress, and so could the Americans. They were all busy, too busy to argue or complain very much, too busy to brood. Schulze, who came as part of the special launch team and then stayed on as one of AMC's eight full-time staffers, remembered those months as probably his happiest in China. He was working ten, twelve, fourteen hours a day installing the new equipment, and he felt he was accomplishing something. The Chinese seemed pleased. They didn't challenge the Americans. They wanted to learn how to use the new technology. They watched the Americans work for hours at a time. Some of the old-time AMC Jeep professionals on short-term duty in China couldn't believe it. Every time the Americans installed a new piece of machinery, it seemed as though they had half the city of Beijing watching them. Later on, Schulze realized that the frenetic work on the launch project had delayed his culture shock. Except for the low-grade hotel he was sleeping in for a few hours a night, he barely had time to think about China.

Late in the summer of 1985, the Americans and Chinese staged their first trial run of Beijing Jeep's new assembly line. The line was clean and spacious, but the results were less than perfect. The first Chinese Cherokee—which had been assembled over the previous few days—had to be pushed off the end of the line because it wouldn't drive. Workers on the line had succeeded in hooking up the Cherokee's engine and transmission, but they had forgotten to tighten the clutch. It was an ominous start.

But on September 26, 1985, the factory was ready for official ceremonies and a press conference to commemorate the launch of the new Cherokee. Once again, just as when Beijing Jeep opened its doors the previous year, workers at the plant banged on gongs and cymbals in ritual celebration. Once again, Chen Muhua, the woman who served as Beijing Jeep's unofficial political patron, and who had recently been promoted from trade minister to the head of China's central bank, did the honors, cutting a ribbon with scissors handed to her on a tray covered with red silk. This time, in the bright sunshine of a splendid Beijing autumn day, Chinese officials graciously added a touch of Western culture, a tape of "Jingle Bells."

Press releases handed out by Chinese officials, written in mind-numbing English, hinted at the strained nature of communications between the Chinese and Americans at Beijing Jeep. "The quality of construction and speed of progress-making of the factory reform are highly evaluated by Chinese and foreign experts," said one Chinese press release. "Our company strictly pursue the reform, develop material civilization and spiritual civilization together motivating employees to be in a good spirit and beautify the company's environment so we are awarded as the civilized company in 1984."

At the press conference, American and Chinese officials made a series of claims, some of which later turned out to be overly optimistic projections or wishful thinking. They were claims aimed at the two sides' domestic constituencies—for the Americans, AMC's shareholders and auto-industry executives, and for the Chinese, the country's Communist Party leadership.

Joseph E. Cappy, AMC's executive vice president, voiced the time-honored Western dream of selling to the most populous country in the world. China was "the world's largest potential market," he said. American Motors hoped to produce 750 Cherokees in China before the end of the year, 4,500 more in 1986, and 40,000 a year by 1990. "Selling that [number of cars] in this country is a piece of cake," asserted P. Jeffrey Trimmer, head of AMC's operations in the Far East.

Cappy and Trimmer were asked repeatedly by reporters how the joint venture would obtain the foreign exchange necessary to import American parts and how AMC would get its profits from China back to the United States. Repeatedly they minimized the problem. "It's not one of those critical issues we have to face at this time," Cappy said. He pointed out that any profits AMC earned in Chinese currency by selling the new Cherokees inside China could be reinvested into Beijing Jeep, increasing American Motors' 31 percent equity in the joint venture to as much as 49 percent. "We are not in this for short-term profit building," he declared. He was confident that Beijing Jeep would be able to export Cherokee Jeeps from China to other countries in Asia and thereby earn foreign currency. "For American Motors, [Beijing Jeep] has meant not only an entry into the Chinese market, but the establishment of a strategic manufacturing base in the Pacific rim of Asia," he explained.

Meanwhile, Chairman Wu told the press conference that he hoped within three years 70 percent of the Cherokee's parts would be manufactured in China. That target turned out to be just as unrealistic as AMC's forecasts of the number of Cherokees it would produce. Chairman Wu also added, "We enjoy strong support from governmental authorities and all the Chinese and foreigners involved in the project," a claim AMC would soon come to question.

In the midst of the celebrations, there were a few notes of realism. Trimmer confessed to reporters that AMC's move into China had turned out to be "a continuing adventure." He said the Americans had learned that "it ain't over when you negotiate the agreement [contract], because that's when the problems really begin. . . . When you sign the agreement, you're dealing with high-level people. Afterward, they're gone." In a special lunch for American and Chinese officials at the Beijing International Club, Chairman Wu sounded a sober note, declaring, "We will confront lots of difficulties in the future. We must keep our heads."

But optimism and playfulness were the order of the day. Inside the factory, in front of photographers, Chairman Wu climbed into a navy-blue Cherokee with a red ribbon on the hood, started up the engine, and proudly drove it off the end of the assembly line. This time, fortunately, the Jeep didn't have to be pushed.

Four weeks later, on October 15, 1985, the ritual was repeated for Vice President Bush, who was visiting China. Bush sat behind the wheel of a new Cherokee and turned on the ignition. "Off to the Beijing Hotel," he shouted, as enthusiastic as if he were driving a snowmobile in a New Hampshire primary. "This represents the wave of the future in cooperation between China and the private sector of the United States."

By that time, the Americans were coming to realize that Beijing Jeep, the wave of the future, was in trouble.

13

The Newcomer

During the disastrous series of meetings in Las Vegas in the summer of 1985 and once again during the launch of the Cherokee in Beijing that fall, the Chinese noticed a new face among the American Motors team, a slightly balding chain-smoker with reddish-brown hair, a ruddy complexion, and a baritone voice. His name was Don St. Pierre. Officially he was listed as the representative of Jeep Japan, the manager of the company's Japanese subsidiary. Unofficially he was AMC's candidate to take over its China operations.

St. Pierre was a shrewd operator, the sort of person AMC's top managers felt could hold his own in China. He was familiar with manufacturing, but most of all he loved the political side of business. He knew that you could build a better mousetrap overseas and still not make any money if the host government or local conditions got in the way. St. Pierre seemed to enjoy meeting with local officials, a job that the heads of manufacturing operations sometimes found tedious and distracting. He liked to quiz diplomats, journalists, and scholars about the vicissitudes of the political and economic situation in China. He was even willing to get mixed up in Chinese intrigues, pushing to advance the careers of those Chinese officials who worked smoothly with his company and to sidetrack the careers of those he thought stood in its way.

He could play the role of a hatchet man when necessary. Before coming to China he had been given the job of closing down two of AMC's overseas operations, first in Indonesia and then in Japan. In Tokyo AMC suspected that a local employee was embezzling money, and St. Pierre spent most of a year dealing with lawyers and private detectives to straighten out the mess.

St. Pierre's introduction to China could not have been less

auspicious. In September 1985, when AMC officials first told the Chinese he was their candidate to be the next president of the Beijing Jeep joint venture, Chinese officials refused even to meet with him. Late one night AMC officials in Beijing called C. B. Sung to ask his help in finding out what the Chinese didn't like about St. Pierre. Sung insisted on meeting St. Pierre first, and St. Pierre passed Sung's inspection. Sung thought he would make a good president.

Within a few days Sung met with Wu Zhongliang, the Chinese leader at BJC. "Why are you rejecting Don St. Pierre?" he asked. "You do not even show good manners by refusing even to see him. That's not fair."

"It has nothing to do with St. Pierre himself," replied Chairman Wu. "In the first place, he is sent here by Renault." Ever since the French auto manufacturer had taken over AMC, the Chinese had been curious about the role the French government played in running the American company.

Sung was stunned. "Where do you get that idea?" he asked.

"He has a French name," Wu replied.

Carefully Sung explained to Chairman Wu that St. Pierre, forty-four, came from Canada and held both Canadian and American passports. His French-Canadian name did not mean he had any connection to France or to Renault. He had been with American Motors for a decade, starting long before the Renault takeover, and had worked at Ford for eleven years before that. St. Pierre had spent his entire career, and almost half his life, working for the American auto industry. He couldn't even speak French, at least not with any fluency.

Wu seemed satisfied but moved on to another objection. "He's not a manufacturing person, and we want someone in manufacturing." Richard Chatterton, the previous American president the Chinese had been so fond of, had been a manufacturing man.

Sung explained that Beijing Jeep needed to learn about more than manufacturing; it needed to know about marketing, international operations, the full spectrum of business operations. Wu refused to budge and offered a compromise: St. Pierre could become the vice president of Beijing Jeep under a Chinese president.

During a walk through the plant, Clare—who was in Beijing for the launch of the Cherokee meetings with Chairman Wu and other Chinese officials—informed St. Pierre of the Chinese pro-

posal. St. Pierre refused to go along. Finally the Chinese side accepted St. Pierre as acting or "deputy" president on probation for
three months. St. Pierre wasn't particularly happy with that, but
he went along. After a month the Chinese factory leaders came to
see St. Pierre, said he was doing a good job, and agreed to make him
president of Beijing Jeep.

In his very first weeks on the job, however, St. Pierre saw that the
joint venture was in trouble. Production of the Cherokees had just
started, and now the Americans were facing up to the realization
that the setup didn't make any sense. More to the point, it wouldn't
make any money, at least not the sort of money that could be taken
out of China.

All through the previous year, both sides had put aside their
differences and left important business questions unsettled. They
had concentrated on the task at hand, setting up the new assembly
line and launching production of the Cherokee. But as they went
about this task, their goals were different.

To the Americans, the Cherokee, assembled from kits sent
from Detroit, was to be the focus of all AMC operations in China.
They realized that the Chinese still wanted them to help design
and produce the new four-door jeep that the People's Liberation
Army wanted, but they hoped their Chinese partners would forget
about that idea. The Americans knew, too, that the Chinese
wanted them to begin producing Chinese-made parts to substitute
for imported ones, and that the Chinese expected them to export
Cherokees from China in order to earn foreign exchange. But the
Americans figured the best approach was just to get production of
the Cherokees under way in China and let these problems work
themselves out later on. They hoped that once the Beijing factory
was set up and running, they could persuade the Chinese to give
permission for the manufacture of large volumes of Cherokees—as
many as 40,000 to 50,000 of them a year by 1990, all made from
the kits imported from Detroit—for sale in China's huge domestic
market. Where China would get the foreign exchange to import
such large numbers of Cherokee kits was something the American
Motors people hadn't really figured out.

For their own reasons the Chinese, too, had been happy to go
along with the start-up of production and leave aside questions
about the future. Chen Xulin, one of the Chinese board members

of Beijing Jeep and eventually its president, later acknowledged to me in an interview that the Chinese aim was simply to obtain American technology. By taking part in the start-up of production, and by gaining access to the assembly-line equipment and the kits of parts used to put together the Cherokees, the Chinese furthered this objective. Nevertheless, Chen admitted, China had intended to import only "a very small volume" of Cherokee kits from the United States—just enough to get a look at the technology.

Both sides had been disingenuous with one another. Now the disagreements were about to emerge at the worst possible time. In the fall of 1985, in the aftermath of the consumer binge and the resulting drop in its foreign reserves, China was imposing severe restrictions on the spending of foreign exchange.

Foreign exchange: U.S. dollars, Japanese yen, French francs, British pounds, West German marks. The Chinese even had their own version, a special currency called foreign exchange certificates (FECs), which were used by foreigners in China and by Chinese importing foreign goods from abroad or exporting Chinese products overseas. All these currencies, including the Chinese FECs, were freely convertible, meaning that they could be traded back and forth for one another on international markets.

But the renminbi, or "people's currency," the regular currency used inside China and on which the economy ran, was not convertible. The two-currency system, one for transactions involving foreigners and one for transactions exclusively among Chinese, became China's principal tool in preventing foreign companies from capturing and dominating its domestic market.

With the import boom of 1984–85 over, China once again began restricting provinces, localities, and departments from spending foreign exchange. Under China's centrally planned economy, each unit submitted an advance plan explaining how it might spend foreign exchange. The general guidelines were that Beijing would approve spending foreign exchange for advanced technology or for items that could help produce Chinese exports.

The need for foreign exchange became the daily obsession for the scores of foreign companies trying to start up business inside China. The problem was simple. In order to import parts from abroad, or to pay for the rent or hotel rooms of foreign business representatives, a joint venture needed foreign exchange. But that foreign exchange couldn't be obtained by selling in China's domestic market, at least not without some special dispensation from the Chinese government. Ordinarily goods sold in China earned renminbi, not foreign exchange.

One way for a company to earn foreign exchange was to export goods abroad from China. That was what China wanted: The Chinese regime hoped the joint ventures would help to create export products. (Indeed, many joint ventures were required by their contracts to export a hefty share of the goods they made in China, even though the foreign businesses would have been happy to sell all their products inside China.) Yet it was hard if not impossible to produce export-quality goods in Chinese factories, particularly in the early years of production. As even senior Chinese officials conceded, the quality was not up to international standards. Moreover, the production costs inside China were surprisingly high.

Of course, foreign exchange wouldn't be necessary if all the required supplies and equipment could be obtained from within China itself. These items could be paid for in renminbi earned from sales inside China. But even when Chinese-made supplies were available, the quality was poor and the costs were high. That was, after all, the reason China had decided to bring in foreign help in the first place. If China had been able to get the industrial quality, the technology, and the management expertise it needed from inside China, it would have had no need for foreign investment.

Two days after the official launch of the new Cherokee, with Cappy and Clare still in Beijing, the top American Motors officials sat down with their Chinese counterparts. St. Pierre, newly arrived in China and preparing to run Beijing Jeep, sat in on the meeting. The Americans wanted to work out some of the unanswered questions concerning the new Chinese Cherokees.

What would the production volume be? How many Cherokee kits would the joint venture import for production in 1986? The initial production in the fall of 1985 was at a token level. No more than seven or eight Cherokees per day were rolling off the assembly line. But the Americans hoped to produce large numbers of Cherokees the following year. What would be the price of those kits—that is, the price that Beijing Jeep, the joint venture in China, would pay to AMC? How much money would the Cherokees sell for inside China, and how much of this money would Chinese purchasers be required to pay in foreign exchange?

In order to plan for the coming year, the Americans needed immediate answers. The Cherokee kits had to be ordered in advance from Detroit, and the decision rested with the Chinese, not only because they held a controlling interest in the joint venture, but also because the Chinese government had to approve import licenses for the kits. The Americans hoped that Beijing Jeep would make 4,000 Cherokees from imported kits in 1986 and as many as 7,000 to 10,000 in 1987. In meetings at the factory, Chinese officials seemed to go along with these targets, at least in the abstract, but were hazy about how these targets would be met.

There were other questions, too—some of them weighty, some mundane, all unresolved.

In order to begin switching from American to Chinese-made parts, the two sides had drawn up an expensive capital budget that included building a new engine factory and a stamping plant in China. Although these new facilities would require a considerable financial investment, there was no agreement on where the money would come from.

Then there was the question of who would pay for the Americans in China. There were only eight AMC representatives in Beijing, and originally their housing costs and other living expenses had been paid by the Chinese joint venture. But the Americans began rebelling against their spartan housing conditions. One by one they began moving out of older places such as the Friendship Hotel and into some of the newly completed joint venture hotels such as the Lido-Holiday Inn. Not only did the Lido cost more, but the rent had to be paid in dollars. The fact that the money was being paid to a joint venture rather than a Chinese state enterprise further annoyed the Chinese officials, and they balked at paying the increased costs for the Americans to live in such luxury.

When the American executives raised these questions, Chinese officials would make no commitments. Whenever the discussions came to money, the Chinese said, "Foreign exchange is a little short here right now." It was clear that China was not ready to start producing the volume of Cherokees AMC had envisioned. The two sides couldn't even come close to an agreement.

The sessions broke up in disarray. Everything was unsettled.

St. Pierre thought it was the most preposterous meeting he had ever witnessed. But AMC executives told him to be patient. "Let's struggle through this thing," they said as they prepared to fly back to Detroit. "We've got no answers, but the answers will come."

Over the next few weeks St. Pierre tried unsuccessfully to get answers. He thought the entire situation was ridiculous. He was supposed to be running Beijing Jeep but was being left hanging on the most fundamental questions about its output and its finances.

Late in the fall AMC dispatched Jeff Trimmer, Clare's assistant and the head of AMC's Far East operations, to Beijing. Trimmer and St. Pierre tried to come up with a full business plan for the joint venture. The problem was becoming increasingly urgent and more pressing: AMC had hundreds of Cherokee parts kits packed and waiting to be shipped to China, but the Chinese government balked at granting import licenses. For the first time, in desperation, they went off, away from their Chinese partners at Beijing Jeep, for a series of meetings with officials of the Beijing government. If the Chinese auto officials at Beijing Jeep couldn't come up with some answers, they thought, maybe the officials in charge of industry and foreign trade for the city of Beijing could help them.

But the city officials were so vague and hazy that they didn't even seem to know what Trimmer and St. Pierre were talking about. Most of them didn't even seem to know what the issues were, much less how they could be resolved. One morning they found a bright young city official, Beijing Vice Mayor Zhang Jianmin, who seemed to listen sympathetically. After two hours Zhang said, "Those are really big problems. I don't know what you're going to do about them."

That noon Trimmer, St. Pierre, and Roger Bruce, another AMC official, considered their plight over a Western lunch at the coffee shop of the Beijing-Toronto, one of the new foreigners-only joint venture hotels. They needed to send a message to the Chinese that would make them realize that AMC could play tough and wasn't going to tolerate this evasiveness. The problems had to be resolved. Before the end of the lunch, Trimmer turned over a paper napkin and took notes as St. Pierre and Bruce began drafting a message to the Chinese, warning them that AMC was planning to retaliate.

The draft on the paper napkin became the basis for what later became known within American Motors as the famous "November telex." It was, in effect, the opening salvo in a nasty, increasingly public battle of wills between the Americans and Chinese.

The telex was sent from American Motors' headquarters in Detroit to Chinese officials of the Beijing Municipality and the Chinese National Automotive Industrial Corporation (CNAIC), the central government agency that oversaw automobile production in China. It described the joint venture's problems and urged that they be settled. China should grant import licenses for the new Cherokee kits, the AMC officials said. If there was no resolution, American Motors would halt all its training of Chinese personnel and all transfer of technology to China.

That threat caught the attention of the Chinese, but it didn't make things any better. The head of China's state-run auto industry, Chen Zutao, was reportedly furious. Not long after the telex was received, C. B. Sung saw Chairman Wu and found that he also was extremely angry. Wu showed Sung AMC's telex. Sung read it and was annoyed, too. He had seen a draft and urged AMC not to send it, at least not in that threatening way. Sung thought it had violated an agreement he had with AMC that every telex and communication with the Chinese would be approved by his office.

From Chairman Wu's perspective, the Americans were being unrealistic about China. Sure, Wu thought, at the board meeting in late September they had all talked about importing four thousand Cherokee kits from American Motors in 1986. But Wu and other Chinese board members had made it clear to the Americans that the volume was not entirely their decision. Wu himself had told the Americans that the final decision would be up to the Chinese government. There were several other Chinese units whose approval was required, such as the Customs Bureau.

China happened to be short of foreign exchange during this period, so the central government was putting pressure on Wu and the Chinese officials at BJC to cut back on its plans to import Cherokee kits. After all, Wu noted, the whole country, all the units in China, had been trying to import foreign cars, along with other foreign products. That was what had led to the foreign exchange problems in the first place. Three years later, in an interview, Wu conceded to me that perhaps the Chinese officials at Beijing Jeep had made a mistake by failing to keep the Chinese government informed about how many Cherokees the Americans were hoping to sell to China. On the other hand, Wu went on, the Chinese government—not Wu and the Chinese team at Beijing Jeep—bore the ultimate responsibility for refusing to grant import licenses for the Cherokees that were packed and awaiting shipment in the United States. Wu was not entirely surprised by the government restrictions that so enraged AMC. It was a fact of life that whenever there was a shortage of foreign exchange, the Chinese government held down on import licenses.

There are few weather changes in the world so drastic or dismal as the quick passage from Beijing autumn to Beijing winter. For a stretch of eight to ten weeks in September and October, Beijing is so sunny and balmy that it could be a concrete-covered California. Then, in the first weeks of November, as the winter cabbages pile up on the streets of the city, the weather turns cold and the sky increasingly gray. Beijing power plants begin burning dirty, low-grade coal, and the air is so sooty that the city is covered with haze. On bad winter days Beijing can be as frigid as Chicago and as polluted as a nineteenth-century British mill town.

The winter of 1985 was particularly grim. In early December Chinese students cancelled their final big anti-Japanese demonstration in Beijing's Tiananmen Square, partly because Communist Party leaders made it plain that they wanted the anti-Japanese protests to stop, but also because the weather was so cold and windy that no human being could stand outside in the square for more than five minutes at a time. During the fall, foreign tourists and businessmen in Beijing had been so numerous that all the hotels were full, and one wing of a newly built Sino-Japanese Friendship Hospital began renting out its rooms for $16 to healthy foreign visitors. ("In China, all our hospitals are subsidized, so the basic fee is not very high," explained Dr. Pan Xuetian, the hospital's assistant director. "In the U.S., a hospital room costs more than a hotel room, doesn't it?") By midwinter virtually all the tourists and most of the business prospectors were gone, and the silvery high rise of Sung's Great Wall Hotel was so empty that at night you could sometimes count on two hands the number of rooms that had lights on inside.

For St. Pierre and the other Americans in Beijing, things went from very bad to much worse. Beijing Jeep's first two hundred Cherokees had been turned over to the State Materials Bureau, a

Chinese government agency, for sale inside China. The State Materials Bureau owed Beijing Jeep approximately $2 million for the Cherokees, but it refused to pay for them. "Don't you know there's a foreign exchange problem here in China?" Chinese officials remarked.

Another 1,008 kits for new Cherokee Jeeps were sitting in the United States, packed and ready to be sent, but St. Pierre had no foreign exchange to pay for them. Chinese officials pointed out that nobody in China could buy Cherokees, because they didn't have any dollars or foreign exchange to spend. The Cherokees were piling up. One Chinese official suggested that they could be sold if St. Pierre would allow Chinese buyers to pay the full cost in Chinese currency. No dice, said St. Pierre. The original idea was for more than half of the $19,000 sales price in China to be paid for in foreign exchange. The kits cost foreign exchange, and the Cherokees had to be paid for at least partly in foreign exchange.

Then one day St. Pierre discovered that his joint venture wasn't even being paid the Chinese currency it was owed for the sale of the old Chinese jeeps. The joint venture was still turning out thousands of BJ212's. These were turned over to the state and allocated, under traditional central planning, to Chinese work units, which paid for them in Chinese renminbi. The Americans' joint venture partner, Beijing Automotive Works, was supposed to collect the money and turn it over to the joint venture. But it wasn't paying up; for BAW, holding the money was like obtaining an interest-free loan. Chinese officials at the joint venture confessed that the Chinese partner, Beijing Automotive Works, owed the joint venture about thirty million renminbi—more than $9 million. As a result, St. Pierre found that he not only didn't have the foreign exchange he needed, but he didn't have much Chinese money, either.

The joint venture was broke. St. Pierre began wondering if he would be able to meet his payroll. One day he found that the joint venture didn't have enough renminbi to pay a Chinese supplier for a new batch of BJ212 engines. St. Pierre had to stop production of the Chinese jeeps for a day. The Chinese finance director for the joint venture, Li Bolin, came to the rescue by loaning Beijing Jeep 6.5 million renminbi, about $1.8 million, from the BJC employees' health and welfare fund.

Until the time of the loan, American officials at BJC hadn't even known that a health and welfare fund existed. It was, in effect, a secret fund that Chinese officials had amassed. Part of the money came from the difference between the $40,000 salaries charged for the eight top Chinese employees and the amounts of less than $100 a month that these employees were given in take-home pay. Separately, Beijing Jeep was also paying 374 renminbi (about $100) per month in salaries for each of the more than four thousand employees in the factory, although the workers themselves received only approximately 40 to 45 percent of this sum in take-home pay. The rest was supposed to go to the Chinese government for welfare benefits. But the Americans were never sure that all of the remaining money was passed on to the government; they believed that part of it was siphoned off into the secret fund run by the Chinese officials at BJC itself. Infusions of loaned cash from Li's health and welfare fund helped keep Beijing Jeep afloat during the prolonged crisis.

St. Pierre asked for a meeting with officials at Beijing Automotive Works to talk about the thirty million renminbi it owed to the joint venture, but officials there refused to come to a meeting, answer his letters, or return his phone calls. It was not as if Beijing Automotive Works were some distant, unknown entity; it was the same Chinese enterprise with which American Motors had struck the Jeep deal originally. Wu, the chairman of the joint venture, was also supposed to be in charge of BAW.

St. Pierre retaliated by telling the Chinese workers that Beijing Jeep had no money and that its future was uncertain. He turned down requests to spend even small amounts of money. The workers were asking for new showers inside the plant. "We don't have the money," St. Pierre replied. He made it plain there would be no bonuses, no increases for lunch money, no new housing, no plant improvements, and no purchases of new equipment until BJC's financial problems were resolved. The workers at Beijing Jeep were earning more money than their counterparts at ordinary Chinese enterprises. St. Pierre thought he was merely telling his workers the truth, making sure they understood that the joint venture was not an endless source of money. He was gambling that after they got angry at him and the other Americans, they might put pressure on their Chinese leaders, too.

The atmosphere became so tense that even the most trivial business dealings between the Americans and Chinese became bogged down in charges and countercharges. Giglio, AMC's chief financial official in Beijing, spent three hours one winter day arranging simple bank transfers between the United States and China. AMC used Chase Manhattan as its banking agent. The Chinese wanted to spread the banking fees around a little and urged the Americans to use the Bank of China, which had an office in New York City. The Americans finally agreed to use the Bank of China for a few limited purposes. Then Chinese officials complained that the Americans were wasting valuable foreign exchange by sending money to China through DHL's courier service. Why not wire it through the Bank of China? the Chinese asked. The Americans pointed out that the bank's wires took ten days and that the money lost valuable interest during the time of the delay. In the end the Chinese agreed to stick with DHL.

In February 1986 the company dispatched Clare and another high-ranking executive, Tom Foley, to try to break the impasse. They got nowhere. The dispute between the Americans and the Chinese within Beijing Jeep was becoming nasty and personal. Before Foley left Beijing, he had one last talk with Chairman Wu. They were sitting on the second-floor lobby of the Great Wall Hotel. "You Americans haven't done anything for this joint venture," Wu said.

"What are you talking about?" Foley shot back. "We gave you a Cherokee. A Cherokee Jeep is a good product, it's sought after around the world."

On the drive to the Beijing airport, St. Pierre turned to Foley and said it was clear that AMC's problems couldn't be solved by talking to people like Chairman Wu or lower-level Chinese bureaucrats. St. Pierre told Foley he was going to start talking to the foreign press and was planning to write letters to high-ranking Chinese leaders. "The shit is going to hit the fan," St. Pierre said.

Foley was silent for a while and then replied, "Yeah. That's a good idea." Foley was a close friend; St. Pierre never told anyone else at American Motors what he was about to do.

14

Of Premiers and Rockefellers

At the beginning of 1986, Mark O'Neill, one of several Reuters correspondents in Beijing, had called St. Pierre and asked some probing questions about the situation at Beijing Jeep. "I'm not talking about that kind of stuff," St. Pierre said. Well, said O'Neill, if you're ever ready to talk, give me a call.

Shortly after Foley left Beijing, St. Pierre called back O'Neill at Reuters. "I'm ready to talk," St. Pierre said.

St. Pierre would make good on his promise to Foley. Over the next few months he raised the stakes by soliciting worldwide press coverage of AMC's difficulties. What had been a private, simmering feud between the Americans and their Chinese counterparts at Beijing Jeep became an international affair, and American Motors' frustration became a symbol and test of the ability of Western companies to do business in China. By May Chinese Premier Zhao Ziyang, David Rockefeller of the Chase Manhattan Bank, Chinese Ambassador to the United States Han Xu, and U.S. Treasury Secretary James Baker, among others, were involved in one way or another in the affairs of Beijing Jeep.

St. Pierre didn't tell Clare and Trimmer, his AMC bosses in Detroit, that he was calling reporters, because he knew they would have ordered him not to do so. He went ahead on his own, explaining to Detroit that the reporters had called him asking questions and that he had felt obliged to give the press the truth.

O'Neill and St. Pierre met over lunch at the Dynasty Restaurant of the Jianguo Hotel, the Western hotel where AMC's China staff regularly dined. St. Pierre volunteered the story of the thirty million renminbi that Beijing Automotive Works owed the joint venture from sales of the Chinese jeeps and the $2 million that the

State Materials Bureau was withholding for the Cherokees. Soon the following story was making its way around the world:

BEIJING JEEP HURT BY FOREIGN EXCHANGE SHORTAGE
By Mark O'Neill

BEIJING, April 2 (Reuters)—Beijing Jeep Corp., a pioneering joint venture auto company, is being crippled by a shortage of foreign exchange and is owed millions of dollars by state concerns, motor industry sources here said Wednesday.

The corporation, almost one-third owned by American Motors Corp., the fourth-largest U.S. automaker, began making four-wheel-drive vehicles last September.

But now it is scrambling to get cash to buy engines and parts and may have to stop production next month unless it gets some of the money it is owed, the sources said.

Beijing Automotive Works owes the joint venture $9.4 million and $2 million is outstanding from another Chinese state concern in part payment for 200 Jeeps, according to the sources. . . .

The corporation's president, Don St. Pierre, conceded that the company was having serious foreign exchange problems that would probably affect planned production unless they were resolved shortly.

"We have not had second thoughts about coming to China. Getting out would be a big step. But we need quick results," he said. . . .

As soon as the Reuters story appeared in Detroit, Clare had Trimmer call St. Pierre. "What are you doing?" Trimmer asked.

"The guy [O'Neill] called me," St. Pierre answered. "He knew all about the thirty million renminbi and the two million dollars, and he asked me about it, so I had to say, 'Yeah, it's true.' I didn't want to lie to him."

Other stories followed. CHINA'S TIGHT FIST MAY SQUEEZE FOREIGN COMPANIES OUT, said *Business Week* in its international editions of April 7, 1986.[1] *The New York Times'* lengthy account, AMC'S TROUBLES IN CHINA, on its business pages was accompanied by a picture of a worker taking a nap on Beijing Jeep's assembly line. Both the *Times* story and the picture of the napping worker appeared in the *International Herald Tribune* under the headline SLEEPY BEIJING JEEP PLANT IRKS AMC; LOW PRODUCTION, DOLLAR DISPUTE THREATEN VENTURE. The picture and headline were embarrassing not only to China, but also to AMC officials in Detroit such as Clare, who had long preached to doubters within his own company about the importance and wisdom of starting up automobile production in China.

On March 22 David Rockefeller flew to Beijing to help celebrate the fifth anniversary of Chase Manhattan Bank's office in the city. Rockefeller, former board chairman of the bank and still head of its international advisory committee, was a guest of the Bank of China and was meeting during the trip with several high-ranking Chinese officials, including Premier Zhao Ziyang.

Accompanied by other senior officials at Chase, Rockefeller stopped in at Beijing Jeep. It was a routine visit. Beijing Jeep was by far the largest single manufacturing joint venture in Beijing, and Chase was American Motors' banker. Rockefeller and his party sat down with American and Chinese officials from Beijing Jeep in the company's spartan conference room on the factory grounds not far from the assembly line. They seemed prepared for the sort of cheery presentation that was standard: slide shows and glowing speeches in two languages praising the progress that had been made and the spirit of cooperation.

Instead St. Pierre let them have it. Looking directly at Rockefeller, he described the predicament his joint venture was facing: its lack of foreign exchange, its piles of unshipped Cherokee kits in the United States, its inability to sell Cherokees inside China.

He was talking fast, sometimes not even bothering to stop for translation from English to Chinese. The Chinese got the drift. Later on the Chinese officials from Beijing Jeep came to their president and asked him, "Why did you tell them all that?"

"Because I'm desperate," St. Pierre replied. "I've got to get some help for this joint venture, or it's down the chute."

After the meeting the Chase visitors went on a tour of the plant's new Cherokee assembly line. Rockefeller walked alongside St. Pierre, quizzing him about the problems of the joint venture. Finally he said to St. Pierre, "Come with me to my banquet tonight.

I want to introduce you to some of the government officials there. You tell them your problem."

St. Pierre showed up at the Great Hall of the People well before the scheduled start of the banquet. He found Rockefeller sitting outside the banquet hall with several Chinese leaders—ministry-level officials, the heads of state planning and economic agencies.

Rockefeller beckoned. "Don, come on over here. I was just talking about you," he said. He turned to the ministers. "This is the guy I was just telling you about, from Beijing Jeep." At Rockefeller's urging, St. Pierre cataloged the problems of his joint venture.

When he was finished Rockefeller gave a brief, polite lecture to the ministers. "You should remember, it's one thing if a business fails because it's a bad business," he said. "It's another thing if a business fails because it doesn't have a chance, it wasn't given the opportunity. And it appears to me that's the case here." He urged the Chinese officials to pay attention to what was happening at Beijing Jeep.

There were no commitments, no promises, just brief expressions of concern by the Chinese officials. Although Rockefeller met with Premier Zhao during the trip, there was no sign that he brought up Beijing Jeep. Still, his involvement was another significant step in St. Pierre's concerted campaign to get around, through, and above the Chinese bureaucracy.

In the United States, AMC's top executives also began stepping up the pressure. Renault was in the process of bringing Dedeurwaerder back to France. Cappy, now AMC's chief operating officer, who was gradually taking over the leadership of the American company, flew from Detroit to Washington to meet with the Chinese ambassador, Han Xu. Cappy outlined American Motors' problems in China and sought Han's help. The Chinese ambassador relayed Cappy's complaints back to Beijing.

St. Pierre also launched a letter-writing campaign. He wrote to Chen Zutao, the head of the Chinese National Automotive Industrial Corporation, in effect minister of the state auto industry; he wrote to the directors or deputy directors of China's State Planning Commission, the State Economic Commission, the Ministry of Foreign Economic Relations and Trade. All the letters described Beijing Jeep's lack of foreign exchange and sought Chinese government help. The letters went unanswered. The more he was ignored, the angrier St. Pierre got. He was convinced that China needed American Motors more than American Motors needed China, yet day in and day out AMC officials were getting the cold shoulder.

Finally he decided to go to the top. He enlisted the help of Hulan Hawke, a Chinese-American woman working in the Beijing office of C. B. Sung's Unison International. Hawke, married to an American businessman and the daughter of an important Communist Party official, knew the ins and outs of doing business in China. She had some high-level contacts in Beijing.

St. Pierre and Hawke talked of writing to Tian Jiyun, the vice premier responsible for economic affairs, but Hawke decided he wasn't high enough. They needed to go to the very top. They toyed with the idea of Hu Yaobang, the Communist Party secretary; but Hu's specialty was Communist Party organization, not the management of the Chinese economy. So finally they settled upon Zhao, the Chinese premier. At the time, Zhao was generally considered the second most powerful official in China, outranked only by Deng Xiaoping.

"If we write to Zhao, can you get the letter delivered to him?" St. Pierre asked Hawke. "Can you get it put into his hands?" Hawke said she could. "Okay, then that's who I want to write the letter to," he said.

They worked together on the letter for several days. St. Pierre would write a draft in English, and then Hawke, who was translating it into Chinese, would suggest revisions. They argued a bit. Hawke thought St. Pierre's style was too simple and abrupt. It might sound all right in English, but when translated into Chinese it sounded rude. St. Pierre thought Hawke was trying to tone down the letter, to make it sound too nice.

"We can make these same points in another way," Hawke told St. Pierre. "We're not changing the meaning, just conveying your meaning in proper Chinese."

Finally, after a couple of rewrites and compromises, St. Pierre said, "I'm not making it any nicer than it is now. It's already too nice. It's going the way it is right now."

Hawke gave the letter to a Chinese friend, a woman who had access to China's top leaders, including Zhao and his staff. She assured the friend that AMC was not in any way asking for special favors from Zhao; AMC was merely trying to call Zhao's attention to a problem that could affect the course of China's policy of opening to the outside world. The woman passed on St. Pierre's letter to a staff aide working for Zhao on the State Commission for Restructuring the Economy, the cabinet-level group overseeing China's economic reform program. Hawke had added a second, formal cover letter urging the aide to pass on St. Pierre's letter to Zhao. The process was reminiscent of the old tradition of sending a memorial—that is, a formal letter warning of problems and giving advice—to a Chinese emperor.

Hawke never told St. Pierre the name of the intermediary who had served as the pipeline to Zhao. St. Pierre wondered whether her friend might have been Zhao's daughter, who had become one of the leading Chinese officials at Sung's Great Wall Hotel. Or, he speculated, the conduit might have been some friend of Hawke's well-connected Chinese family.[2] Hawke also didn't tell Sung about the letter to the premier until well after it was sent, since Sung might not have approved of taking such a drastic step.

Hawke's quiet, well-timed help proved crucial to AMC's future in China. Within a day or two she got a message back. St. Pierre's letter had been passed on to Zhao personally, and Zhao would act upon it. St. Pierre should be patient. That was wonderful news, the first encouraging sign St. Pierre had had.

Weeks more went by and nothing happened, no meetings, no changes.

One day in the midst of the crisis, a Chinese official named Ji Chunhai came to St. Pierre's office. To the Americans, Ji was known as the head of the trade union for the four thousand Chinese workers at Beijing Jeep. He was not part of the Beijing Jeep management team; he was not among the group of Chinese officials, such as Chairman Wu and Vice President Zhao Nailin, who held executive responsibilities at the joint venture. But as St. Pierre and the other Americans were to learn later on, Ji had another title. He was the party secretary, the general secretary of the Communist Party organization within the factory.

"Look, you'd better stop this, all this talking to the press," Ji told St. Pierre through a translator. "Putting all this pressure on is not going to work. You're going to get yourself in trouble, and you'd better not do that. I'm serious."

St. Pierre erupted. He later remembered this occasion as the one time in his entire stay in Beijing when he had lost his cool. He yelled. It was the old game of role-playing between foreigners and Chinese, and St. Pierre had worked up enough outrage to be willing to play the time-honored role of the angry barbarian.

Ji was dead wrong, St. Pierre told him. "This is the only way, the only thing that is going to solve our problem," he said. "And I'm going to continue to do just what I'm doing."

Ji looked at him intensely. "You're lucky you're not a Chinese, because you'd be in big trouble," he said.

St. Pierre threw Ji out of his office with the most direct language he could summon. "Get the fuck out of here!" he shouted. The Chinese translator softened the words, but Ji got the message.

In March, as the Beijing winter was coming to an end, St. Pierre drafted a long telex to AMC headquarters in Michigan, summarizing the joint venture's plight.

Marketing of Cherokees? Beijing Jeep had delivered 450 of them to China but had not been paid any of the foreign exchange it was owed for 200 of these. At least 200 more Cherokees built from imported kits were sitting unsold at the plant, with no sales in sight.

Foreign exchange? Beijing Jeep had none available—none to pay for importing more Cherokee kits from the United States, none to pay for housing the AMC people in China. And Chinese customers had no foreign exchange to buy Cherokees. "There are currently no prospects for the required foreign exchange," St. Pierre concluded.

Finances? "BJC is basically out of funds and barely surviving day to day," he wrote. "We have no renminbi." Worse, the joint venture faced upcoming debts, including ten million renminbi for capital projects. And the labor union was seeking hefty wage and bonus increases for 1986.

Living costs for American Motors staff in China? "BJC has no means and our partners no desire to pay [foreign residents'] costs, which are increasing rapidly," St. Pierre said. Housing costs had gone up 38 percent in the prior two months, and at current rates rent for the five Americans living at the Lido-Holiday Inn would cost a total of $360,000 in 1986.

The Chinese partners? St. Pierre told his bosses he thought that the joint venture "has been used as a dumping ground for excess inventories and bad equipment. . . . The leaders are sadly lacking in business experience. They appear to have no influence with the government, and there have been numerous attempts to deceive."

Exports? "Beijing Jeep has no real prospects of exporting any significant volume of automotive components or vehicles in the next few years," the memo said. "Our stated goal of BJC becoming a low-cost source of components and vehicles is probably not attainable in my lifetime.

"I do not see the situation changing drastically in the next few years, because the problems are deep-rooted and complex," St. Pierre continued. "My overall conclusion is that BJC will be a cash drain on AMC for some considerable time without a basic change in our agreement."

St. Pierre proposed the most radical solution, the one that many other Western companies in China had quietly fantasized: to pull out of China.

"My recommendation is that we withdraw, as gracefully as possible, but immediately," he said. "We should advise the government that we want to negotiate a new agreement that includes a CKD [Cherokee kit] program and guarantees foreign exchange availability." There would be no need to have AMC people living in China during the time it took to negotiate a new agreement, St. Pierre said. Instead, AMC could send negotiating teams in and out.

St. Pierre sent off his telex, and in early April he flew back to Detroit to discuss with Clare, Trimmer, and other AMC officials what steps the company should take next. He made sure his trip home was as public as everything else he had done in the previous weeks. Reporters in Beijing were told that St. Pierre had "returned to the United States for consultations."[3] St. Pierre and other AMC officials also announced, in advance, that the assembly line for the new Cherokees at Beijing Jeep would close down in June because of a shortage of supplies. Without any deal on foreign exchange, AMC was not shipping new parts kits for the Cherokees to China.

It seems doubtful that a telex such as St. Pierre's would have remained secret from the Chinese. St. Pierre knew that the information-gathering system within his factory was remarkably effective. Chinese officials at Beijing Jeep often seemed to know everything going on with remarkable speed. Many other foreigners

in China—particularly diplomats and journalists—believed that
their phones were tapped and their offices or homes bugged. St.
Pierre wasn't sure about that. But he had left a copy of the telex
recommending a pullout from China around his office, and he had
sent the telex through the Chinese telecommunications system, to
which Chinese security officials had access.

St. Pierre was sitting in Clare's office, arguing for some strong
new action by American Motors, when a telex arrived from Beijing.
It was from Zhu Rongji, an official of China's State Economic Commission. Zhu said he had been entrusted by Premier Zhao to resolve the problems at Beijing Jeep. He asked AMC officials to send
a high-level delegation to Beijing for negotiations as soon as possible.

The months-long stalemate was coming to an end. China was
finally ready to talk.

15

An Outpouring of Grievances

AMC's misfortunes were hardly big news to Beijing's foreign business community. At watering holes such as Charlie's Bar and the Bell, the pub on the grounds of the British embassy compound, other businessmen and -women had for years been swapping grievances similar to AMC's. The outside world might think the business prospects in China were wonderful, but the foreigners working there from day to day didn't share the optimism.

Yet if the world was unaware of the difficulties of doing business in China, they, the foreigners living in Beijing and their companies, were at least partially to blame. Few of them—and certainly very few, if any, of the major companies—had been willing to voice any of their complaints publicly. It was taken for granted that silence and private negotiations were the best policies.

The businesses were willing, indeed happy, to see a few abstract studies published about the rising costs of doing business in China or about the difficulties of obtaining foreign exchange. But for the most part, until St. Pierre and AMC spoke out, individual businessmen and their companies were afraid to be publicly identified as criticizing China's treatment of foreign businesses.

Why were the foreign companies so unwilling to complain? Each company feared Chinese retaliation. China had successfully created a climate in which favoritism was expected. If Coca-Cola complained that it was being unfairly restricted, Chinese authorities might counter by making life tougher for Coke (or better for Pepsi). In a sense, this was what had already happened to AMC. Its toughly worded November 1985 telex had led to a worsening, not an improvement, of its situation in China.

Of course, the foreign businesses wouldn't have worried so much about retaliation had it not been for the fact that they still held high hopes for future business in China. Despite rising costs and uncertain profits, they didn't want to do anything that might jeopardize their long-range prospects.

Moreover, foreign companies failed to complain because of their own internal tensions and disagreements, generally between the local representatives in China and the headquarters back home. The head of a company's Beijing or Shanghai office might want to take a strong public stand against exorbitant costs, unpredictable fees, protracted delays and severe market restrictions in China, but chances were that the home office didn't want to rock the boat. The board chairmen and chief executives who lived in the West didn't confront the daily frustrations of life in China. On their visits there, things didn't seem so bad.

Foreign correspondents doing stories on business conditions in China regularly found that unhappy local representatives were willing to voice bitter complaints, but only in private. They might talk to the press, but only on background or off the record. For any official, on-the-record comments, the correspondents would generally be referred to headquarters back in the United States, Western Europe, or Japan. And executives at the home offices didn't want to say very much. Few news articles were written about difficult business conditions in China, and the ones that appeared had a remote, abstract feel to them. They contained few names or concrete examples.

In the spring of 1986 American Motors' dispute with China changed the situation. AMC was desperate. And unlike many other foreign companies, AMC wasn't in a particularly competitive situation. AMC had been one of the few auto companies to invest in a manufacturing venture in China. The other companies to do so—the Western European carmakers, Volkswagen, Peugeot, and Fiat—were producing passenger cars and trucks, which weren't interchangeable with AMC's Jeeps. As St. Pierre's memo pointed out, AMC was beginning to reconsider the value of its long-term prospects in China. St. Pierre, by taking it upon himself to go public with his complaints, had overridden the usual reluctance of the home office to speak out.

The AMC dispute crystallized the general dissatisfaction with business conditions in China. Indeed, once St. Pierre had complained, other foreign businessmen in China found it much easier to do so, too.

Thus, the American Motors case became the vehicle for a full-scale reexamination of Western business prospects in China. By April and May 1986, within weeks after AMC's conflict with China became public, newspapers and magazines in the West began publishing feature stories focusing not specifically on AMC, but more broadly on how Western companies were faring in China. Invariably, the thrust of these stories was that China was a disappointment.

SWEET IS TURNING TO SOUR. FOREIGN CAPITALISTS IN CHINA RUN INTO A HOST OF TROUBLES, declared *Time*. BLUSH FADES FROM CHINA INVESTMENT BLOOM, announced *The Washington Post*. INVESTORS THINK AGAIN ABOUT CHINA, said the *International Herald Tribune*. Worst of all was a front-page story in *The Wall Street Journal*, the most widely read newspaper of the American business community, which told readers: FIRMS DOING BUSINESS IN CHINA ARE STYMIED BY COSTS AND HASSLES. THEY COMPLAIN OF RED TAPE, POOR ACCESS TO MARKETS, EVEN A SHORTAGE OF LABOR. [1]

These stories included the names of several businessmen, women and companies willing to recount the obstacles to doing business in China. Cardio-Pace, a St. Paul company making heart pacemakers at a plant near Xian, told *Time* that local officials had tried, unsuccessfully, to have it hire a number of unnecessary Chinese "assistant managers." Otis Elevator told *The Wall Street Journal* it had productivity and quality-control problems at its elevator plant in Tianjin. Mats Engstrom, president of Tsar Nicolai, a San Francisco food company, was quoted in the *Herald Tribune* as saying that after buying two $19,000 Cherokee Jeeps for his Beijing caviar operation, he had had to fend off repeated Chinese demands to pay "rental" fees of $100 per day for the Jeeps he already owned. "I told them, 'They're my Jeeps,'" said Engstrom. David Chang, the top China consultant to Nike, which was having serious difficulties in a venture to export footwear from China, told *The Wall Street Journal*: "The big problem is attitude. Profit is still a four-letter word in China."

The companies began airing their gripes through other channels as well. One group of businessmen sent a private letter to Vice President George Bush. Others began lobbying their embassies and consulates in China and important visitors arriving in Beijing from abroad.

In this long suppressed outpouring of grievances, the busi-

nesses listed a number of general problems. The first was the lack
of foreign exchange, or more specifically the inability to take in as
much foreign exchange as they were required to spend. One newspaper survey found that out of the 139 joint ventures in Canton in
1985, only 46 were able to keep a balance of foreign exchange.[2]

Another common theme of the businesses was the high and
rising cost of doing business in China. The private letters and press
accounts told of the $6,000-a-month rents for expatriates, the end-
less lists of fees, tariffs, taxes, and other charges imposed upon
foreigners. In addition, the myth that China was a source of cheap
labor for manufacturing was finally being questioned. Many other
businesses, particularly oil companies involved in offshore drilling,
had been required, like American Motors, to pay Western salaries
of $40,000 or more for Chinese managers who themselves took
home less than $100 a month. Manufacturing ventures had been
required to hire three, five, even ten times as many workers for
their China operations as they felt they needed. By 1986 many
companies had had time to look not only at the Chinese wage rates,
which at first glance seemed low, but also at the bonuses, the
health and welfare fees, and the other costs they paid for their
workers. Beyond all these personnel costs, the businessmen complained that supplies and raw materials for their China operations
were surprisingly expensive. When you added it all up, said Roger
Sullivan, president of the National Council for U.S.-China Trade,
it cost Nike more to make a pair of shoes in China than it did in
Maine.

The foreign businessmen pressed several other complaints,
too. It was hard to find skilled Chinese personnel for management
or technical work, they said. The productivity of labor in China
was low and the quality of output was poor. Companies found it
difficult, if not impossible, to export, because potential buyers saw
that the products from China weren't very good; the Western companies in China were reluctant to jeopardize their reputations by
exporting shoddy products. China's government bureaucracy was
so cumbersome that foreign businessmen could wait for months,
or even longer, for officials to reach even a relatively simple decision. On the other hand, the Western companies never knew when
officials from some Chinese ministry, department, province, municipality, or state enterprise would show up with some new tax or
fee, some new regulation. Doing business was utterly unpredict-

able, and they felt that Chinese officials were constantly testing how much they could pay, how hard they were willing to fight. "Doing business in China is like being staked to an anthill," one American told *Time*. "They nibble away all the time."

In their long lists of complaints, there were a few points the Western businessmen overlooked. They ignored the fact that they themselves had entered into deals based on the premise that they would export from China. If they suffered from a shortage of foreign exchange, it was often because, like American Motors, they had discovered they could not export and had failed to get solid answers as to how they would earn an adequate supply of foreign exchange in China's domestic market. It was true that the foreign companies had no way of predicting many of the rising costs, hidden fees, and bureaucratic obstacles that they were now facing in China. But it was also true that in their rush to start up operations in China, many of them had simply misjudged the conditions there. They had overestimated their ability to produce export-quality products in China. And they had also overestimated China's ability to produce inexpensive locally made parts, supplies, and raw materials that would obviate the need to import these from abroad.

The U.S. government was ambivalent about the businesses' complaints.

Internal documents that have been declassified and released to me under the Freedom of Information Act show that U.S. officials had little sympathy for American Motors. One memo by officials of the U.S. embassy in Beijing noted disapprovingly that AMC's critical comments about business conditions in China had been "aired in press reports." The memo also pointed out that when AMC had persuaded the Chinese in 1984 to switch from manufacturing a new Chinese jeep to assembling Cherokees from imported kits, "no written contract describing this agreement was ever signed or approved." The suggestion was that China wasn't violating anything in writing when it refused a year later to pay the costs of importing Cherokee kits.

The U.S. embassy concluded: "AMC's problems seem based in: 1) failure of both parties to get all the relevant terms of their agreement in writing, with the full approval and backing of the appropriate government authorities; 2) assumptions by each side that the other would be able to take care of the foreign exchange needs of the joint venture; [and] 3) poor anticipation and overreaction to problems."[3]

Nevertheless, despite their irritation with American Motors, U.S. officials tended to agree with the general thrust of the Western companies' grievances. According to another internal document, during a meeting of the U.S.-China Joint Commission on Trade and Commerce in May 1986, Melvin W. Searls, Jr., a Commerce Department official, told Chinese officials: "The bottom line on investment is whether U.S. companies can have profitable operations in the People's Republic of China." His Chinese counterpart, Zhang Qi of China's Ministry of Foreign Economic Relations and Trade, responded that "the increase in foreign investment in the PRC demonstrates that the environment has improved in the last few years."[4]

Furthermore, the spate of newspaper stories, magazine articles, and private letters by businessmen encouraged some senior American policymakers to echo the companies' complaints. In May 1986, at the height of the American Motors controversy, Treasury Secretary Baker met with Chinese officials in Beijing. "We had frank talks about some current difficulties faced by American businesses in China," he told a press conference. "There are serious problems to doing business here." Baker also said that Chinese Premier Zhao Ziyang had specifically mentioned American Motors' problems in Beijing and had told Baker that China wanted to settle the controversy. Another high-ranking official, U.S. Ambassador to China Winston Lord—who had replaced Hummel in late 1985—devoted a May 1986 speech to the frustrations confronted by foreigners doing business in China.

Some present and former government officials in the West jumped to China's defense, unwilling to entertain any unpleasantness that might disturb relations. At one press conference in Phoenix on June 10, 1986, former Vice President Walter Mondale urged American companies to consider investing new money in China. "This is one of those cases where good business is good for our country," Mondale said.[5]

For China, the public airing of the businessmen's problems was a public relations disaster. Not since the beginning of the open-door policy in the late 1970s had there been such a fundamental Western reevaluation of the business prospects in China. The public discus-

sion would make it much more difficult to attract Western investment and to negotiate new deals on favorable terms.

There were hints that a few conservative officials within the
Chinese Communist Party would have been happy to hold the line
and not make any new concessions to Western businesses. If the
foreigners wanted to leave China, let them go, they argued. AMC
officials later concluded that some officials at the Chinese National
Automotive Industrial Corporation (CNAIC) would have been
happy to see AMC pull out of China.

But in the spring of 1986 the prevailing climate within the
Chinese Communist Party still favored reform-minded officials,
such as Premier Zhao, who stressed the importance of continuing
Western investment in China. China couldn't afford to let the foreigners go; it had to modify its own instincts and traditions to
accommodate them and to get their technology.

From the Chinese perspective, the foreigners who had come
into their factories were an unsettling presence; they were still
suspect, as were the Chinese working for and with them. The
Chinese reformers were still trying to overcome these deeply
rooted cultural fears. In the spring and early summer of 1986, in
the midst of the AMC controversy, the most widely discussed
movie in China was called *The Black Cannon Incident*. The film
was so politically daring that some leading officials within the
Communist Party were said to have sought to prevent it from being
shown.

The plot of *The Black Cannon Incident* revolves around a
Chinese factory obtaining new technology from West Germany.
The Germans send in a stout, impatient adviser named Hans
Schmidt, who works closely with a middle-aged Chinese translator
named Zhao Shuxin. In order to impress the Germans, factory officials give Zhao the first Western attire he has ever worn—an ill-
fitting suit borrowed from a nearby song-and-dance troupe. "You're
representing our country now," they tell him as he goes to see the
German.

But Chinese security officials suspect the translator may be
spying for foreigners. The Chinese security apparatus reports an
incident that eventually turns out to be utterly innocuous: Zhao
has sent a friend a telegram that says, "Black Cannon Missing."
While the police think the message might refer to secret arms or
documents, it turns out Zhao is merely a devotee of Chinese chess

referring to a lost piece in his chess set. For much of the movie, Communist Party officials at the factory and China's much feared Public Security Bureau carry out a fruitless secret investigation of Zhao. He is moved away from all contact with foreigners, yet never told what he has done wrong. Zhao's replacement is an unskilled tour guide whose language skills are so poor that his mistranslation of technical documents causes a fire at the factory.

Despite the film's not-so-veiled attack on the Chinese security apparatus, the regime allowed *The Black Cannon Incident* to be shown. The Chinese leadership wanted to send the nation a message not to be so mistrusting of foreigners and of the Chinese working with them. The regime wanted China to try harder to come to terms with the foreigners in its midst.

16

Inside the Plant: The Cultural Divide

It was the Newtonian law of doing business in China. For any Western reaction there was an equal, and often opposite, Chinese reaction. At Beijing Jeep Americans and Chinese frequently gave different meanings to the same events. They had different attitudes toward work, toward management, toward money, toward the importance of foreign advisers, toward nearly everything.

Amid the large business disputes over the future of Beijing Jeep were smaller daily conflicts inside the factory. The Chinese and Americans had been trying to coexist and adapt to one another, but it wasn't easy. Both sides found that the cultural differences were even greater than either had expected before the joint venture opened its doors.

To the Americans, the photograph of a worker sleeping on the assembly line—which was published in the spring of 1986 along with the Western news accounts of troubles at the joint venture—perfectly illustrated China's lassitude. The Americans always wanted the Chinese to move faster, to be alert, to wake up. "Time just ain't important to them," growled Ed Schulze, who was in charge of production and maintenance at Beijing Jeep. Schulze had seen a Chinese worker punching a dozen time cards at a time for himself and his friends. In theory the Chinese workday began at 8:30 A.M. and ended at 5:30 P.M., but in practice production started later, stopped for a long lunch, and ended early, perhaps an hour and a half before closing time. Realistically, Schulze figured, the average Beijing Jeep worker put in four and a half to five hours a day.

But to the Chinese, the same photo showed a good guy and, ironically, a good worker, too. On the afternoon that picture was taken, there had been nothing more for workers to do on the assem-

bly line. In fact, most of the workers had quietly slipped off and
gone home. The worker in the photo had been too conscientious to
leave early. Instead, with no task to perform, he had decided to take
a quick nap while remaining on the job. Most factories in China
were overstaffed; workers took it for granted that sometimes there
would be little if anything to do.

Among the Chinese workers on Beijing Jeep's assembly line, there
was an extraordinary degree of resentment and hostility. The feelings were directed toward all authority, both Chinese and foreign.
The workers were quick to say they were victims of exploitation.
The Chinese regime was exploiting them, and the outside world
was exploiting China.

Along the assembly line, Chinese workers complained that
American auto workers were being paid $12 per hour. (That guess
was in fact too low but seemed astonishingly high to the Chinese
workers.) They compared that American figure with their own
wages. At Beijing Jeep the average wage was about 200 yuan, or
$54, per month, and that sum was itself more than other workers
in Chinese enterprises were making.

Communist Party leaders sometimes explained that China's
low wage figures were misleading, because the state paid for medical care and education and subsidized rents so heavily that Chinese
workers often paid no more than $2 to $4 a month. Americans kept
in mind that in the United States houses cost $150,000 and a year
of college up to $20,000. But the Chinese workers didn't bother
with such nuances. They just felt they were being exploited.

Once, when a group of Chinese workers on the Beijing Jeep
assembly line complained to an American visitor about the low
wages in China and the high ones in the United States, the visitor
pointed out that they were at that moment in the middle of a
seemingly endless afternoon tea break. If they worked in an American factory, they would probably have some boss complaining or
disciplining them if they took a break as long as even twenty minutes.

"That's okay," said one worker. "We Chinese know how to
endure hardship. We can do that better than anyone else in the
world."

Give the Chinese workers a chance to be like the rest of the world, and they would work harder. Their sense of oppression was an all-purpose ideology. It gave them both a belief in their ability to do hard work and at the same time a justification for not working very hard. The Chinese workers might agree in principle with some of the government's reforms, such as the idea of higher pay for better workers, but they were also cynical enough to think that the way China operated, the money would always go to the wrong people.

The workers along the Beijing Jeep assembly line were tough and embittered. In talking to them, it was easy to see why the Chinese leadership was always nervous about possible social unrest among factory workers. And it was also easy to see why, as China opened its doors to the outside world, foreigners still were rarely permitted to walk through a Chinese factory without some high-ranking Chinese official escorting them.

The slowness was just one example of what Schulze saw as a lack of discipline inside the Chinese factory.

The work rules were a farce, Schulze felt. Safety regulations were ignored. Some welders worked without safety glasses. Workers smoked in nonsmoking areas, even near flammable materials in the paint shop. Schulze's own office was near the paint shop, and he became increasingly nervous that he would get caught in some industrial accident.

Attention to maintenance was also minimal. Equipment at the plant fell apart rapidly. And when it broke, production would usually have to stop because there were no spare parts. Moreover, Schulze found, when they didn't have some job to perform, workers sat in the unfinished Cherokees, listening to the radios and smoking cigarettes. Sometimes they damaged the new vehicles. They threw garbage on the floor of the plant.

What irked Schulze most of all was the fact that the Chinese leaders inside the plant wouldn't do anything to control the workers. If the workers didn't want to do something, nothing on earth could make them do it. No Chinese leader wanted to play the role of disciplinarian; if the Chinese workers didn't like one of their supervisors, they could often get rid of him. Chinese shop directors spent their time mostly on personnel and welfare matters—housing, schools, funerals, family feuds. Inside the walls of the factory, the Communist ideal of worker control was not entirely a myth. After a while the American Motors people learned to shrug and tell one another: Just remember, you're in the People's Republic.

"It wears you down," mourned Schulze. "I'm a tough son of a bitch, but it wears you down. Sometimes you just get to the point where you don't give a shit."

The Chinese—assembly-line workers and office cadres alike—grumbled about the American Motors staffers in their midst.

The Americans were much too expensive. In 1986 their salaries and $70,000-a-year rents, their trips home, their vacations and phone bills, added up to about $220,000 for each of the American Motors people working in China.[1] Chinese people could handle some of the work the Americans were doing. One of the AMC people was just sitting in his office reading novels. Another always seemed to be asleep.

Some of the American Motors people were arrogant, the Chinese thought. They talked differently to Chinese than they did to other foreigners. Some of them completely ignored Chinese suggestions. They seemed to think that anything the Chinese said was foolish.

The Americans also used bad language a lot, some of which was so crude that Chinese interpreters would refuse to translate it. In the United States swearing could be a sign of strength and masculinity; an American politician who used the euphemism "deep doo-doo" instead of "deep shit" had to fight the public perception that he was overly refined and weak. But the United States was an obsessively antiseptic place, and China already had its nightsoil. Coarse, scatological speech ran against the grain of Chinese culture; in the Chinese view it meant, most of all, that you were not very well educated. Chinese people could never respect someone who used bad words.

The Chinese felt that the quality of the advisers AMC sent to Beijing Jeep wasn't high enough. Some of the American advisers seemed to come to China to escape problems back home or because of the financial rewards that came with working in China. Furthermore, China had no control over the American personnel. The American company decided which employees would be sent to China. Those assigned to Beijing Jeep continued to get their paychecks from American Motors. Beijing Jeep paid a flat sum of money for each employee from AMC, but it was up to the American company to decide individual salaries and yearly raises. Thus the Chinese had no method of providing financial incentives for the Americans they thought were performing especially well. The Americans' loyalty wasn't to Beijing Jeep; it was to American Motors.

Ironically, in making these complaints about a lack of control over the foreigners, the Chinese at Beijing Jeep were echoing the oft repeated grievances of Western companies doing business in China. Western businesses regularly complained that they had to accept the Chinese employees sent to them by China's state-controlled personnel agencies, who remained more loyal to the Chinese agencies than to the Western businesses.

The Americans felt the Chinese leaders inside the factory just weren't tough enough. The Chinese factory managers were intimately involved in every aspect of their workers' lives—their pregnancies, their children's education, their housing assignments and recreation. The Chinese managers spent far more time with workers on the factory floor than management people did in American plants.

Yet all these other responsibilities tended to take the Chinese managers away from running an efficient factory. Clare thought that a Chinese plant manager was like an American summer camp director: the guy with a whistle who says, You go there and you go there, everybody go to bed, okay lights out. At Beijing Jeep the Chinese leaders were so busy solving problems of mothers-in-law having to share bedrooms with daughters-in-law that they couldn't understand the role the Americans wanted them to play. In the United States and other countries Clare had worked in, important policy questions were solved by dealing with the plant manager. In China, Clare observed, you couldn't do that. To solve policy questions, you had to go to the higher-level officials in the subministries or the municipal governments. The plant managers, really, were social directors.

Other Americans at Beijing Jeep thought of the Chinese leaders in the factory mostly as good-natured bumblers who were particularly eager for privileges.

Many of the Chinese leaders had their wives on the payroll. Chairman Wu's wife worked at Beijing Jeep, as did the wives of

Vice Chairman Zhao Nailin and Vice President Chen Xulin. Most of the leaders' spouses had vague responsibilities in the strategic planning department, which was run by a Chinese official named Mr. Ma. The joke among the Americans was that Mr. Ma was in charge of finding Beijing Jeep's strategic plan.

Working in Beijing Jeep's computer rooms was another cushy job. The factory had two mainframe computers, one bought from Burroughs and the other from East Germany. Neither of them seemed to be used very much. But they were kept running in air-conditioned rooms, which were kept cool and free of dust. The computer room employees, not surprisingly, were often the relatives of high-ranking Chinese officials. When personal computers were introduced at Beijing Jeep, Chairman Wu asked for one in his own office. He never seemed to use it, and the Americans decided he wanted the computer so that he could have an air conditioner.

More than anything else, the Chinese cadres wanted to travel overseas, the Americans noticed. One of the dates the Americans remembered best was April 25, 1985—a landmark in Chinese history, the Americans joked. On that day the Chinese government lowered the amount it would reimburse officials for overseas travel from $32 per day to $25. In the weeks before the cutoff, the Americans were besieged with travel requests from Beijing Jeep officials eager to get abroad before the deadline. Once overseas, the Chinese travelers tended to live and eat as cheaply as possible in hopes of pocketing the money they saved.

The Americans couldn't believe the way their Chinese counterparts handled money. They were, alternately, wildly extravagant or impossibly penny-pinching, depending on where the money was going. Once, Beijing Jeep was hit with a bill of more than 180,000 yuan (roughly $50,000) for gardening, and when the Americans asked why the bill was so high, they were told the work had included trimming, as though that explained everything. Yet on another occasion Li Bolin, Beijing Jeep's finance director, refused to pay for a few phone calls on the Americans' hotel bills. When one AMC staffer, Dennis Noonan, ordered a few printed calendars in Hong Kong, Li and his associates unaccountably refused to pay the bills.

To the Americans, the refusal to pay for Dennis Noonan's calendars was evidence of their Chinese partners' miserliness and unpredictability. The Chinese, however, saw the matter differently. Noonan had paid money in Hong Kong to have a calendar printed. That simple work could have been done in China; Beijing Auto Works had calendars printed every year. The quality of the printing work in Hong Kong wasn't even particularly good. Maybe the Chinese couldn't make export-quality cars, but they certainly knew how to print a calendar.

The workers had nicknames for many of the Americans. St. Pierre, for example, was called *Dadu'*. It was a short form of the Chinese expression *Daduzi*, which means, literally, "Big Belly" and, figuratively, "Pregnant." In China pregnant women were supposed to stay inside and rest. When the workers called St. Pierre (who was not overweight) *Dadu'*, they meant that he seemed to stay in his office like a pregnant woman.

Weeks could go by without St. Pierre visiting the assembly line. St. Pierre felt he was looking after business and politics, the important aspects of keeping Beijing Jeep viable, and leaving the problems of the assembly line to his subordinates. But in the Chinese view, factory managers were supposed to spend time with the workers. The Chinese leaders at Beijing Jeep always spent time out on the shop floor. St. Pierre's predecessors, MacGregor and Chatterton, had both been more visible to the workers than St. Pierre.

The Chinese workers even had a nickname for the office building at the factory where St. Pierre, the other Americans, and the Chinese factory leaders worked. They called it the *Bai Gong*, the White Palace. The Americans thought the building was filthy and dilapidated: it had concrete floors, no paint, and bad lighting. The Americans couldn't believe that the building was only a few years old. But to the Chinese workers, the building was palatial. By their standards, the building gave Chinese leaders plenty of space and comfort.

On a typical summer day in the White Palace, Chen Xulin wore a plain white shirt, dark slacks, sandals with green socks, and a boyish, smiling face determined to show only expressions of harmony and content. With his dark, heavy eyebrows and slender build, Chen bore a slight resemblance to China's longtime premier, Chou En-lai. Indeed, like tens of thousands of other Chinese cadres, Chen seemed to fashion himself after the premier: he was so seemingly modest, so self-effacing, that he could make strong points without ever seeming to be aggressive.

Chen seemed able to get along with whoever was in charge, under any political regime. The Americans considered Chen to be, by their standards, the most competent cadre within the Chinese leadership at the factory. Unknown to the AMC people, though, Chen's revolutionary credentials were also excellent: he had been a star young worker at the jeep plant during the Cultural Revolution. Photos taken by an American reporter during a tour of the factory on President Nixon's 1972 trip to China shows a smiling Chen Xulin, then thirty years old, posing along the assembly line, on display as one of the factory's model employees.

Chen had blended well with the American Motors people, yet he retained a Chinese perspective on all things American. On his first trip to the United States, he had stared up at the American Motors corporate headquarters building in Southfield, the gleaming high rise with the AMC logo on top, and had been deeply impressed. But once inside, Chen was surprised and less impressed. American Motors only occupied a small portion of this high rise. The company shared its own corporate headquarters with other companies. In Beijing, a city of walls and enclosures, each individual enterprise functioned within its own, self-contained space. No Chinese work unit would want to share a part of its own building.

When he talked about American Motors, Chen sprinkled his speech with the usual, obligatory Chinese invocations of friendship and cooperation. The American and Chinese partners were solving their problems through mutual efforts, he would say. The atmosphere was good.

Nevertheless, when Chen talked about the different working styles of American and Chinese managers, he could be surprisingly blunt and critical of the Americans. The Chinese leaders had to worry about things that the Americans could ignore, he pointed out. Chen Xulin spent much of his life carrying out the sort of work Tod Clare had compared with that of an American summer camp director.

"Almost every day, I receive visitors at my home," Chen once told me in an interview. "They talk about housing, about their troubles at home, about their families. The housing problems of the employees take up a lot of space in my mind. Mr. St. Pierre lives too far from the plant. His hotel has a guard at the front gate, so that stops a lot of problems, too. But me, I live only five minutes from the south gate of the plant."

For the Chinese, housing was the most pressing problem at Beijing Jeep.

The Americans didn't believe their joint venture should have to worry about building or distributing housing for their employees. The Chinese, however, took it for granted that workers should get housing from their employer, their work unit. Who else would do it? Ironically, in this socialist society, there were few social benefits outside those provided by the work unit.

The four thousand Chinese at Beijing Jeep earned, on the average, 50 percent more money in salaries than did their counterparts at their old Chinese unit, Beijing Automotive Works. However, each year BAW provided some new housing for its workers. By contrast, during the early years of the joint venture, there was no new housing at all. High-level cadres like Chen Xulin lived in apartment buildings nearby the factory. Other workers were scattered all over Beijing. Some workers at Beijing Jeep could find no housing at all. There were stories of two or three families sharing an apartment, of young single people postponing marriage and staying at home with their parents because of the lack of an apartment.

When the Chinese first suggested to the Americans that they should pay the costs of new housing for Beijing Jeep's workers, the Americans felt the Chinese were simply testing the depths of their pockets. Providing housing wasn't in the contract. Clare and other AMC officials argued repeatedly that providing housing was the job of the state, or of the Beijing municipal government, not of Beijing Jeep.

Beijing Jeep workers seeking apartments went to see Chen Xulin, sometimes bursting into tears in his office. Chinese employees also showered favors and presents upon those in charge of distributing the housing. The Beijing Jeep unit of Chinese officials in charge of allocating apartments was said to be corrupt, so that apartments were obtained on the basis of friendship or "gifts," rather than the actual need for housing.

Housing was the most important but not the only welfare benefit on which the Beijing Jeep workers felt they received second-class treatment by working at a joint venture instead of a Chinese state enterprise. Beijing Jeep had no kindergarten, hospital, or cafeteria of its own. If Beijing Jeep workers wanted medical care, or if they wanted to send their children to kindergarten, they had to use facilities run by BAW, the state enterprise from which they had come. Beijing Jeep paid BAW for these services, but the Chinese enterprise gave priority to its own employees. Sometimes the Beijing Jeep employees found that there was no space for their children in the kindergarten. They often grumbled that by working at Beijing Jeep, they got inferior medical care.

The Chinese had come to expect that the place that employed them would take responsibility for—and, indeed, supply on its own —virtually everything they would ever need in their lives. The Americans had no intention of shouldering that responsibility.

At one point Chen Xulin came up with his own idea for improving the quality of the Americans sent to Beijing Jeep. Chen suggested to AMC that it send some of its retired employees to China. The American retirees would be experienced. Because of the Chinese reverence for age, the retirees would be well respected in China. They might be easier to work with than the younger, more ambitious, hard-driving Americans. Most important, the retirees would be cheaper.

The Americans refused to go along with the proposal. St. Pierre argued that the retirees would have health problems in China and would not be up to speed with developments at the home company. Moreover, the Americans didn't want to lose control over their people at Beijing Jeep. People eligible for a pension, and unconcerned about promotions, might not care what management thought at headquarters in Detroit.

At the root of most of the cultural differences, of course, was the extraordinary gulf in living standards between the Chinese and the Americans. Every once in a while the AMC people would run into some jarring reminder of the scarcities and deprivation to which their Chinese partners were accustomed. When Schulze's wife sent him a Sears catalog from the United States, he brought it to the factory one day. Workers would sit and read it for hours at a time, staring endlessly at the range of products it offered.

Once, Chinese officials at Beijing Jeep approached St. Pierre with a special request. China was temporarily short of wood and paper, and as a result there was a severe shortage of matches. Whenever you're in those fancy Western hotels and they have match-books lying around, the Chinese officials asked St. Pierre, could you please bring them over to Beijing Jeep?

So St. Pierre, the president of a multimillion-dollar business, regularly picked up some of the free matchbooks at the Jianguo, the Great Wall, or the Lido-Holiday Inn hotels. Inside the factory, the matchbooks were a prized item.

17

Showdown in May

On May 8, 1986, Zhu Rongji, vice minister of China's State Economic Commission, welcomed a phalanx of AMC executives, most of whom had flown from Detroit for a new round of talks aimed at resolving the crisis at Beijing Jeep. No one wanted to phrase it quite so bluntly, but everyone knew the question by this time was whether American Motors was going to stay in China or not.

The first meeting was held on what might pass in Beijing for neutral territory: the International Club, a dilapidated complex that the Chinese had erected two decades earlier as a recreation facility for foreign diplomats. It was a relic of the era before Deng, before the days Beijing had a Sheraton, a Holiday Inn, and a Shangri-La Hotel. Outside the International Club's drab low-rise building were some tennis courts and a swimming pool whose greenish-brown water was changed once every few weeks. The Club was not nearly as Western as Beijing's artificially elegant new hotels, yet not nearly as Chinese as the formal reception rooms of Beijing state enterprises.

Zhu, fluent in English and one of China's brightest officials, quickly made clear that he was in charge. He called the meeting to order; he served as its moderator and controlled the discussions. Zhu was not going to bargain on behalf of the Chinese. He was going to remain above the fray while other, lower-ranking Chinese officials carried out the negotiations. For the Chinese, the negotiators were two senior officials: Chen Zutao, the head of the Chinese automobile industry, who had helped negotiate the original American Motors contract; and Zhang Jianmin, the vice mayor of Beijing. For the Americans, the top two negotiators were Clare and Timothy R. Adams, AMC's director of forward plans and programs.

At the outset the Americans were given a sacrificial offering, a classic, old-fashioned Chinese self-criticism. Two days earlier Chairman Wu, the Chinese head of Beijing Jeep, had suddenly disappeared from the scene. (He was said to be ill, in the hospital, and the Americans did not see him again for nearly a half year—so long, in fact, that they believed he had been quietly fired.) The second-highest Chinese official at Beijing Jeep, Zhao Nailin, offered the American and Chinese negotiators an abject apology. Zhao said he had failed to inform China's central government of the 1984 switch from the newly designed Chinese jeep to the production of the Cherokee from imported American parts. He had neglected to tell authorities in the central government that the Americans were planning to make large numbers of Cherokees in China and had failed to alert these authorities that Beijing Jeep had absolutely no way of earning on its own the foreign exchange necessary to import the American parts for these Cherokees.

In one sense, some of the Americans thought, Zhao's self-criticism was phony and preposterous. It was a way of dumping blame onto an individual, while letting the Chinese government off the hook. How could the central government not have known what was happening, and what was being planned, at Beijing Jeep? Wasn't China the sort of place where everybody in positions of authority knew everything with remarkable speed? It wasn't as if higher-level Chinese officials had been kept in the dark. After all, the September 1986 ribbon-cutting ceremonies for the launch of the Cherokee—during which the Americans had talked of producing forty thousand Jeeps a year by the end of the decade—had been witnessed by the head of the People's Bank of China, the nation's central bank, and by Chen Zutao, the same auto industry official now sitting before them at the International Club. The Americans weren't just dreaming that these senior Chinese leaders were there. They had pictures of them that day, smiling benignly upon the Cherokee deal.

On the other hand, the Chinese officials at Beijing Jeep could be held personally responsible for leading the Americans to believe that they would be allowed to produce large numbers of Cherokees in China. They were the ones who had sat in on the board meetings and business strategy discussions. Zhao Nailin had put his own name on a detailed business plan for Beijing Jeep which called for producing 4,000 Cherokees in 1986 and at least 7,000 in 1987. And

Beijing Jeep had failed to get formal approval for such large-scale production from China's state planning apparatus. These transgressions provided enough material to make Zhao Nailin's "confession" plausible. (At the time, some of the Americans thought this self-criticism meant that Zhao Nailin, whom they considered one of the most difficult members of the Chinese team, would be fired. As usual, their predictions turned out to be wrong.)

Once the self-criticism was over, Zhu Rongji gave Clare twenty minutes for an overview of the Americans' case. Clare was prepared for a flashy corporate presentation, a slick, American-style dog-and-pony show. The Americans had even brought slides. But Zhu Rongji reined them in. Clare wasn't even permitted to put up his screen and slide projector. Zhu told him to just make his presentation without visual aids. Clare started talking, warming up to his points, but after precisely twenty minutes Zhu cut him off in midsentence, telling him his time had run out.

The Chinese official then delivered a little lecture aimed at both sides. Zhao Nailin had made some serious mistakes, he said, but the Americans had made some, too. Now, Zhu went on, he wanted the two sides to start negotiating a settlement. The sessions were to start the following morning, not at the International Club but at Beijing Jeep. "I am entrusting Chen Zutao and Zhang Jianmin to represent me," he said. The Chinese and American sides were to keep on talking until they resolved the crisis. With that Zhu adjourned the session, hosted a luncheon, and vanished.

When the talks on Beijing Jeep's future began the following day, it became clear that a settlement would not be easy.

The crucial issue was volume, the number of Cherokee Jeeps to be built in China from imported American kits. Chinese officials made clear that they were willing to come up with enough foreign exchange to import the American parts for at least a few Cherokees. That promise of foreign exchange was a crucial Chinese concession.

But for how many Cherokees? The Americans had originally been hoping for 40,000 annually by 1990. Throughout most of the talks, the Chinese were holding the line at a figure far below this: they were offering to guarantee foreign exchange for only 2,000 Cherokee parts kits in the first year and another 2,500 the following year. The Americans were willing to give up their hopes for 40,000 Cherokees annually, but the hard-liners on the American side were holding out for guarantees that China would pay to import parts kits for at least 15,000 Cherokees over the next four years. The two sides weren't even close.

Meanwhile, the talks also reopened many of the oldest and touchiest issues between American Motors and China. It became clear that China had never given up the idea of obtaining a newly designed Chinese jeep. In fact, Chinese officials described in lavish detail once again the special sort of jeep that China needed. That new vehicle was what China had expected to obtain from the Americans when it first signed the deal for the joint venture, said Chen Zutao, who had helped negotiate the 1983 contract. Why couldn't the new Chinese jeep be designed and produced from the Cherokee? Finally Adams, one of the AMC officials, told Chen he was dreaming. You just can't use the Cherokee to make the kind of jeep you have in mind, he said. It just won't work. Chen, the head of the Chinese automotive industry, was furious.

It became clear that there were tensions and differences within the negotiating teams. On the Chinese side, Chen Zutao was particularly hostile to American Motors. Some of the Americans believed Chen was hoping that the talks would fail, that he wanted to end the joint venture and throw the Americans out. It was Chen Zutao who had received, and disregarded, AMC's first telex of complaint the previous November. It was Chen Zutao, too, who gave public speeches criticizing foreign companies for failing to do enough to help China develop its own national automobile industry. Chen didn't like the idea of CKD production from American parts. He was particularly incensed that AMC had gone to the international press and to Premier Zhao Ziyang.[1] By contrast, the Americans felt that Beijing Vice Mayor Zhang Jianmin was more reasonable and more eager to keep the joint venture going. The two men's differences seemed genuine, not some feigned good-cop, bad-cop routine.

The Americans, too, were torn by internal disagreements. Each evening, after leaving the talks at Beijing Jeep, they would return to their rooms at the Lido-Holiday Inn Hotel for long strategy sessions and stay up much of the night debating and arguing among themselves.

For Adams and St. Pierre—the hard-liners—it was time to take a tough stance. China needed American Motors at least as much as American Motors needed China, they contended. "We've got to stick to our guns," St. Pierre told Clare. "They can't afford to let us walk out of here. You've got to stay tough in there."

Clare didn't want to take a hard line. He was willing to make concessions to the Chinese in order to keep Beijing Jeep alive, as he had been all along. China was important to him and, Clare felt, to American Motors. He just wanted to get the project moving. He had eight years invested in Beijing Jeep, and he felt that holding out for higher numbers of Cherokees certainly wasn't worth taking the risk that the Chinese would close it down. Clare wasn't going to haggle, as long as AMC got a guarantee of some foreign exchange to operate and a promise of some significant volume of imported kits. Clare wanted Beijing Jeep to be an enterprise that would be successful for both sides.

Years later Clare would reflect bitterly that in these talks to settle the crisis, Adams, his fellow negotiator, was looking for some sort of hero badge. Clare felt Adams had his own personal stake in the negotiations, that he wanted to get the credit within AMC's top management back home for extracting more guarantees from the Chinese.

Throughout the week of talks the Chinese didn't budge, and Americans like Adams and St. Pierre weren't willing to give in, either. Even C. B. Sung, AMC's consultant, who usually played the role of middleman between Americans and Chinese, was urging Clare to hold out and not to give up. Each night Clare would phone home to AMC headquarters in Michigan to tell Cappy, who by now was running American Motors, where things stood. Things are looking bad, he would say, the Chinese won't budge on volume. St. Pierre thought this was probably the worst week of Clare's life.

In the midst of everything, AMC got an offer to help from a curious source, a man who had spent more time across the bargaining table from American Motors than the Chinese had.

Leonard Woodcock, the former head of the United Auto Workers, who had served as President Carter's ambassador to China, was visiting Beijing that week. While serving as U.S. ambassador, Woodcock had taken an interest in the Chinese auto industry. Touring the big Chinese truck plant at Changchun in Manchuria, he had told officials that it would be a mistake to try to obtain the latest, most advanced Western technology; if they were to receive it, Woodcock said, they would have to find new jobs for 30 to 40 percent of their work force. In return for that advice, Woodcock was told he was a colonialist, that he was treating the Chinese as second-class citizens.

Woodcock probably had spent more time with Chinese leader Deng Xiaoping than any other American. In 1978 the two men had negotiated face to face the details of the agreement under which the United States and China reestablished diplomatic relations. Now, Woodcock called Clare and offered his aid. If AMC wished, Woodcock could see Deng and talk with him about Beijing Jeep's plight.

Even if Deng agreed to help, Woodcock said, that might not solve American Motors' problems. Chinese bureaucracy had a power all its own. And if Deng refused to help, the rebuff might make matters worse.

The Americans thought Woodcock's last-minute offer was too risky. The Chinese negotiators were tough, but Premier Zhao Ziyang, Deng's protégé, had indicated he wanted to reach a settlement that would keep AMC in China. And it would have been an embarrassment for American Motors to have its deal rescued by a stalwart of the UAW.

In their hotel strategy sessions, the Americans devised a few schemes aimed at shaking up the Chinese. On what was supposed to be the next-to-last day of the talks, Clare arrived late to show the Americans' displeasure. It was well after ten in the morning when Clare showed up, but he overplayed his act. He stormed into the room, banged his fist onto a table hard enough to rattle the teacups, and shouted: "There's a worker sleeping out there! When are you people *ever* going to learn?" The Chinese weren't impressed. Their two negotiators, Zhang Jianmin and Chen Zutao, packed their briefcases and quietly walked out. It was left to Sung to smooth over the differences, to talk with both the Chinese and Americans and bring them back for a last day of talks.

On Friday morning, May 12, Clare told the Chinese team he had a plane reservation that afternoon. "We're leaving," he said. "I'm not going to stay any longer, because we keep saying the same things over and over." It was a tactic he'd learned years earlier doing business in Iran; he had discovered that the Iranians would keep on negotiating for as long as you stayed, considering it almost a discourtesy not to do so.

But on this final day the two sides were still deadlocked. Some side issues had been resolved, and the Chinese had agreed in principle to provide some foreign exchange to import the American kits for the Cherokees. But they still had no deal on how many Cherokees would be produced. The Chinese were still talking about a guarantee of 4,500 over two years, and although Clare was willing to compromise, other Americans were still holding out for 15,000 over four years. The meeting broke up without any agreement.

The two sides milled around in the lobby outside the conference room at Beijing Jeep. Clare's car was to leave for the airport in fifteen minutes.

Suddenly Sung called St. Pierre into a corner and asked, "Don, what would it take to settle this thing? Will you take ten-thousand [Cherokee parts kits]?"

"Nope," said St. Pierre. "It's not enough."

Sung persisted. "What'll you take?"

"Twelve thousand five hundred," St. Pierre replied. At AMC's price of close to $9,600 for each Cherokee kit, that volume would require China to guarantee spending $120 million in foreign exchange.

"Done," said Sung. He walked over to consult with the Chinese officials, spoke to them briefly, and hurried back. "They accept," he said. St. Pierre, meanwhile, told Clare of the last-minute offer. Clare, who would have accepted less, thought it was wonderful.

They all went back inside Beijing Jeep's conference room. Sung, who through the week had been sitting near the end of the table, now moved to a middle position, between the two sides. He asked for a blackboard; Chinese staff aides brought him a whiteboard with a black grease pencil. On it Sung wrote out the key elements of what was to be the deal: Beijing Jeep would import 12,500 of AMC's Cherokee kits over four years, with China guaranteeing $120 million in foreign exchange to pay for them. Zhang Jianmin immediately announced that he would accept the plan. Chen Zutao was more reluctant but said he would go along, too.

American Motors was paying Sung handsomely for his services. Sung's consulting firm, Unison, was getting as much as $5,000 to $6,000 a month for its services—and, in addition, one percent of all the money AMC would earn by selling CKD parts kits to China, to a maximum of $700,000.

Thus Sung had a considerable financial stake in brokering a deal for the Cherokees. Years later St. Pierre was still marveling at the role Sung played and wondering about his relationship to the Chinese government. It had turned out that Sung was an old friend of Zhu Rongji, the senior official on the State Economic Commission assigned by Premier Zhao to work out a settlement. On that last day Sung had barely consulted with the Chinese negotiators. He had said, "Done!" first and checked with the Chinese officials afterward.

The following day the deal was put in writing.

For the first time, nearly eight months after the launch of the Cherokee, the Chinese government officially accepted in writing the idea of assembling Cherokees from imported American kits. In fact, the new model jeep that the Americans and Chinese had agreed to produce in the original 1983 contract was redefined as a Cherokee. "A new vehicle, and particularly a four-door, soft-top derivative, will *not* be developed," the new agreement said. The Chinese thus abandoned their hopes of getting the Americans to help the People's Liberation Army make a new military jeep.

The two sides also agreed that the proportion of the Cherokee manufactured from Chinese parts would be increased by at least 10 percent each year until 1990, by which time 80 percent of the content of the Cherokees was to come from parts manufactured in China.

China committed itself to buying AMC's parts for at least 2,000 Cherokees in the first year, 3,000 the second year, 3,500 the third year, and 4,000 in the fourth—thus, a total of 12,500 in the four years until May 1990.[2] (After that time, it was assumed, there would be little need to import American parts for the Cherokee, because China would be making most of its own parts.)

Under the deal, China agreed that Beijing Jeep could try to obtain the dollars to import the American parts by selling the Cherokees for foreign exchange in China's domestic market. But of far greater importance, the Chinese negotiators promised that whenever these sales inside China didn't earn enough foreign exchange, Beijing Jeep could keep on importing the 12,500 Cherokees by converting its renminbi earnings into dollars at the official rate of exchange. The agreement promised, in writing, that the joint venture would have a foreign exchange budget of $120 million, enough to cover the costs of importing the Cherokee kits.

For AMC, it was an astonishingly good deal. At the time, the official exchange rate was 3.2 renminbi to the dollar. But that rate overvalued the Chinese currency, and most business transactions were carried out at unofficial rates closer to 5.0 renminbi per dollar.

Furthermore, in the four-page settlement, the Chinese government agreed for the first time to provide the money necessary to pay for major new capital projects at Beijing Jeep. One of the continuing, underlying sources of friction between the Chinese and Americans had been the question of who would put up the huge new sums of money necessary to begin manufacturing auto parts in China. More than $100 million was needed for projects such as engine, stamping, and axle plants and a new paint system. The Chinese had been arguing that AMC should come up with the money. AMC, which had its own financial problems, refused. The American corporation had also turned down Chinese suggestions that AMC guarantee loans to Beijing Jeep. The Americans argued that major new projects such as an engine plant would be of long-term benefit to China. Indeed, after the end of the joint venture in the year 2003, the physical plant would belong to China.

Now, in the May agreement, China agreed for the first time to finance these capital projects. If Beijing Jeep could not find loans or new investors, the Chinese government would put up the money. The Americans were off the hook.

Years later St. Pierre thought that if American Motors had bargained a little harder, the company might have obtained a commitment from China for higher numbers of Cherokees. The guaranteed minimum of 12,500 Jeeps wasn't much. It wouldn't turn China into the huge sales market AMC had once thought it would be. Still, 12,500 Cherokees was enough for a nice business. AMC would make money both by selling the American kits to Beijing Jeep and by selling the asembled Cherokees inside China. The Americans also had permission to try to increase the volume above 12,500, if they could figure out how to export Jeeps, sell some to expatriates in China, or speed up the program to produce Chinese components.

From the Chinese perspective, AMC had gotten a deal that was remarkable, perhaps unprecedented. Not only had American Motors been guaranteed the right to trade the renminbi it earned inside China for dollars, it had also been given the additional privilege of making that currency exchange at the official rate. The Americans didn't know of any other Western business in China, at least not any major corporation, with as good an arrangement.

The Chinese didn't want any other Western companies to ask for such a deal, either. The final section of the written agreement swore both sides to secrecy.

"Both parties agreed that this is a highly confidential document that should not be released to the press," said the text of the signed accord, a copy of which I later obtained. "The press release matter should be submitted to higher authorities, who will discuss the content and timing of the joint press release."

After a delay of ten days, AMC and the Chinese government issued a short press release. It said only that the two sides had "agreed in principle to actions which will enable Beijing Jeep to continue the Jeep Cherokee program. . . . "

A few days after the deal was struck, St. Pierre instructed Beijing Jeep's finance director to go to the Bank of China and trade in fifteen million Chinese renminbi for U.S. dollars. Some of the staff, both Americans and Chinese, thought there was no way it could be done. The finance director didn't even want to make the trip. He thought Chinese banking officials would tell him he was crazy.

But it worked. Bank of China officials simply deducted the Chinese currency from Beijing Jeep's renminbi account and put nearly $5 million into its dollar account. The joint venture's foreign exchange problems were over. The following day St. Pierre opened a letter of credit for $4.3 million to begin paying for the Cherokee kits back home that had been sitting for months in boxes waiting to be shipped to China.

Beijing Jeep was back in business.

Over the next few months American Motors discovered it was able to settle a series of other important disputes with astonishing ease. Chinese officials even gave AMC the right to convert into dollars and bring back to the United States some of the profits the joint venture earned from the BJ212's, the old Chinese jeeps.

China had long insisted that American Motors could not bring home any profits from China until after Beijing Jeep earned enough foreign exchange to pay for these dividends. Such a policy would have meant that AMC would wait at least another three or four years before it took any profits from Beijing Jeep. But in the autumn of 1986, after talks in Beijing and Detroit, the Americans won the right to convert some of Beijing Jeep's renminbi earnings into dollars to bring home as dividends. The amount was small: AMC was to be paid $300,000 in dividends for 1985. But the precedent was important.

Executives like Clare knew that the dividend payment had important practical consequences for AMC. Under U.S. tax law, once American Motors had obtained at least a token dividend payment in dollars, the company could declare all of its earnings from China, including those in Chinese currency, on the corporate books in the United States as paper profits. In 1985 AMC had earned forty-seven million renminbi in profits in China from the sale of the BJ212's—an amount that would have been worth close to $15 million if it could have been traded for dollars.[3] Those China profits helped the bottom line. AMC didn't broadcast that some of the company's earnings were in the form of nonconvertible Chinese renminbi.

During the meetings in the fall of 1986, Chinese officials also guaranteed that Beijing Jeep could obtain $32 million in foreign exchange for the expensive projects in its capital budget by trading in renminbi it earned inside China. The joint venture was given authority to obtain $16 million by trading in renminbi at the official rate, which by then had gone up to 3.7 to the dollar, and another $16 million by trading in renminbi at unofficial rates of around 5.0 or more.

There were other Chinese concessions. Chinese officials agreed for the first time that Beijing Jeep would pay all the expenses for the eight American Motors employees in China. Those costs, which included salaries, trips home, and other benefits, added up to $1.3 million a year. They all had to be paid in foreign exchange; China's newer hotels, its airlines, and even its grocery stores generally prohibited foreigners from paying for services in renminbi. Until then American Motors had been paying roughly half these costs, primarily because China had refused to go along with the huge new sums required when the American Motors people moved, on their own, into new Western-style hotels and apartments.

The change meant that the joint venture would begin paying the $72,000-a-year rent for rooms at the Lido-Holiday Inn Hotel. Moreover, Chinese officials at Beijing Jeep dropped their longstanding demand that the American company should pay for the costs of new housing for its Chinese workers. Instead, they agreed to spend just over $1 million from Beijing Jeep's 1985 profits and 10 percent of the joint venture's future profits on Chinese workers' housing. China was even willing to make down payments to American Motors for the Cherokee kits five months before they were shipped. Before the May meetings, Chinese officials had refused to consider any form of advance payments.

American Motors had succeeded because it had managed to turn the future of Beijing Jeep into a test of China's open-door policy. The Americans had gone over the heads of their Chinese partners and attracted the attention of Premier Zhao. They had managed to convince China's top political leadership that the future of foreign investment in China was at stake—that if American Motors left China, other Western companies might follow and few others would come in. During the May meetings the Chinese negotiators bargained hard, but only to minimize the costs they would have to pay to keep AMC in China. Indeed, St. Pierre remained convinced that if the Americans had only bargained a little harder during the May meetings, the Chinese would have agreed to fifteen thousand Cherokees.

The Chinese leadership was now eager for AMC to stay. China wanted to cast American Motors in a new role, as a model foreign investor. Beijing Jeep was going to become a model joint venture.

18

Model Company

INVEST IN CHINA, SAYS CAR CHIEF, read the headline of the *China Daily*, the Chinese government's English-language newspaper. The car chief in question was Don St. Pierre, the president of Beijing Jeep, who several months earlier had been talking about pulling his company out of China. He offered his investment advice at a gathering of foreign businessmen and Chinese officials during ceremonies sponsored by the Chinese government to mark the beginning of the spring festival, the Chinese new year, in January 1987. "I see the coming Year of the Rabbit as one of unlimited potential here in China for foreign investment, and I do not hesitate to advise others to jump in. The water is fine," he said.

The deal to keep AMC in China transformed both Beijing Jeep and St. Pierre. Once China's most problematic joint venture, Beijing Jeep was rapidly becoming a government-approved symbol of success. And St. Pierre had become the spokesman for that success. He was quoted frequently in the official Chinese press. One winter day he was interviewed by forty Chinese reporters at once and another day that same week by another thirty. When the city of Beijing set up a new "joint venture club" to counteract negative publicity about China's investment climate, St. Pierre became its chairman.

St. Pierre felt that he was turning into what he privately termed China's pet white face. Chinese officials liked to show him off. At one point, when he was invited to two separate Chinese receptions on the same day and couldn't appear at both, he offered to send another AMC staffer in his place to one of them. "Okay," said Beijing Jeep Vice Chairman Zhao Nailin, "but he has to pretend he's you. He can wear your name tag and sit in your spot at the table." St. Pierre said he thought that would be a problem. The stand-in they had chosen, Bob Steinseifer, didn't look like St. Pierre, and he weighed almost as much as two St. Pierres. Someone would be bound to notice Steinseifer was an impostor. All right, said Zhao, but then Steinseifer has to tell people that you couldn't come because you're really, really sick. Sure enough, when Steinseifer attended, several people came up, asked about St. Pierre's health, and sent their wishes for a speedy recovery. To justify St. Pierre's absence, Chinese officials had already spread the news of his "illness."

Among foreigners, too, St. Pierre had become probably the single best-known businessman working in China. In the fall of 1986, when Katherine Graham, the chairman of the Washington Post Company, visited Beijing and wanted to talk with someone doing business in China, a *Post* correspondent arranged a meeting with St. Pierre. When NBC's *Today* show broadcast a week-long series of programs from China the following year, its cohost Jane Pauley interviewed St. Pierre. In the West as well as inside China, St. Pierre was achieving a level of fame well beyond that of the ordinary Western businessman in Beijing.

Privately St. Pierre acknowledged that these changes were the result of an implicit understanding between American Motors and the Chinese, certainly as important as any of the financial agreements that had been set down on paper the previous May. In return for getting the foreign exchange the company needed to make the Cherokees, American Motors was expected to spread good news about China. After all, China's primary motivation in making the AMC deal had been to demonstrate to foreigners that American Motors could survive and that business conditions in China were improving. Now, China wanted to reap the benefits of that deal.

This understanding on publicity was never expressed in such blunt terms. It was more indirect. Chinese officials would say, "Let's tell everybody how well things are going." But AMC officials certainly grasped the point, and they were happy to oblige.

In August 1986, when the newly ordered Cherokee parts kits had arrived and the dormant Beijing Jeep assembly line resumed production, St. Pierre had held a press conference in honor of the occasion. "Barring a natural disaster, we won't shut down the line again," he said. "We are in business to stay." He expressed optimism that the joint venture could begin exporting some of the

Cherokees soon, and that it would gradually begin replacing American parts with ones made in China. That autumn, when China cleared the way for American Motors to bring home its first dividends, St. Pierre again gave the event maximum publicity. On none of these occasions did he or other AMC officials divulge the details of the secret deal of the previous May, guaranteeing Beijing Jeep $120 million in foreign exchange.

St. Pierre persuaded himself that his help in these publicity efforts was, to some extent, merely a matter of fairness. When things weren't going well for American Motors, he had been rough on China in the international press. Now things were going well for AMC, and he was willing to give China a little good publicity. He wasn't really telling the press anything inaccurate. It was certainly true that the situation for American Motors had improved. (Although St. Pierre was telling the truth, he also wasn't telling the whole truth. In his press conferences and interviews, he wasn't revealing the details of how or why AMC's China venture had improved. The written agreement signed the previous May barred him from doing that.)

St. Pierre's principal motivation, though, was not one of altruism or theoretical fairness toward China. He felt that praising Beijing Jeep was good business for his company. If China benefited from turning Beijing Jeep into a model joint venture, then so did AMC. Every time the Chinese leadership used Beijing Jeep as a shining example of how well a joint venture could work, China's political stake in the fate of Beijing Jeep increased. The greater China's stake in Beijing Jeep, the higher the costs if American Motors were to pull out. And the higher the costs were for China, the more Chinese leaders would let American Motors have its way.

Certainly, in the fall of 1986, St. Pierre was getting his way at Beijing Jeep. The joint venture was having no difficulty trading its renminbi earnings for foreign exchange. American Motors was being sent its $300,000 dividend, the company's first return on the $8 million AMC had invested in Beijing Jeep.

Moreover, Chinese officials seemed to be making management and personnel changes at Beijing Jeep in an effort to accommodate the Americans. Wu Zhongliang, the chairman of the board of Beijing Jeep, had disappeared. Just before the May meetings, the Americans had been told he'd had a heart attack. He was still said to be ill, but St. Pierre was certain that higher-ranking Chinese officials had forced him out. Wu had been Clare's close friend, but St. Pierre was happy to see him go. He was a nice man, St. Pierre thought, but he didn't understand the first thing about making automobiles or running a business. He felt Chairman Wu was a typical Chinese bureaucrat, conditioned by socialist central planning and unable to adapt to Western management techniques. Chairman Wu knew only how to do things the way they had been done in China for years.

St. Pierre was so emboldened by AMC's new, favored status that he began lobbying for a new Chinese candidate to take over for Wu—even though AMC's Chinese partners held 69 percent of the equity and thus the controlling vote on who would be chairman of Beijing Jeep's board of directors. Within the Beijing city government there was a unit in charge of the automobile industry, which oversaw Beijing Jeep. Early that fall the office's vice chairman, a middle-aged woman named Wang Mei, had traveled to Detroit with other Chinese officials from Beijing Jeep for a series of business meetings. St. Pierre thought she was aggressive and tough, but reasonable, and she knew enough about the industry to understand what the AMC people were talking about.

St. Pierre had another motivation for wanting Wang Mei as chairman: he believed her appointment might help AMC outmaneuver its American competition. At the time, Wang Mei was the lead negotiator for the city of Beijing in its talks with General Motors about making pickup trucks in China. American Motors was itself trying to persuade Chinese officials to buy another AMC vehicle, the Comanche truck. The General Motors truck would compete with the Comanche, and St. Pierre thought it wouldn't hurt to have the official in charge of the talks with General Motors committed to Beijing Jeep. St. Pierre began doing some politicking for her, mentioning to Chinese officials that he would like to see her become chairman of the board.

At the same time, within the factory, St. Pierre was steadily promoting and grooming Chen Xulin to succeed him as president after his term ran out. The contract called for the Americans to hold the presidency of Beijing Jeep for its first three years of operations and the Chinese to hold the presidency for the following three years.

Chen had developed a close personal relationship with St.

Pierre. "It's so critical to the success of this company," Chen explained. In fact, Chen said, the public dispute between AMC and China over foreign exchange for the Cherokee kits would have been much worse than it was, if he and St. Pierre had not been on such good terms.

In late 1986 Chen was forty-four, virtually the same age as St. Pierre but young by Chinese standards for such an important job. He was a loyal Communist Party member, who had been working at the jeep factory for twenty-one years. After graduating from industrial college in his hometown of Hefei, he had been assigned to the Ministry of Machine Building, one of Beijing's most important bureaucracies. Chen was sent first to the jeep plant for a year of factory training. During that year the Cultural Revolution broke out, and amid the chaos Chen found he couldn't transfer back to the ministry. He stayed on at the factory, becoming the deputy director of one of the factory shops. In the first years of the joint venture, he headed the supply department. A few months after St. Pierre arrived, he was promoted to vice president. Chen became, in effect, St. Pierre's man, his closest Chinese confidant.

Some of the other Americans found Chen's promotion ironic, because Chen was said to have been among the faction within the factory leadership that originally opposed setting up the joint venture. At the last minute, when the joint venture was about to start operations, Chen was said to have switched sides and joined Beijing Jeep, choosing a senior position within the joint venture management instead of a lower-ranking one within the remaining all-Chinese unit, Beijing Automotive Works.

In turning Beijing Jeep into a model joint venture, the regime was following an old, well-established Chinese tradition. China often held up certain select people, places, and institutions as models for the rest of the nation. Under Mao the entire Chinese nation had been urged to emulate a model soldier named Lei Feng, a selfless proletarian hero whose ideal had been "to be a small cog in the machine" working for Chairman Mao and the Communist Party. So, too, during the Cultural Revolution, the slogan "Learn from Dazhai!" was spread all over rural China. Dazhai was a model commune that was said to have dramatically increased agricultural output by encouraging the political consciousness of Chinese peasants. Only later, after Mao died and Deng Xiaoping came to power, was it disclosed that Dazhai's stunning output figures had been fabricated.

Though Lei Feng and Dazhai were intended as symbols for Chinese audiences, China also set up models for foreign consumption, models that often bore strong resemblance to Russia's old Potemkin villages. Foreign visitors were often brought to the same model store, model factory, model village. If they asked to see something else, they often found themselves turned down.

Under Deng's leadership, many of the models were different. There were model factories where reform-minded managers had increased production through bonuses and other incentives. China even set up a "model bankruptcy" in the Manchurian city of Shenyang—an example for the nation of how a failing enterprise could be allowed to go out of business within a Communist state that had permitted no bankruptcies for decades. (It was of course said that with the help of the state, most of the Shenyang workers quickly landed other jobs; in a model bankruptcy, unemployment was not a serious problem.)

Models sometimes served as a legitimate channel for experimentation. If the regime was reluctant to adopt a policy for the entire nation, it could set up a "model" in a single location and see how it worked. Setting up a model, though, could also sometimes reflect the leadership's inability to win political support for a more concerted, nationwide program of reforms. At various times during the 1980s, many people mistakenly believed that bankruptcies, stock exchanges, rent reforms, and other, similar changes had been adopted throughout all of China when, in reality, the regime had only set up models in a few isolated locations.

Beijing Jeep became a model joint venture, an officially approved example of successful cooperation between Western business and Chinese socialism. Visitors, both foreign and Chinese, were regularly escorted through the plant. The Chinese press hailed its operations and told how the joint venture had overcome serious difficulties. That story fit in perfectly with the message that the regime wanted to convey to Western companies: If one remained patient with China, all problems, even big ones, would get resolved.

Beijing Jeep was not a Dazhai or a Potemkin village. Its production and profit figures were not fakes. It was a real factory, in which real workers produced real jeeps for real wages. And yet Beijing Jeep was, in its own way, as false as these other models. It was succeeding because of the secret financial support it was getting from the Chinese government. Beijing Jeep had its own unique deal, the $120 million fund provided by China to supply the foreign exchange needed to keep on importing parts from abroad. And Beijing Jeep could draw on that fund by exchanging Chinese currency for dollars at the official rate. China wasn't giving that kind of special help to other joint ventures.

The special deal transformed the entire nature and thrust of AMC's joint venture. Beijing Jeep became a business different from what either side had planned. The original idea had been to phase out production of the old Chinese jeeps. Now, with the new foreign exchange deal, the Americans realized they could make more money by continuing to produce the BJ212's. The Chinese jeeps were much cheaper than the Cherokees, and the joint venture produced over twenty thousand of them a year, more than five times the number of Cherokees. The BJ212's could be sold in China for renminbi, and these Chinese profits could be converted into dollars. The Americans didn't even have to worry about overseeing production of the old Chinese jeeps. The Chinese had already been manufacturing them for years without American help. Within the existing technology, there was little to change.

Those old Chinese jeeps became Beijing Jeep's principal, steady source of income. It was the ultimate irony: An American corporation that originally expected to reap huge profits by bringing modern technology to China and by selling its superior products to the Chinese found itself surviving, indeed thriving, by selling the Chinese old Chinese products. When there was some renewed discussion among both Americans and Chinese about the possibility of phasing out production of the old Chinese jeeps, St. Pierre found himself arguing against the idea. Let's keep the BJ212's alive, he said. We're making good money here.

While St. Pierre's interviews were full of optimism about China, he was sounding a very different note to his bosses at AMC. Privately he was saying that the long-range future for Western companies in China was dim.

By the fall of 1986 St. Pierre had served as president of Beijing Jeep for a full year. The pace of life in China was slow. He had plenty of time to reflect, and the more he thought about it, the more certain he was that Western companies weren't going to stay in China for long. The regime was going to close the joint ventures and kick out the foreigners, probably within a decade. Any Western business that hoped to capture China's market for the twenty-first century was doomed to disappointment. Anyone who gave up profits now for future dreams was going to end up with only dreams.

All China wanted from Western businesses was their technology, St. Pierre concluded. As soon as China obtained what it needed for modernization, there would be no reason to keep the foreigners around. Whenever he talked with his Chinese partners or government officials about business, that was obvious. Even money for investment capital was a secondary concern. The possibility that American Motors might pull out of China and that other companies might follow suit posed a serious threat to China's strategy. China needed another five or ten years to obtain and master the technology. After that, its own technicians and engineers, including some of the thousands of Chinese being educated at American universities, would hopefully take over.

The technology that China sought was not the most advanced in the world. It was the Western technology of the early and mid-1980s, to replace the equipment and techniques China had obtained with the aid of the Soviet Union and Eastern Europe in the 1950s. St. Pierre thought China would keep this technology for at least two decades. China couldn't afford to regularly buy more advanced technology from abroad and in any case probably didn't want to do so. Why would the nation with the largest labor force in the world need industrial robots?

St. Pierre also didn't see any sign that China intended to become a great exporting nation, as Western investors had hoped. The Chinese automobile industry had no long-range export plans; Chinese officials weren't wondering what would sell on the world market or developing products to meet these needs. Exports were important to China only insofar as they helped generate the cash that was needed for modernization. China didn't need to follow Japan, Taiwan, or South Korea—in part because it couldn't and in part because it didn't feel taking such a path was necessary. Chinese industry didn't need the world market, because it had its own giant market. Really, when you came down to it, St. Pierre felt, his Chinese counterparts were thinking only about the domestic market. The lure of the fabled China market was most tempting of all to China itself.

His experience at Beijing Jeep reinforced St. Pierre's conclusions. AMC's plans to export Jeeps from China had been cast aside. China didn't have the money or capacity to build a new jeep for export. And the new Chinese Cherokees were too expensive. The costs of buying American parts, shipping them to China for assembly, and then shipping them overseas again for export made the Chinese Cherokees far more costly than other four-wheel-drive vehicles.

Under the original contract, AMC had guaranteed to buy or arrange purchases for a minimum of $70 million in exports from Beijing Jeep in its first seven years. (The language was carefully qualified: Beijing Jeep's vehicles had to meet American Motors' quality standards and to be "competitively priced" in world markets.) By mid-1986 there had been no exports at all, and the original target seemed well beyond reach.

Soon after the secret foreign exchange deal, Chinese officials began pressuring the Americans to begin exporting at least a few Jeeps, so that the joint venture could earn some foreign exchange. In the fall of 1986 American Motors and China announced, with considerable fanfare, that the joint venture would export its first Jeeps overseas. In China the *People's Daily* proclaimed that Beijing Jeep would export thirty-one Jeeps to Latin America. In reality, as the Chinese knew, the purchaser of the Jeeps was American Motors itself. The Americans agreed to buy back thirty-one Chinese Cherokees for $10,800 apiece, but only after quietly negotiating down the price so its financial loss on each vehicle was only $1,000. St. Pierre felt the deal was a public relations gimmick with great political value for AMC inside China. After reading the news, several Chinese government and trade officials told St. Pierre how proud they were that Beijing Jeep had begun exporting. AMC finally located a distributor in Miami who was willing to sell most of the thirty-one Chinese-assembled Cherokees in Central and South America and the Caribbean.

If exporting from China was difficult, St. Pierre was discovering, the process of localization—that is, of replacing imported parts with ones made in China—was even harder. American Motors, like other Western companies manufacturing in China, had assumed that as it found more and more Chinese parts, its costs would decline. But that common Western assumption turned out to be wrong. Finding Chinese parts was no easy feat: They were both expensive and of poor quality.

When Beijing Jeep could make auto parts on its own, the work wasn't too bad; but when the joint venture had to rely on outside suppliers, the quality was poor and the prices too high. St. Pierre found that on the average, Chinese-made auto parts cost approximately twice as much as those produced in the United States. Because of the low quality of Chinese steel, rubber, and other raw materials, the Chinese suppliers had to import them. They also had to import equipment in order to manufacture the parts. Moreover, St. Pierre believed, some of the suppliers were charging exorbitant prices, aware that the joint ventures were under heavy pressure to obtain Chinese-made parts.

The Cherokee kits that AMC shipped to China contained more parts than the kits sent anywhere else in the world, because there were no decent parts available in China at any price. The kits included batteries and tires, glass and sandpaper. Even Clare, who was far more optimistic about China than St. Pierre, found it unbelievable that his company was putting sandpaper into China's Cherokee kits, for a profit. But there was no sandpaper in China, at least none that could be used at Beijing Jeep. Clare wondered how any modern culture could survive without sandpaper.

After living a year in China, St. Pierre thought it was a joke that he couldn't even obtain such basics as tires and batteries from inside the country. Beijing Jeep ordered batteries from a local supplier, but production had to be delayed because the samples leaked and weren't built according to specifications. An order for tires from an enterprise called Beijing Tire was canceled because the tires were poor. Despite political pressure from officials in Beijing to stick with Beijing Tire, the joint venture finally purchased some tires from a factory in the port city of Qingdao.

One of the underlying problems was that there was little Chinese effort to develop a national automobile industry. There were few if any Chinese factories that could produce parts and components in volumes high enough to supply the nation and thus achieve economies of scale. Moreover, each enterprise purchased parts from within its own city or province: Shanghai state enterprises, for example, were pressured or ordered to buy from within Shanghai. This system was rooted in China's regional traditions, its Maoist ideology of local self-sufficiency and its antiquated transportation network. It seemed ironic that the government of South Korea, a capitalist nation, wielded enough control over its private enterprises to plan and nurture the development of a world-class automobile industry. By contrast, China, a Communist nation with a huge central planning apparatus, couldn't make its own state enterprises do the same thing.

Despite all the difficulties, St. Pierre thought, there was money to be made in China—but the profits had to be earned now, by selling technology at a time when China desperately needed it. You couldn't sit and wait for the twenty-first century.

In the early fall of 1986 St. Pierre put some of these thoughts into a confidential two-page memo. Entitled "Proposed Strategy for China," it was distributed to AMC officials in Detroit less than four months after the special foreign exchange deal.

"My main premise is that China wants to modernize [its] auto industry," St. Pierre wrote, "and when they feel they have sufficient technology and know-how, they will throw us out in one form or another. . . . This will happen in five to seven years.

"I believe our strategy should be developed recognizing that we only have five to seven years to make any money," the memo continued. "And we will make that money mainly through the sale of CKD [American kits] and service parts, with a minor contribution from Beijing Jeep dividends. . . ."

Since the strategy was to make money in the short term, the memo argued, American Motors shouldn't worry too much about how much money Beijing Jeep borrowed for capital projects. Nor should the American company make any great concessions for long-term exports. American Motors should do nothing to block or obstruct Chinese efforts to have more parts for the Cherokees manufactured in China, St. Pierre said; these efforts would go slowly in any case. "AMC kit content will remain high for the next five years," he said. In addition to its kit profits, American Motors should "keep service parts pricing high. As [the number of Cherokees] increases, significant volumes will be necessary, especially crash parts (the Chinese can't drive)."

St. Pierre also recommended a public relations strategy: "Continue to spead the 'good news' [about Beijing Jeep], emphasizing the government's involvement and cooperation. This gets them more and more 'on the hook' and will result in higher CKD volumes and probably approval of the Comanche." (In this last prediction, St. Pierre himself fell victim to misguided optimism.)

The confidential memo cast aside all the conventional hopes that China represented the wave of the future, and that American Motors and companies like it should be positioning themselves to capture China's domestic market over the next few decades.

Some of St. Pierre's allies at AMC headquarters, such as Foley, the company's main strategic planner, told him they tended to agree with him. His own boss, Clare, however, reacted coolly. When St. Pierre was home in Detroit, Clare didn't mention the memo at all for four or five days. Just before St. Pierre was about to return to China, Clare told him, "By the way, I read your paper. Very interesting."

Clare didn't care too much what St. Pierre thought about China's future. He thought St. Pierre was in China to run a business and not to figure out where China was heading or even what American Motors' future there should be. St. Pierre could harbor his deep, dark suspicions, Clare thought, but frankly, if Clare were trying to divine his company's future in China, there were other people whose opinions he would solicit before St. Pierre's. Clare wanted to hear from St. Pierre about operations. How many cars did you build yesterday? How many are you going to build tomorrow? Where are your shortages? Is the paint system working? These were questions more important for St. Pierre than the future of China, Clare thought.

St. Pierre tried once, briefly, to tell U.S. Ambassador to China Winston Lord his views on the long-term prospects for Western businesses in China. St. Pierre felt that U.S. government officials had become cheerleaders for business in China and that they really didn't know what ordinary businessmen faced.

Lord, a National Security Council staff aide to Henry Kissinger during the Nixon administration, had accompanied Kissinger on his secret 1971 visit to China. He had sat in the front of Kissinger's plane as it crossed from Pakistan and was therefore the first U.S. official in China for two decades. St. Pierre thought that as ambassador, Lord wasn't giving American businessmen a realistic portrait. Every time there was a going-away party for some American businessman leaving China, every time there was a briefing for businessmen at the U.S. embassy, Lord talked as though American companies had a glorious future in China.

Much of this came from the fact that Lord's interests were more geopolitical than economic. The word *geopolitical* crept regularly into Lord's conversations about China. Like his mentor Kissinger, he viewed China, with its huge landmass and population, as an important buffer against the Soviet Union. Lord recalled that during the Nixon-Kissinger days, American officials paid little attention to the commercial benefits of improved Sino-American relations. Even when the Nixon administration loosened some trade restrictions on China, the motivation was strategic, not commercial. It was one way of sending a message to the Chinese leadership about the U.S. interest in rapprochement.

In the late 1970s and early 1980s, after Deng was in power and the United States had officially recognized the Chinese Communist regime, Lord observed that commercial relations between the two countries took on a life of their own. By 1985, when he was preparing to come to China as the American ambassador, Lord recognized that Sino-American business relations had become extremely important, not only to the private companies involved, but to the whole strategic relationship. The more trade and investment ties the United States had with China, Lord felt, the more the Chinese were going to be politically linked to the United States.

Lord didn't intend to be a cheerleader for China. He wasn't naive; he knew there were some difficulties in doing business in China. He would never advise an American businessman to invest in China just for the sake of the government-to-government relationship. The businessmen would have to make their own profit calculations on a case-by-case basis. As a matter of fact, his own advice to American business leaders was to have patience and realistic expectations, and not to make too large an investment in China. Lord was, instinctively, a cautious man who always qualified what he said, always pausing near the end of his sentences to avoid saying anything too categorical.

Still, Lord freely acknowledged believing that American companies should view China for its long-term potential. American companies, at least fairly large ones, should have at least a symbolic toehold in China, he argued, because the country was too important to ignore. And Lord hoped that the companies already in

China wouldn't leave. The Chinese were working to improve the investment climate.

In short, the ambassador's own conclusions were directly the opposite of St. Pierre's. He believed that in another seven or eight years things would be better for Western businesses. China would have more foreign exchange, more of a legal system in place, and more experience in dealing with the Western companies. Lord doubted there would be any dramatic improvement for the American companies over the next couple of years, but eventually, perhaps in seven or eight years, things would get better.

The U.S. embassy in Beijing held occasional briefings for the American business community. The embassy's commercial and political officers, and usually the ambassador, sat down with business representatives, both to listen to complaints and to exchange views on the significance of China's political and economic policies. At one of these sessions, Lord was asked whether he foresaw long-term benefits for U.S. companies in China. Yes, said the American ambassador; he spoke once again about the long-term future in China, about the prospects in the coming decades, in the twenty-first century.

St. Pierre spoke up. You might be right, he said, but you ought to consider the possibility that it might be a lot less than that, that the prospects for American companies are *only* over the next seven to ten years. You ought to consider that the Chinese are going to close down to the West. Maybe not completely, but they're not going to need us around anymore.

Well, I don't agree with that, Lord told St. Pierre.

19

Outside the Model

Americfan Motors was rewarded for singing China's praises, keeping its complaints quiet, and saying nothing about the details of the May agreement. Yet while American Motors' joint venture improved markedly, the situation for other Western companies in China did not. Other companies couldn't get the sort of financial deal that American Motors had. They still faced the same obstacles: the same foreign exchange shortages, the same delays, and the same bureaucracy.

Consider, for example, the travails of the Beatrice Companies, Inc., one of the largest American food companies, at its joint venture on the outskirts of Canton. Beatrice, along with a Canton state enterprise, had formed the Guangmei Foods Corporation. The aim was to produce soft drinks, ice cream, and other snack foods both for sale inside China and, it was hoped, for export throughout East Asia, particularly to nearby Hong Kong and Macao. The joint venture bore the personal imprint of Beatrice Chairman and Chief Executive Officer James Dutt, who boasted that his company had obtained a good deal in China because of his "unique, personal relationship" with Chinese officials.[1]

By the spring of 1987 Beatrice's venture in Canton was awash in problems. Some of them were caused by day-to-day frustrations of operating in China. Hector Veloso, the Beatrice employee serving as Guangmei's president, found that it was difficult to get electricity in Canton, where the demands for power were so severe that many areas of the city lost their electricity at least two or three days per week. The Chinese-made soft-drink bottles were made of a lower standard than the ones used in the United States, and they tended to explode in the new bottling machine Beatrice had installed. When Beatrice officials set up a plush new training room for the Chinese staff, complete with videotape facilities, they found that the room was being used by Communist Party officials to carry out indoctrination and rectification campaigns for Party cadres inside the factory.

Veloso gave vent to his frustrations in an artfully worded article for an official Chinese publication. "Managing a joint venture in China," he wrote, "takes a positive outlook on life, patience, a healthy sense of humor, a willingness to learn, and a very understanding wife and family. . . . It's not so much that there are no systems in China, because there are. But it is necessary to modify existing ones to produce the desired results."[2]

Beatrice's main problem in China was the same one that plagued the other joint ventures: the difficulty of obtaining foreign exchange. The deal that Dutt, Beatrice's chairman, had approved required Guangmei to earn foreign exchange through exports. And Guangmei was finding it difficult, if not impossible, to export. The price of sugar, the principal ingredient in soft drinks, ranged between fifteen and twenty cents a pound inside China, compared with seven to eight cents a pound on the world market. Even on price alone, Guangmei couldn't compete. Moreover, in Hong Kong, Macao, and other Asian markets, the company was running up against Coca-Cola, Pepsi, and other well-established international giants.

Inside China, however, Guangmei was doing well, indeed better than expected. Using local vendors, it was selling its soft drinks and ice cream virtually everywhere on the streets of Canton. It was making large profits in Chinese renminbi. Unfortunately the joint venture needed more than $1 million a year in foreign exchange to buy foreign supplies, such as the milk products used for Guangmei's ice cream. Repaying loans and paying the salary of Veloso, Beatrice's lone employee in China, also required dollars.

Veloso found that he was spending 80 percent of his time in China scrounging around for foreign exchange. Because he had no special guarantee like American Motors, he had to find an enterprise, or person, willing to part with dollars for Guangmei's renminbi.

Once in a while an enterprise or company was willing to trade. Some of the new, Western-style hotels catering to foreign tourists, for example, took in dollars and needed renminbi to pay their

Chinese staff and food costs. But because foreign exchange was in such demand, no one was willing to trade at anything near the official rate of 3.7 renminbi to the dollar. The Chinese government had authorized some currency markets where joint ventures could legally trade in their renminbi for dollars, but the exchange rates were negotiable. In the spring of 1987 Veloso couldn't buy any foreign exchange at rates below 5.3 renminbi to the dollar. Because of its sales inside China, Guangmei had earned a profit in 1986, and Beatrice expected to be paid dividends. But the profits were in Chinese currency, and Veloso had little hope that they could be turned into dollars and sent back to Beatrice.

Starting in the fall of 1986, imitating the example of American Motors, Beatrice started to complain in public about its problems in China. "Our partners have to realize that the world is not wait-ing for Chinese ice cream or soft drinks," Veloso told one Hong Kong newspaper.[3]

Beatrice was too late. China was going to allow only one Amer-ican Motors, only one model success story. No one else was going to get the AMC deal.

On October 28, 1986, the first anniversary of the contract that launched Orlando Helicopter Airways Inc.'s operations in China, Arthur E. Bates sat in his Hong Kong office, the picture of dejection. Bates's fortunes in life were tied to those of Orlando, the American company he represented. A year earlier, at the time Vice President George Bush had helped celebrate Orlando's contract, Bates and Orlando executives had expected everything to move quickly.

Bates epitomized the hard life of the Hong Kong middleman, the breed of traders who tried to make a living by putting together deals between Western businesses and Chinese enterprises. He worked out of a tiny, dilapidated office in one of the lowest-rent buildings in the highest-rent district of Hong Kong. He had a view of Hong Kong harbor, but also of an expressway. The ground floor of Bates's building was occupied by the Club Dai-Ichi, a Japanese hostess club.

Several years earlier Bates had been enlisted by Fred P. Clark, the chairman of Orlando, to get his company into China. Orlando was a small, family-run company in Sanford, Florida, with fewer than forty employees. Its main line of business was taking surplus U.S. military helicopters, Sikorsky S-55's, and rebuilding them for commercial use. Often Orlando would install new engines on the copters that could run on automobile gasoline.

Orlando's copters were cheap. The company's vice president for sales, Troy Simmons, boasted that you could buy one of Orlando's helicopters for $1 million, perhaps a quarter to a fifth the cost of Britain's lush Wesson helicopters. To counteract any qualms about buying a refitted helicopter, Simmons boasted that Orlando's products "have gone through the growing stages. They've proven themselves."

Roughly half of Orlando's business was in exports; Orlando had sold copters in Haiti, Thailand, Norway, Venezuela, Taiwan, and Australia. In the mid-1980s it turned its attention toward China. Orlando's business was perfectly suited to the Chinese work style and habits. The Chinese were not accustomed to throwing things away. When Boeing sold its 707's to China, it ran into serious maintenance problems because thrifty Chinese crews cleaned and reused the filter cartridges in the hydraulic system— even though the filters, which cost $30 apiece, were stamped "non-reusable" on both ends.[4]

At first Orlando wanted simply to sell helicopters to China. But China didn't want to buy helicopters; it wanted to learn how to make them and, particularly, to remake them. Chinese officials suggested that Orlando consider rebuilding helicopters inside China, together with Chinese workers.

Bates, who had done some other aviation work from his base in Hong Kong, agreed to help Orlando find a Chinese partner in exchange for a 10 percent share in the joint venture. After a search, he put Orlando in touch with a state enterprise on the outskirts of Canton called Canton Number Three Machine Tool Factory, which had no experience with helicopters but seemed to be eager to learn.

There was the usual reciprocal entertainment and cross-Pacific tourism. In early 1985 Clark and his wife had gone to Canton to meet officials of the machine tool factory. They invited their hosts back to the United States. Three months later ten Chinese officials visited Florida. Over a two-week period the Chinese delegation was given the royal treatment. It was escorted through Orlando's factory, flown around on a helicopter, and given free tickets and tours of Walt Disney World and Epcot Center and the National Aeronautics and Space Administration (NASA) headquarters.

Soon the two sides worked out an agreement for a joint venture to rebuild helicopters. At first they were to be assembled in China from American bodies and parts, and later on helicopter parts were to be made in China. The new joint venture was to get a loan from the government-run Bank of China for working capital of $700,000, and Chinese officials assured Orlando the loan would be no problem.

By the early fall of 1985 the contract was ready to be signed. The small American company was eager to impress its Chinese partner with high-level political support. Orlando officials first got a tentative commitment from then Florida Governor Bob Graham to fly to China for the signing ceremonies, but Graham canceled out. In desperation Simmons began calling other politicians. He was finally steered to Bush's office, where he was told that the vice president was about to travel to China and would be willing to attend ceremonies for the new helicopter joint venture.

In October 1985 Bush traveled to China, bringing with him a huge entourage that included two old Bush aides from the CIA, Donald Gregg and James Lilley, who were his China experts; Bush's press aide, Marlin Fitzwater; National Security Council staff aide David Laux; at least twenty other White House staffers; twenty-four members of the U.S. Air Force for transportation, eleven White House communications experts; and forty-nine Secret Service agents.

By this time the Chinese were used to the foibles of the traveling White House. When Secret Service agents arrived at the Canton Trade Fair twenty minutes before Bush was scheduled to appear there, they looked at the throngs of plainly dressed Chinese wandering around on the floor and said to Chinese security officials, "We can't allow the vice president to walk through a crowd like this. You've got to clear this place! Who are all these people?"

"Relax," said the Chinese cops. "Half of these people are ours." It was a momentary, startling glimpse at the huge size and pervasiveness of China's security apparatus.

One of the main themes of Bush's trip to China was the importance of U.S. trade and investment, both for China and for the United States. While in Canton, he met with representatives of the thirty-seven American companies, most of them oil-related, which were then operating in the city. "The more business we do here [in

China], the more it is in the self-interest of the United States, and I think it is in the self-interest of China as well," he told them.

On the night of October 17, soon after his arrival in Canton, Bush went to a reception at the White Swan Hotel honoring the Orlando Helicopter deal. It was only a short appearance, no more than fifteen minutes or so. But the vice president happily posed for pictures and wished Orlando officials well. Barbara Bush came, too, and charmed Clark's wife with her earthy sense of humor. They compared notes about dyeing hair, and Barbara Bush complained about the tour she had just been given of Canton's Ching Ping Market, where a variety of live, caged animals, including dogs, were on sale to satisfy the eclectic Cantonese palate. Try as she might to accept cultural differences, Barbara Bush told Mrs. Clark, she couldn't get used to the idea of eating a dog. "I sleep with the dog, and I don't mean George," she joked.

Clark's son Brad, not quite thirty, who also worked for Orlando, came with his parents. He had been designated to move to the factory in Canton when the new joint venture started operations. The Orlando officials thought that would be within three months, by the beginning of 1986. Chinese officials assured Orlando that their $700,000 loan—needed for shipment of the first three helicopter bodies from the United States—would be approved within six weeks after contract was signed.

Instead, to Bates's dismay, by the first anniversary of the signing, Orlando still hadn't been able to start operations. At first, every time Bates had asked about Orlando's loan he was told that it would be coming next month. Months went by. Bank officials then told him they couldn't approve the loan until the new joint venture was fully capitalized, meaning that Orlando would have to put up more than $1 million at the outset. Then the Chinese officials reversed themselves and told Bates Orlando wouldn't even be permitted to put in new capital until after the loan was approved.

Bates devoted most of his time to obtaining the loan. He commuted up to Shenzhen to meetings with Orlando's Chinese partners, and to Canton to negotiate with Chinese banking officials. After twelve months Bates thought he finally had the loan worked out.

On the wall of Bates's Hong Kong office was a picture of Bush and the Orlando officials at the ceremony in Canton the previous year. Underneath the picture were photocopies of newspaper articles about the problems of doing business in China, which Bates offered to visitors and prospective clients. Bates was trying to put together other China deals, but it wasn't bringing in enough money. He was trying to make some small change on the side by selling shares in a small investment fund. When I stopped by to interview Bates about Orlando, he tried to interest me in his fund.

At the time the contract had been signed, Bates had thought a 10 percent equity in the China venture seemed like a good deal. It was a chance to earn big money. When I interviewed him in the fall of 1986, he regretted it. He should have asked Orlando for a simple monthly or yearly retainer and repayment for his expenses, he thought.

"I've invested three years of my time on this, and I haven't earned a penny from it yet," Bates said. "I wouldn't do it again. If anybody came to me with the same deal again, I'd say no."

In the spring of 1987, after the loan came through, Brad Clark moved to Canton to supervise the beginning of the joint venture's operations. The first helicopter was loaded onto a ship and carried from the United States to Shanghai. There, it was to be transferred onto another boat for shipment to Canton. While the helicopter was being moved in the Shanghai shipyard, workers banged the helicopter into the overhang of a warehouse, damaging the rotor head and the fuselage. The shippers called Clark from Shanghai with the bad news.

The next helicopter sent from the United States was damaged in shipment, too. Clark told the Chinese shipper that Orlando hadn't seen damage like that anywhere else in the world.

Celestial Yacht Ltd. entered China with the usual hopes and the usual hoopla. The Hong Kong company, which makes pleasure boats for export, set up operations along with a Chinese shipbuilding enterprise in the pleasant, sleepy port town of Xiamen (Amoy) on the South China coast. In September 1985 former President Richard Nixon—who was traveling through China at the time with former Treasury Secretary John Connally, a friend of one of the principals in the yacht company—attended the ceremonies for the opening of the joint venture.

That same month Anthony Lewis of *The New York Times*

visited Xiamen and used Celestial's joint venture as a springboard for an uplifting column about the economic changes taking place in China. "The skeptics have reason for wondering whether China can really change, but in this beautiful place, there is a feeling of hope," Lewis wrote.

By the spring of 1987 Celestial was in such deep trouble that officials were thinking of closing the joint venture. Company officials had been confounded by a recurring problem. Materials brought into China from abroad would mysteriously vanish. "You can't leave anything lying around for half a day," David Edinburgh, the firm's production manager, told me when I visited that spring. "It's not just petty thieving. It's important stuff—shiploads of teakwood and resin. We'd get a shipload in, $2,000 worth, and a day later, half of it would disappear." (Employees of some other joint ventures in China, such as Eastman-Kodak, made similar complaints, though they did so privately.)

Celestial had another problem. It had paid to send its Chinese workers to Japan and the United States for special training. After they returned, Chinese officials assigned at least six of these newly trained workers to work in a nearby Chinese shipyard. "Instead of being able to use the experts we trained, they took them away to work in their shipyard," Edinburgh said.

Su Jinzhui, the deputy director of the bureau of foreign investment for Xiamen, acknowledged that the specially trained Chinese workers had been pulled out from Celestial, though he said the actual number of transfers had been five, not six. "The Chinese enterprises are quite busy, so they borrowed the workers [from Celestial] for one or two months," Su explained to me. He said Xiamen would make new efforts to improve the supply of trained personnel for foreign companies operating there.

"We have done a lot of work in these areas, but we have a long way to go," Su said. "We were so isolated from the outside world that we cannot make everything perfect in a day."

China was becoming increasingly uneasy. The American Motors dispute had served as both symbol and catalyst for a change in the relationship between China and the Western companies. In the late 1970s and early 1980s, when Western companies were falling over one another to gain a toehold inside China, it was China that had the upper hand. But by 1986 China found itself increasingly in the role of the suitor, and Western businesses were playing the role of skeptical, reluctant coquettes.

For the remainder of the decade China found itself dispatching officials on tours of the United States and Western Europe, seeking to drum up investment. Again and again these Chinese officials would voice ritual reassurances that China was a safe place to invest; that its open-door policies would never change; that it remained the world's most important future market.

Although China had signed contracts for approximately $17 billion in foreign investment from 1979 to 1986, no more than $4.7 billion of this money had actually been spent or committed. The rest was investment envisioned for the future. During the first half of 1986, the amount of foreign investment China obtained in new contracts slumped to $1.24 billion, a drop of about 20 percent from the previous year. It was a worrisome turnaround, the first such decline since China had opened its doors to foreign businesses in 1979.

While the money was important for China, it was not the main reason the regime was concerned about a downturn in foreign investment. The Western businesses' slackening of interest in China threatened the regime's modernization program and, particularly, its plans for obtaining technology.

There were a number of factors underlying this change, some of which stemmed from international economic forces that were unrelated to the business conditions inside China.

One was oil. In the late 1970s China and the rest of the world had expected that there were huge reserves of oil as large as those in the North Sea or Alaska's Prudhoe Bay beneath the waters off the South China coast. Western companies believed that offshore oil production would provide China with billions of dollars in foreign exchange, which they hoped would be spent on their companies' products. "Even the most conservative estimates are staggering," gushed *Newsweek* magazine in 1975. "Some Western oilmen and intelligence experts even equate Chinese reserves with those of the entire Middle East."

It didn't turn out that way. In the early 1980s, when Western companies began leasing tracts and drilling for oil in the South China Sea, they found little of value. British Petroleum drilled fourteen wells and came up with fourteen dry holes. "The biggies that seemed possible are almost certainly not there," concluded George V. Wood, general manager of BP's China operations. "Rather than Prudhoe Bay–sized discoveries [of about ten billion barrels], we're talking about fifty to one hundred million barrels of recoverable oil at best." Esso China did only marginally better than BP; it drilled nine wells and found only one of them even worth calling encouraging. "We think any discoveries are likely to be small," said the company's president, Murray Hudson. To make matters worse, by the mid-1980s the price of oil had dropped, so that even if there had been as much oil as was expected, the income to China would have been less than anticipated. Its lack of oil revenue meant that China was no longer viewed in the West as a potentially wealthy customer, as a young man about to inherit a fortune.

China was also affected by currency changes that increased the prosperity of its East Asian neighbors, Taiwan and South Korea and made these countries more attractive to foreign investors. In September 1985 the world's leading economic powers had negotiated an agreement under which the dollar's value was to be permitted to drop sharply in comparison with the Japanese yen and West European currencies. This agreement provided a huge economic windfall for Taiwan and South Korea, which were under no obligation to have their currencies appreciate as much as the yen.[5] Exports from Taiwan and South Korea suddenly became much cheaper in the United States than similar, competing products from Japan or Western Europe. Money from abroad, especially Japan, poured into Taiwan and South Korea; foreign investors bought low-priced companies there and set up factories that would earn huge profits through exports.

China suffered by comparison. It wasn't nearly as dynamic as these other Asian countries and couldn't offer foreign investors the same prospect of quick rewards. Moreover, as AMC's experience showed, China seemed a much less appealing place to invest than had been expected. China didn't have much foreign exchange to spend. Foreigners' access to the China market was still severely restricted.

Beginning in mid-1986, the Chinese regime launched a drive to reassure Western businesses of both the wisdom and the safety of putting their money into China. The campaign had several distinct elements: public efforts by top Chinese leaders, a massive propaganda drive, and some changes in the laws and rules covering foreign investment in China.

Among China's senior officials, Premier Zhao Ziyang took the lead. In June 1986 the premier told a delegation of American investors headed by former Democratic Party Chairman Robert Strauss that they could invest in China "without worries." The premier promised the Americans that China would always honor its contracts. That summer Zhao invited a group of businessmen, ambassadors, and other diplomats from the United States, Japan, West Germany, and Britain to his seaside villa at Beidaihe and told them China was preparing to improve the business climate. "Some foreign firms," Zhao acknowledged, "are complaining that investors in China feel disappointed at the relatively high costs."[6]

The premier assigned Zhu Rongji, the official who had settled the Beijing Jeep dispute, to oversee China's efforts to woo Western corporations. Zhu, fifty-seven, was a fluent English speaker who had been trained in electrical engineering at Beijing's elite Qinghua University. At a press conference in October 1986, he offered an unusually frank acknowledgment that China had made some mistakes in its treatment of Western businesses. "Some of our comrades are always thinking of taking a bite at joint ventures, and even sucking them dry," Zhu said. He conceded that the regime needed to provide new assurances that foreign companies could make profits inside China and that the firms could somehow get these profits out of the country. Zhu promised that the situation would change.

The Chinese regime knew the importance of a good publicity stunt. For publicity no one was more important than Deng Xiaoping. Moreover, there was no image or idea as avidly greeted in the West, as guaranteed to attract the attention of the Western press, as the illusion of China, the world's largest communist country, embracing capitalism.

So in November 1986 Deng welcomed a delegation of investment bankers, financiers, lawyers, and executives from the United States. The group came mostly from Wall Street and included John J. Phelan, Jr., the chairman of the New York Stock Exchange. Foreign businesses "cannot find a safer investment than China," Deng told them. He predicted that China's open-door policies would continue "through the end of this century and through the next century as well." Deng added that he hoped American investors would "have more courage" in making investments in China. Phelan, evidently awed by his meeting with Deng, responded exactly as the Chinese leadership wanted. "I would hope the U.S. business community would win a gold medal in terms of investment in China in the future," the stock exchange chairman told the press after the meeting.

To reinforce these overtures from the leadership, the Chinese press published a barrage of articles aimed at reassuring foreign investors. SINO-FOREIGN JOINT VENTURES ARE FLOURISHING trumpeted the *People's Daily*. WE URGE FOREIGN ENTREPRENEURS TO FEEL RELAXED AND INVEST said the *Economic Daily*, another official, Party-controlled paper.[7]

Along with the propaganda campaign, China made genuine efforts to change some of its rules covering Western businesses.

On October 11, 1986, the Chinese government issued a series of new provisions designed to improve the business climate. The list was aimed at two kinds of foreign businesses operating in China: those that produced goods for export and those that supplied "advanced technology" to China. For these companies, the regime offered some new tax benefits, lower land-use fees, special preferences in obtaining water and electricity, and priority for loans from the Bank of China. In addition the government promised greater autonomy in recruiting, hiring, or firing Chinese workers. And in an implicit recognition of the widespread price gouging of Western businesses, the regime announced that foreign firms facing "unreasonable charges" could refuse to pay and could appeal the fees up to the State Economic Commission.

But these new rules failed to bring about any dramatic change. The vague wording of the rules left Chinese ministries, provinces, and local governments great latitude in interpretation. There was, for example, no definition of what constituted "advanced technology." Was a Swiss watch company providing advanced technology to China? How about a fast-food company?

Moreover, the new rules failed to address the fundamental problem: Although Western businesses wanted to sell as much as possible in China's domestic market, the regime wasn't willing to let them do this. Whatever money they earned from their limited sales inside China still was in nontransferable Chinese currency.

Indeed, at his press conference in October, Zhu admitted that
China simply didn't have the money to allow the conversion of
renminbi for foreign exchange. "If all the joint ventures were allowed to sell in China, they would have no difficulty marketing
their products," he said. "But the problem is, we would have no
foreign exchange for them to repatriate [that is, to take home] their
profits."

Finally, the new rules didn't help much because Western companies had begun to learn firsthand one of the enduring realities of
Chinese life: The regulations handed down by China's central government and the broad policy statements of its leaders often had
little impact on daily life.

What was said in Beijing didn't always matter. Many of the
problems Western businesses faced were at the working level: with
the local officials charging a joint venture five times as much for
its phone bill as the state-owned factory next door; or with a
Chinese enterprise refusing to deliver supplies on time unless it
was paid a special service fee.

After the new rules were adopted, He Chunlin, a high-ranking
Chinese official touring the United States, boasted to a group of
American businessmen about China's improved investment climate. The Americans were openly skeptical. One of the American
businessmen told He that the rules didn't seem to matter much for
his own company's existing operations in China. The existing rules
had promised foreign businesses that they would have the same
access to electricity as Chinese companies, the businessman said.
Nevertheless, his own company had recently been told that in
order to obtain power, it would have to buy new "bonds" in the
local electrical enterprise to help repay it for the additional output
required to service the foreign company.

"That's illegal! That's against the law!" exclaimed the Chinese
official earnestly. "Of course, those of us in the central government
in Beijing can't control everything that goes on in the country. But
we do set policy, and when we hear of instances where it's not
being carried out, we try to stop that. Now, where was this utility
located?"

"Beijing," replied the businessman.[8]

20

Reforming Beijing Jeep

One day, after Beijing Jeep had taken on the status of a favored joint venture and tensions had begun to ease, Ji Chunhai called St. Pierre into his office.

"You want to know how the Party works around here?" Ji asked. St. Pierre realized that Ji, officially the head of the factory trade union, was Beijing Jeep's Communist Party secretary, but beyond that he knew very little about the internal structure or activities of the Party within the factory. He told Ji that he would love to find out.

So Ji spent four hours outlining the Party structure. Within Beijing Jeep there was an elaborate Communist Party organization. An eight-member Party Committee for the factory supervised the network. Chen Xulin, officially the highest-ranking Chinese manager, was one member of this Party Committee. Ji made St. Pierre guess who the other members of the committee were. St. Pierre managed to get five names out of eight. In fact, six members of the Communist Party Committee were among the joint venture's top Chinese managers.

There were two hundred to three hundred Party members among the four thousand workers at Beijing Jeep. As Ji explained it, the Party's organization spread into every shop and department of the factory. The chassis shop, for example, had both a shop director and a Party representative.

In these respects Beijing Jeep mirrored every other factory and enterprise in China. In the confused world of China in the 1980s, the lines of authority of the Communist Party within each factory were unclear. Under Mao, the Communist Party secretary had run the factory. By the 1980s Chinese leaders such as Premier Zhao Ziyang had called for Chinese factories to be run by professional managers—that is, by skilled technicians and engineers whose primary concerns were production and efficiency, rather than politics. Yet at the same time the Party organizations remained in place within the factories.

In theory the Party leaders were responsible for politics, propaganda, and social welfare within a factory, while the managers were in charge of day-to-day business operations. In practice these distinctions blurred. Selecting a factory personnel director, for example, was a management decision, but it was also a decision in which the Party had a strong interest. Deciding how much to pay the workers or whether to build new housing for them involved both management and the Party.

The situation was further complicated in the 1980s because many of the best engineers and technicians, the likely candidates for factory managers, were also senior Party members. The result was confusion. In some Chinese factories the Party secretary actually *became* the factory manager. In others the Party secretary turned over daily operations to a weak manager yet remained the most influential figure in the factory. Elsewhere a factory manager controlled the show, relegating a weaker Party secretary to minor tasks like organizing May Day celebrations and the study of Party circulars.

One of the Communist Party's most important jobs within each factory was monitoring birth control and enforcing China's limits on population growth. At one point officials at Beijing Jeep informed St. Pierre that they were carrying out a new policy under which workers who gave birth (or whose wives gave birth) to a second child would have their salaries reduced by 40 percent. St. Pierre thought the penalty was staggering. He also learned indirectly of a separate, secret regulation under which women who had already had a child and became pregnant again would be given a bonus of two months' salary if they agreed to have abortions.

The Party was not particularly popular at Beijing Jeep, particularly with the tough, alienated younger workers. In 1987 the median age of the entire Beijing Jeep work force was thirty-five. That meant roughly half of the workers had had their education disrupted by the 1966–76 Cultural Revolution. Those were the "ten years of turmoil" when classes often went untaught, when defiance of established authority was a way of life, and when politics was conducted in such a way that many Chinese never wanted to hear about politics again.

Inside Beijing Jeep the Party held regular "political study" meetings. Some of these sessions were on Saturday afternoons and some early on weekday evenings. At the meetings leaders read Party documents aloud to the workers or had them read articles from Party newspapers. Sometimes Party leaders asked workers to write down on paper what had happened during their workday or to report to them anything they felt was improper at Beijing Jeep.

Workers had to pay small fines, amounting to a few pennies, when they missed political study. The fines were deducted from the workers' monthly paychecks. Despite the fines, some workers still refused to attend. They didn't want to be bothered with politics, and they figured the time they saved was worth the money.

Some of the younger workers complained that Ji Chunhai, Beijing Jeep's Party secretary, talked down to them in the old style. I am the father, so you had better listen to me, he seemed to say. That approach might have worked twenty years ago, one young worker said, but not for our generation.

St. Pierre was a realist. This was China. The Communist Party was running the country, so he wasn't particularly surprised that the Party played a powerful role at Beijing Jeep. He tried to meet regularly with Ji Chunhai. Although Ji was not part of Beijing Jeep's management team, he was permitted to attend all the board meetings, ostensibly in the role of the head of the trade union. St. Pierre thought the combination of Chen Xulin, his vice president, and Shao Ligong, his personnel director, who was also the second-ranking Communist Party official, probably were together more powerful than Ji, the Party secretary. But he wasn't sure.

Even after Beijing Jeep had achieved the status of a model joint venture, American Motors wasn't able to get everything it wanted. The joint venture's overall financial situation was excellent. The relations between Americans and Chinese improved greatly. Yet when AMC sought to make major new changes at Beijing Jeep, the company often found itself stymied. Several American proposals for reform were delayed, diluted, or defeated. Although the government was eager to keep AMC happy, it did not give the Americans carte blanche.

The Americans slowly discovered some of the realities of Chinese office politics. In China there was little job mobility; both workers and managers tended to stay in the same work unit for life. As a result, victories and defeats were often temporary; personnel changes were slow; and after an interoffice conflict, those who lost out were likely to stay around and wait for years for rehabilitation, revenge, or vindication.

Although the Americans believed Chairman Wu had been forced out, he was never officially replaced. Wang Mei, the woman St. Pierre had hoped would become board chairman, was said to have declined; some Americans were told she was too smart to get involved in a political mess like Beijing Jeep. Zhao Nailin—whose self-criticism of the previous May led St. Pierre and other AMC officials to think he would be stepping down—remained Beijing Jeep's vice chairman.

Chinese officials never bought AMC's Comanche pickup truck, as the Americans had hoped. During one board meeting in late 1986, Chinese board members at Beijing Jeep agreed to consider buying the Comanche, but a few months later they turned down AMC's truck in a terse report that said the army didn't have the foreign exchange to pay for it.

St. Pierre discovered how hard it was to change things when he pressed the idea of salary reform.

As the vice president of Beijing Jeep, the top Chinese manager, Chen Xulin was paid approximately 270 yuan, or about $73, per month. China's wage system remained so egalitarian that even some ordinary, unskilled workers at Beijing Jeep made very close to that salary, if they had enough seniority. By contrast, some of the talented younger Chinese with little seniority, the men and women in their midforties whom the Americans were pushing into management positions, were being paid no more than the average wage at Beijing Jeep, about 200 yuan, or $54, a month.

It galled St. Pierre that there was little difference between the wages of Beijing Jeep's highest-ranking managers and its most unskilled workers. In order to provide stronger incentives, St. Pierre believed, it was necessary to create much wider gaps in income, particularly between management and workers. Why should someone in China work hard to become a boss and deal with all that grief, all those problems, for no more money? He was particularly eager to give big raises to those Chinese managers, engineers, and directors who were most important to the company. The top people like Chen Xulin, he thought, should have their salaries at least doubled, up to around 600 yuan ($162) a month.

For more than a year, during the 1986–87 period, St. Pierre campaigned for a system of new pay scales at Beijing Jeep. But the Chinese proved remarkably resistant. In fact, Chen Xulin turned out to be one of St. Pierre's biggest obstacles. Chen professed agreement with the general principle of salary differentials but kept urging that they not be made very large. "If we go too far and create too much of a gap between white-collar workers and other workers, then people here won't be able to accept it," Chen told me. Chen himself didn't want such a big raise. In fact, he kept trying to give extra money back. During one New Year's festival, the city of Beijing had given Chen an award of 100 yuan as a "model manager," and Chen had promptly donated the money to the Communist Youth League. He felt that if he made too much money, he would have a harder time dealing with the workers. At Beijing Jeep everyone knew what everyone else's salary was. A big salary increase would just cause resentment.

Some ordinary workers felt the same way. Their attitude, reinforced by a quarter century of egalitarianism, was that the people using their hands to make the product deserved the rewards. The managers just sat, talked, and spent money. One young Chinese employee at Beijing Jeep who was promoted and given a raise of 10 yuan (about $2.70) per month found that workers became cool and unfriendly toward him. He began to wonder if the 10 yuan was worth it; he would rather have had friendlier, happier relations with his peers.

St. Pierre took his proposals for salary differentials outside the factory to top Chinese officials in the State Economic Commission and the city government. They encouraged him to go ahead with the idea. But at lower levels of the bureaucracy, such as in the Beijing Labor Bureau, officials told him that his factory workers would never accept the plan. In the end St. Pierre was able to win approval for the general concept of a new system of salary grades, but only after he watered down his original proposal so much that little remained of it. He never was able to get the large salary differentials he had been seeking.

After the plan finally took effect, Chen Xulin, as vice president, was given a raise to 370 yuan, or $100, per month. By contrast, St. Pierre's salary (paid by American Motors) was $100,000 per year, plus a 25 percent hardship bonus and housing and food benefits.

St. Pierre said he would not have been too surprised to find out that Chen was secretly giving his raise of 100 yuan ($27) per month to the Communist Youth League.

One day at the factory, St. Pierre heard a commotion outside his office. A worker named Wang was asking to see him. Wang, covered with bloody bandages across his forehead, on the back of his neck, and on his wrists, looked terrible. Chinese officials were trying to hustle him away, telling Wang that he had no right to talk with the American president. But St. Pierre—who had much less regular contact with the day-to-day life of the Beijing Jeep workers than his production manager, Ed Schulze—was intrigued.

"Sure, he's allowed to talk to me," St. Pierre said. He waved off the Chinese intermediaries. Wang came inside and sat down, followed closely by his wife.

Five days before, a worker named Li beat up Wang. It happened in the early afternoon, at the start of the two o'clock shift, as Wang was about to punch in for work. Wang claimed he hadn't been doing anything at all. He said Li was drunk and had jumped him and hit him on the head with a beer bottle. When the beer bottle broke, Li jabbed Wang in the neck and wrists. Afterward he picked up a large thermos bottle and began pummeling him with that, too.

Wang had come to St. Pierre in anger. He had reported the incident to Chinese authorities but found that nobody was planning to do anything about it: Li's father was a leading security official at the Beijing Automotive Industrial Corporation, the city-run agency that oversaw Beijing Jeep. Wang had been told that the American president already knew all about the incident and had decided to do nothing. Wang had come to tell St. Pierre that he thought St. Pierre's decision was wrong.

Wait a minute, said St. Pierre. What they told you was untrue. I didn't know anything about this.

St. Pierre found himself interviewing Wang about the incident. "You must have done something to provoke this guy," he told Wang.

"Nothing," said Wang. "Absolutely nothing." Moreover, he

went on, after the incident Li's father, the security official, had come to see Wang and told him he should keep quiet about the whole affair.

Wang seemed sincere. So St. Pierre ordered Chinese officials to look into the incident. Li was temporarily suspended. Within hours other Chinese officials at Beijing Jeep began visiting St. Pierre's office. I heard you were told about what happened with Little Wang and Little Li, they said. Don't worry. We'll take care of it.

After a week Chinese officials investigating the incident told St. Pierre that Wang's story had checked out. Li had attacked Wang without provocation. He had been drinking since ten o'clock in the morning and had been thoroughly intoxicated.

Working with Chinese officials, St. Pierre decided to punish Li severely. He gave Li an official reprimand, the most serious disciplinary action short of firing, and put him on probation. In addition, Li's pay was cut in half for three months, and he was required to pay Wang's medical bills and lost pay. Finally St. Pierre ordered Chinese officials at Beijing Jeep to inform Li's father of the disciplinary action and tell him they expected no further interference from him.

St. Pierre and other American officials were told that Li's father had apologized. As far as they were concerned, that was the end of the incident. They were proud to have upheld the principles of fairness and equality. The Americans felt they had scored one small victory over the Chinese system of *guanxi*, in which those with personal connections got special treatment.

What the Americans didn't know was that, according to Chinese workers, once the incident had blown over, Li's family connections still bailed him out. Li's punishment was reduced, his pay was not cut as much as had originally been announced, and he was allowed the unusual privilege of transferring to another department within the factory.

From the distance of the United States, it was easier to imagine that the Americans ran Beijing Jeep. Americans who saw television stories of Chinese eating at Kentucky Fried Chicken, playing golf, and listening to Wham! concerts could fall victim to the false impression that all of China wanted to Westernize—and that Chinese did whatever Westerners asked.

But in China the AMC employees working at Beijing Jeep

learned how marginal their role was. There were only eight Americans, compared with four thousand Chinese. Inevitably the Americans operated on the fringes of daily life at Beijing Jeep; they were the *waiguoren*, the foreigners, and mistrust of foreign influences remained strong.

From the Chinese perspective, AMC's Jeep, the Cherokee, still remained only a sideline venture, and so were the marketing and sales techniques AMC valued so much. For 1986 Beijing Jeep produced a total of 24,500 jeeps. Of these, only 2,000 were American Cherokees. All the rest were the old Chinese jeeps, the BJ212's on which no Americans were working and which AMC had originally intended to phase out.

Only 3,000 of those BJ212's could be sold on the free market. The other 19,500 had to be turned over to the Chinese government for distribution under the standard, decades-old method of central planning. That was the factory's quota. State planning remained the dominant form of distribution.

Each year Beijing Jeep was permitted to sell some more Cherokees on the free market. Yet significant as the changes were, they tended to obscure the underlying continuities of economic life at Beijing Jeep. The reality was that most of Beijing Jeep's four thousand workers still spent their days manufacturing the same jeeps the factory had made before the Americans arrived, and that the overwhelming majority of these jeeps were distributed through the same central-planning techniques set up in China in the 1950s.

The Americans were important to Beijing Jeep not so much for their Cherokees or their knowledge of sales and markets, but because of the technology and modern equipment they brought. The Chinese could have lived without the Cherokee, but they were eager, indeed desperate, for the tools, equipment, and techniques the Americans used to manufacture it.

Beijing Jeep certainly wasn't like the AMC factory where Schulze had worked in Kenosha, Wisconsin. In the time-honored manner of American efficiency experts, following the industrial traditions of Henry Ford, Schulze measured the output of Beijing Jeep's workers in numbers of man-hours per car. Back in the United States, it took roughly twenty-six man-hours of labor to build each car; there were a few plants running at levels of about twenty man-hours per car or less. Auto factories in Mexico and Venezuela ran at about the same efficiency. At Beijing Jeep, on the assembly line producing the Cherokees, the figure was around eighty-six man-hours per car. The Cherokee assembly line had 108 workers producing ten Jeeps per day.

Chinese workers have too much ass time, Schulze said. They sit around too much. In American factories like Kenosha, each worker did less per vehicle, but the production volumes were high enough so that the American worker was always busy. A Chinese worker at Beijing Jeep had more tasks to perform on each car, but the volume was so low that they had more down time. No wonder absenteeism was so high. The Cherokee assembly line was averaging ten to twelve absentees per day, an unusually high rate, Schulze found, because workers had little trouble getting a doctor's permission to take a week off.

Schulze concluded that the workers' indolence was due not to some cultural trait, but to the Chinese system: There were too many Chinese workers and too few incentives to work hard.

After two years at Beijing Jeep Schulze decided to recommend a change in factory operations that he thought would benefit the workers, save money, and cut down on the waste of energy. He decided to press for a five-day workweek.

Beijing Jeep's assembly line ran six days per week, with Sundays off. Schulze was convinced Chinese workers didn't have enough time for themselves. He proposed giving all workers an extra day off. The factory could still make the same number of Jeeps, Schulze figured, because the workers were now only putting in at most five hours a day of actual labor. He was sure they would be able and willing to increase the speed of production if they were given an extra day off. Switching to a five-day week would also save Beijing Jeep more than $325,000 a year in costs for water, gas, electricity, and steam, plus smaller amounts for lunch subsidies, Schulze calculated.

In a memo to management, Schulze contended that the extra day off work would reduce the high level of absenteeism and make for happier, better-rested workers with more free time. "The employees will gain more time for their housework and still have time for rest and social activities," he said, making it sound as though Chinese workers, like Americans, had big houses with lawns to mow and leaves to rake.

It was, in its way, a typically American approach to China. It placed a high premium upon the values of time and efficiency. It recommended for China the American ideal of regularly alternating hard work and leisure. In practical terms Schulze's proposal made sense, but it also called for fundamental changes in the entire rhythm of Chinese life. Its chances of adoption were so slim that even St. Pierre, Schulze's boss and close friend, wouldn't stake any political capital on the five-day week. Schulze was no sophisticated executive, and he was too low-ranking to carry influence on his own. Still, he pushed hard.

Schulze talked to as many Chinese officials as he could. He found that they were attracted by the idea of saving energy costs. But they balked at giving workers a second day off. Virtually every factory in China was on a six-day week. One Chinese official recommended that Schulze revise his proposal: The assembly line could be closed on Saturdays, but the workers would come into the factory that day for special training. Of course, that approach undercut Schulze's initial purpose of giving the workers an extra free day.

Gradually Schulze realized that Chinese leaders didn't like the idea of giving workers more free time. They were nervous about the social consequences. In the United States factories were merely for production, but in China, where apartments were tiny and streets overcrowded, the factories also served the purpose of social control. Having workers in the factories kept them off the streets.

Schulze viewed the issue in political terms. "This shows you the inefficiency of the country," he told me. "I never realized how much I hated communism until I came to this country. What they do to these people is unbelievable."

21

The Return

In early March 1987, Chairman Wu Zhongliang suddenly reappeared at Beijing Jeep. Chairman Wu had been away for nearly ten months, since he was reported to be ill on the eve of the talks to settle American Motors' financial problems. St. Pierre believed he had been quietly dismissed. Yet the Chinese had never appointed a replacement.

Now, Chairman Wu was said to have recovered from his ailments. He didn't look as though he had been sick. Whereas previously he had worked out of his office in the city of Beijing's automotive department, this time Chairman Wu moved into a new office inside the White Palace.

Chairman Wu soon began giving the Americans new headaches at Beijing Jeep. He complained that AMC wasn't transferring enough of its technology to China. While most of the Americans were off at a meeting in Detroit, he launched a sudden investigation of service problems with the Cherokees. He also hosted three meetings at which he accused the Americans of moving too slowly on the process of substituting Chinese-made parts for American-made ones.

St. Pierre felt that Chairman Wu was stirring up trouble. If this kept up, St. Pierre thought, he would have to make use of his own political connections in China to counteract Chairman Wu.

It may have been just a coincidence, or perhaps not. The Americans never knew for sure. But the unexpected return of Chairman Wu ran parallel to the momentous political changes taking place in China in the first months of 1987.

Throughout the previous year the reform wing of the Chinese leadership, led by Chinese Communist Party Secretary Hu Yaobang, had been fostering a new climate of political liberalization. Hu and his aides permitted unprecedented intellectual discussion of such subjects as the meaning of freedom and democracy, the right to dissent, and the necessity for a system of checks and balances upon the power of the Chinese government and the Communist Party. At one symposium some Chinese intellectuals contended that "the relationship between Marxism and non-Marxism should not be one between the ruler and the ruled."[1]

In early December 1986, encouraged by this new climate of tolerance, students at some of China's leading universities began demonstrating for democratic freedoms. Some of the students borrowed American symbols such as the Statue of Liberty and slogans such as Patrick Henry's "Give me liberty or give me death." The demonstrations spread to other cities. Within less than two weeks tens of thousands of Chinese students were jamming the downtown streets of Shanghai.

On January 1, 1987, defying an official ban on demonstrations, students in Beijing marched through Tiananmen Square, the place that had served in the twentieth century as the starting point for many of China's most important political movements. "Please make the rest of the world know what we are doing here," said one young participant that day. "We want public elections. We want to elect our leaders."

The leaders of the Chinese Communist Party reacted swiftly. Shortly after the student demonstrations erupted, China's top military leaders convened for a special series of meetings. A few days later the *People's Daily* said the student protests were the result of "the spread for several years of bourgeois liberal thought." From now on, the paper said, the Chinese regime would insist upon rigorous obedience to the "four cardinal principles": socialism, the dictatorship of the proletariat, the absolute leadership of the Communist Party, and the ideology of Marxism, Leninism, and the thought of Mao Tse-tung.

On January 16, 1987, Hu Yaobang, Deng's right-hand man and heir apparent, who had served as general secretary of the Communist Party for six years, was ousted from power.[2] The Party leadership accepted Hu's resignation at what was called "an enlarged session" of the Communist Party Politburo—a special meeting stacked with elderly Party leaders who were not officially Politburo members. Premier Zhao Ziyang was named the Party's acting secretary.

To dramatize the return to orthodoxy, the television anchorman who informed the nation of the news that night wore a Mao jacket rather than the customary Western suit and tie. Seeing this sudden sartorial change, and observing the somber expression on the anchorman's face, some ordinary Chinese later said they had momentarily feared that the anchorman was going to announce China had been invaded by the Soviet Union. (A few weeks later the Chinese regime volunteered a convoluted, sexist explanation for the Mao suit. Originally a woman had been scheduled to anchor the news that night, Chinese officials said, but the story of Hu Yaobang's resignation was so important that it required a man. The only male anchorman available in the studios of China's state-run television network that night hadn't been planning to go on the air and didn't have his usual Western clothes with him.[3])

In the following weeks there were suggestions that some China leaders favored a return to the old virtues of the Party's early days under Mao. Ordinary Chinese were once again urged to imitate the model soldier, Lei Feng, the "cog in the machine" who unquestioningly followed the Party's orders. Writers and artists were told to reread the lectures given by Mao in 1942, in which he said intellectuals should be "oxen for the proletariat and the masses." Two prominent intellectuals—the writer Liu Binyan and the astrophysicist Fang Lizhi—were purged from the Communist Party for advocating democracy and the right to dissent. Liu's offense was to have written a book, *A Second Kind of Loyalty*, which challenged the wisdom of blind loyalty to Communist Party leaders.

The Party encouraged Chinese university students to gain "practical experience" by working in the Chinese countryside, a reminder of the mass upheavals of the Cultural Revolution. Chinese newspapers carried denunciations of Westernization. "We're full of confidence that socialism is bound to defeat capitalism," declared one Communist Party paper. The United States was once again characterized as a nation ruled by "the monopoly capital class."[4] The leading Party newspaper in Beijing published a front-page story about a Chinese college student who was said to have murdered a girlfriend and then committed suicide after being corrupted by reading Western philosophers like Jean-Paul Sartre and Friedrich Nietzsche.[5]

There were signs that China's political shift might be accompanied by new economic changes as well. The regime put its price reform proposals on hold, thus freezing China's steps toward a market economy. Rules were issued urging Communist Party organizations in factories to "aid" plant managers in making decisions, thus undercutting the recent policy of giving the managers a degree of independence. Chinese Communist Party circulars criticized Hu Yaobang for having pressed too hard for more consumer goods for the Chinese people.

Moreover, some of the Party leaders who had engineered the ouster of Hu began calling upon older, semiretired cadres to return to their old factories and offices in order to help guide China back in the right direction.

Until Wu reappeared, St. Pierre hadn't noticed any dramatic changes at Beijing Jeep stemming from China's political turbulence. Shortly after the student demonstrations had erupted, Chinese officials at the factory held a large meeting to give the workers the Party's version of what was taking place. When American officials tried to ask their Chinese counterparts about the ongoing campaign against "bourgeois liberalization," the Chinese clammed up. They didn't want to talk about it. Among the Chinese officials and workers at the factory, there was no sign of any anti-Western or antiforeign sentiments.

A month after his return, Chairman Wu started pressing for a major change in Beijing Jeep's management. He suggested that Chen Xulin, the man the Americans had been grooming to succeed St. Pierre as president, might not get the job. During a trip to the United States, Chairman Wu began preparing American Motors officials for the possibility that Zhao Nailin—the Beijing Jeep board member who had made the abject "self-criticism" during the talks to ease the joint venture's financial crisis—would become the first Chinese president.

As soon as he heard what Wu was doing in Detroit, St. Pierre began his own maneuvering in Beijing. He passed the word to Beijing city officials like Vice Mayor Zhang Jianmin, a strong supporter of the Jeep venture, that he was unhappy with Chairman Wu.

. . .

Within only a few months the political climate in China changed once again. With the student demonstrations under control and the advocates of greater political liberalization neutralized, Deng and Zhao did an abrupt about-face. They attacked the orthodox Marxists within the Party who seemed to be threatening a rollback of China's economic reforms.

In late May Deng reminded the nation that China had suffered from "leftist errors" from 1957 through 1978 and that the result had been stagnation. Zhao decried "rigid thinking" within the Party and said that "the problem of having too many elderly people in leading positions has not been fully overcome." Those within the Party who favored further economic reforms managed to regroup under Zhao's leadership, though they were eventually obliged to accept Li Peng, the candidate of the older traditionalists, as the next premier. Thus, the Chinese Communist Party put aside, for a time, its internecine factional disputes between reformers and conservatives. The intraparty frictions were to reemerge once again following an upsurge in inflation the following year and, most dramatically, after the student demonstrations began at Tiananmen Square in 1989.

Similarly, at Beijing Jeep AMC's new difficulties ended just as mysteriously as they had begun. Chairman Wu's power suddenly evaporated. During a visit to the factory in May, Vice Mayor Zhang told St. Pierre that Wu had been acting on his own, not for the Chinese government or the city of Beijing.

Nothing at the factory was going to change, the vice mayor said. Chen Xulin was going to be the next president. In fact, St. Pierre was told, the city was in the process of reorganizing the Beijing Automotive Industrial Corporation, which supervised auto production in Beijing. Wu, who until then had been head of BAIC, would be losing this powerful city post.

The return, the rise, and the fall of Chairman Wu at Beijing Jeep may have been connected to the broader political swings in China that spring. Or perhaps not. To the Americans, it was a mystery.

The regime's campaign against bourgeois liberalization did nothing to improve China's standing with foreign investors. Indeed, the political campaign of early 1987 overshadowed the regime's at-

tempts to overcome the negative publicity caused by the American
Motors dispute.

The propaganda efforts and new rules issued in the summer
and fall of 1986 had had little effect. By the end of that year some
struggling Western companies in China had begun to cut back in
earnest.

Even the determinedly optimistic U.S. embassy in Beijing acknowledged the deteriorating situation. "Several major U.S. corporations reduced staff in China, and U.S. government agencies like
the Overseas Private Investment Corporation continued to encoun-
ter resistance in their efforts to drum up interest in China among
U.S. companies at home," reported the U.S. embassy's commercial
section in a year-end cable to Washington.[6] The U.S. Department
of Commerce's annual report on China in late 1986 included this
gloomy note for the American businesses: "Recently . . . there has
been rising discontent among foreign businessmen and investors in
China. Complaints center around the high costs of doing business
in China, murky regulations and official secrecy, lengthy negotiations, complex bureaucratic procedures, difficulties in obtaining
foreign exchange, and the lack of control over local personnel."[7]

The 1986 year-end figures showed that new investment in
China had dropped by nearly 50 percent. The previous year China
had attracted $6.3 billion in new contracts; in 1986, according to
official Chinese figures from the Ministry of Foreign Economic
Relations and Trade, the figure was $3.3 billion. It was the first
such decline since China had begun accepting foreign investment
after Deng came to power.

In the past, the hard-luck stories of the foreign business community involved delayed deals, unsigned contracts, and lost money.
Now there were layoffs. By the spring of 1987 some Westerners
who had come to do business in China were out of work.

I met Herbert Liu, a young, college-educated Chinese-American, in April 1987, when he was staying in a $2.70-per-night youth
hostel for foreigners on Canton's Shamian Island. Most of the other
occupants were freewheeling foreign adventurers, part of the international backpacking army preparing for its annual spring invasion
of China and Tibet. Liu wasn't like the others; he was sleeping in
the hostel because he needed to save money. Each day he donned
a suit and tie and made the rounds of Canton's new, expensive

Western-style hotels, trying to meet Western businessmen who had gathered for the semiannual Canton Trade Fair. Liu was looking for work. He had been laid off and left stranded in China.

At the beginning of 1986 Liu had come to Beijing as a salesman for a leading American computer company.[8] Only a week after his arrival Liu was sent out on the road to sell the company's computers. There had been no time to learn the products or the territory. The company was in a hurry to get salesmen out into the field.

Liu's timing was terrible, and so was his deal with the company. When he first arrived, the American company had sixty people jammed into its Beijing office. The firm had made its plans for a large sales operation in China during the 1984–85 period of consumerism when it seemed as though China had plenty of foreign exchange. By the time Liu started work, the economic situation had changed; it soon became clear that Chinese provinces, municipalities, and enterprises wouldn't be able to buy as many computers as the company had hoped. Liu came to China with no contract or job security. Within a few months he was laid off, along with most of his coworkers. Over the course of a year, from early 1986 to early 1987, Liu's company reduced the size of its Beijing office from sixty employees to twenty.

At the height of the domestic political turmoil, the Chinese leadership tried to reassure foreign countries and investors. Zhao, in his first speech as the new Communist Party secretary, stressed that China would continue the policy of opening to the outside world. Ironically, he was blazing the path that would be followed, two years later, by his own successor. After Zhao himself was dismissed as Communist Party secretary in June 1989, Jiang Zemin, the man who replaced him, similarly attempted to reassure the world that there would be no changes in China's open-door policy.

In the aftermath of Hu's ouster, U.S. officials sought to minimize the significance of the event. At the U.S. embassy in Beijing, American diplomats suggested to correspondents that Hu had lost his job primarily because of his mercurial personality and shortcomings as a leader, rather than because of policy disagreements or a resurgence of orthodox Marxism in China. A few weeks later, as Secretary of State George Shultz prepared for a visit to China, senior State Department officials told Washington reporters that Hu's ouster was "a little bump on the road, but perhaps no more than that." (Much later, in a 1988 report to Congress, the CIA acknowledged that as a result of Hu's fall from power, "reformers [in China] lost one of the most vocal and powerful supporters of faster political liberalization and greater reliance on consumer-driven economic development."[9])

Nonetheless, the student demonstrations and the replacement of the Party secretary touched off a new round of anxiety among Western companies. The events revived old memories of China as a nation prone to sudden political change. Moreover, despite the efforts by Zhao and others to limit the damage, at the height of the political campaign some Chinese officials and newspapers for the first time in a decade explicitly questioned China's policy of attracting foreign investment.

"We must rely on our own efforts," said one Party paper, the *Workers' Daily*, in a front-page commentary. "Capitalists are capitalists. They will never be so generous as to assist a country like ours without benefiting themselves." While China should continue to bring in some foreign investment and technology, the newspaper went on, the nation should adhere to a policy of "self-reliance"—the same economic policy that Mao had propounded.[10] During the peak of the political campaign, Vice Premier Li Peng said China planned to depend mostly on its own resources. "You must be psychologically prepared for some projects to be rejected or restudied," Li informed one visiting delegation of French officials.[11]

Such statements increased the reluctance of Western companies to put new money into China. In 1987 the Chinese regime failed to attract any significant increase in foreign capital from the low level of the previous year. The amount of foreign investment for 1987 remained approximately the same as the previous year and well below the 1985 level.[12] The U.S. Department of Commerce estimated that American investors signed contracts worth approximately $400 to $500 million in China in 1987, slightly less than in 1986 and far below the $1.1 billion in contracts signed in 1985.[13]

"China has never been an easy place to do business. It has always been tough, and it is going to continue to be tough," concluded the U.S. embassy's commercial section in a cable from Beijing to Washington after the fall of Hu Yaobang. "However, the suddenness and seriousness of the current political shift, which is the most important in ten years, creates an impression of disorder and of an unstable and uncertain China. And the one thing the business person looks for most, in order to plan, is predictability."[14]

Even amid all the gloom, Western businesses were still dispatching scouting expeditions to China, with ideas ranging from the ingenious to the grandiose to the bizarre. Those who made the trips now, however, came with much more skepticism than their predecessors five or ten years earlier. And they tended to propose different sorts of business schemes, ones that did not depend on being granted access to a market of a billion Chinese.

In April 1987 Chinese officials in Shanghai were invited to a wine tasting sponsored by the Wine Institute, the organization representing the California wine industry. On a rainy spring day, at the U.S. consulate in Shanghai, located in what was formerly a millionaire's mansion, Chinese officials stood in line to sample glasses of Domaine Chandon and 1982 Almaden Premium Red. They peered at English-language brochures that described Rutherford Hill Sauvignon Blanc as "a refreshing wine, with hints of herbs and grasses followed by tropical fruit complexities in the nose."

U.S. officials from the Shanghai consulate clustered around a cheese fondue, swapping stories about film director Steven Spielberg, who had been filming *Empire of the Sun* in Shanghai. Even Spielberg had gotten a taste of the vagaries of doing business in China, the Americans said. After giving him the authority to film in Shanghai's grimy downtown streets, city officials had at the last minute demanded that his company pay a fine of more than $10,000 for polluting the environment with the smoke used in his battle scenes.

That spring the Wine Institute conducted similar tastings in three other Chinese cities. The California wine companies had asked Rory Callahan, director of the Wine Institute's New York City office, to investigate the prospects for new business in China. Callahan—who realized that the prospects for selling wine to the Chinese weren't great—hoped the American wineries might be able to launch a major new effort to sell wine to some of the millions of Western tourists traveling through China each year.

During his trip, Callahan found that a single Chinese enterprise controlled the importation of all wine into China, and that it imposed markups of 100 percent on the price of each bottle. The enterprise sold the wine to hotels and restaurants, which then added their own markups. The result was that a bottle of Paul Masson Cabernet Sauvignon that sold for $5 in the United States cost $45 at hotels in Shanghai and Canton. At those prices Callahan found that even he was switching to local beer. Callahan also found that meals for Western tourists on packaged tours were so programmed that there was no real time for the tourists to have what the Wine Institute considered "a dining experience," a leisurely meal with a bottle of wine.

When Callahan returned to the United States, he informed the California wine companies that there were too many hurdles for any company to try to enter the market in China. "Mainland China is not that promising at this moment," he told them.

22

Corporate Takeover in the People's Republic

On the fateful morning of Monday, March 9, 1987, Don St. Pierre had just arrived at AMC headquarters with Chen Xulin and some other Chinese officials from Beijing Jeep for what they all had expected to be an unusually peaceful and uncontentious visit. The crises of the previous year had passed, things were going well at Beijing Jeep, and both Americans and Chinese were looking forward to a relatively quiet week. They were going to work on routine plans for the following year. AMC wanted to explain to the Chinese its credit policies and some new procedures for ordering American parts.

That morning St. Pierre was in Clare's office when another company official stuck his head inside the door and interrupted their conversation. "Chrysler just bought us," he said.

Everyone laughed; rumors like that had been around AMC for a long time. "No," said the informant at the door. "It's true."

The news stopped all ordinary work, both in Clare's office and everywhere else at American Motors. Soon someone brought in a copy of a press release. It was official. Chrysler had signed an agreement with Renault to buy Renault's 46 percent controlling interest in AMC for $200 million; Chrysler had also offered to purchase the remaining shares in AMC from other stockholders.

AMC's struggle to survive as a relatively small American auto manufacturer, separate from the Big Three, had come to an end. In all, AMC had 19,000 employees, 1,300 American dealers, and four plants with a combined production capacity of approximately 700,000 vehicles a year. In his public statements that day, Chrysler Chairman Lee Iacocca made it plain that some of AMC's assets were more important than others, and that AMC's Jeep was on top of the list. "For Chrysler, the attractions are Jeep, the best-known automotive brand name in the world; a new assembly plant at Bramalea, Canada; and a third distribution system giving us access to a larger market," Iacocca said.

The Chinese were extremely nervous. Merger mania had not yet reached the Middle Kingdom. In China, in those rare instances when one state enterprise took over another, it was a sure sign that the purchased enterprise had failed. Chinese officials had found it unsettling enough in 1979 when Renault had first bought its stake in American Motors. Now, AMC was being taken over by another American corporation, one about which the Beijing Jeep officials knew very little.

On the Monday night of the sale, Chen Xulin began getting phone calls from Beijing. Similar calls came in nightly for the remainder of his time in Detroit. Chinese officials wanted to know what had happened to AMC and what Chrysler's purchase might mean for Beijing Jeep. The first news of the Chrysler takeover had been given considerable display in the Chinese press. Chinese government officials urged Beijing Jeep's Chinese board members to find out from the Americans what was going on. Chrysler might not be as interested in China, or as tolerant of its foibles, as American Motors had come to be.

There would be a six-month interim before the takeover became final. The deal required government approval in the United States, France, and Canada, where AMC had plants at Bramalea and in Brampton, Ontario. Chinese officials began suggesting that the Chrysler-AMC deal might require the authorization of the Chinese government as well before Chrysler took over Beijing Jeep. They pointed out that the 1983 contract between AMC and China contained a clause prohibiting American Motors from selling or transferring its shares in Beijing Jeep without the approval of its Chinese partner and without offering China a chance to buy out AMC's 31 percent interest in the joint venture.

Hurriedly, American Motors had its lawyers issue an opinion for the benefit of the Chinese that said the Chrysler takeover would have no effect on AMC's shares in the China venture. AMC took the position that its shares in China weren't being sold to Chrysler. American Motors would still retain the shares; the takeover meant that Chrysler would own AMC. Chinese officials listened to this explanation and said little. St. Pierre thought the Chinese were looking for a new angle in order to obtain something better for China out of the Chrysler deal.

On Wednesday, two days after the announcement, St. Pierre brought in Chen Xulin for a private meeting with Joseph E. Cappy, AMC's president and chief executive officer. Cappy had been surprised by the acquisition: Chrysler and Renault officials had negotiated the deal in Paris and hadn't informed AMC's top management until the day of the announcement.

Now Cappy, the head of a major American corporation, poured out his disappointment about the takeover to Chen, a loyal cadre of the Chinese Communist Party. Cappy was distressed that American Motors had been sold without his having been told beforehand. He felt that in his year as president, AMC had turned the corner. He had pushed along the new products that were on the verge of coming out and that might make AMC more profitable. Now Cappy and AMC wouldn't get a chance to show what they had done. Left unsaid was the idea that what had just happened represented the workings of the capitalist system: AMC had failed to earn enough profits for Renault or to win it a strong position in the American auto market.

Finally Cappy turned to the question that most concerned Chen Xulin: What would the Chrysler deal mean for Beijing Jeep and China? Cappy told Chen that Chrysler had more resources and products than American Motors; it was a bigger, wealthier corporation, and it had the capacity to do more for Beijing Jeep. Cappy, who had lunched with Iacocca the previous day, also told Chen that the Chrysler chairman had seemed tremendously interested in China.

The Chinese delegation completed its scheduled rounds in Detroit. With AMC's top management suddenly preoccupied by the merger, only lower-level American officials showed up for most of the sessions with the Chinese. The Chinese visitors were getting a firsthand look at the upheavals caused by a corporate takeover in America.

Despite AMC's reassurances, the Chinese returned to Beijing still worried about the effect of the takeover. The legal questions over what would happen to AMC's shares in the joint venture came up again that spring in Beijing. St. Pierre wondered whether General Motors, which had been exploring the possibility of setting up its own joint venture in China, was trying to make life difficult for AMC and Chrysler by creating uncertainty among the Chinese about the takeover.

In April Chairman Wu announced he was traveling to Washington to participate in ceremonies at which a Chinese-made Jeep was being given away. Since he was going to be in the United States anyway, he said, he might as well stop off in Detroit and see Clare and Cappy. The American Motors officials believed Wu was trying to arrange to stop by at Chrysler for a private meeting with Iacocca. Beijing Jeep was still AMC's joint venture, and the AMC executives made sure the Chrysler people kept the Chinese at arm's length. Chrysler executives needed little persuading; they were busy with the larger aspects of the takeover and weren't ready to zero in on AMC's China venture. Chairman Wu made the Detroit stopover but didn't get to see Iacocca.

Meanwhile the AMC executives were also frightened. Their worries extended far beyond the future of Beijing Jeep: their own jobs and futures were at stake. How many vice presidents from American Motors was Chrysler going to need? Chrysler had its own international division. In May news accounts in *The Wall Street Journal* quoted Chrysler officials in ways that suggested they intended to eliminate duplication of jobs after a takeover and to lay off some American Motors executives.[1] Copies of such stories attracted considerable attention in American Motors' management offices.

At Beijing Jeep the Americans found that as the time for the takeover approached, it was becoming increasingly hard to deal with their bosses back home. It was a surprising reversal. Suddenly AMC headquarters was taking hard-line positions on business with China. The Americans working in Beijing, who had for years urged headquarters to be tougher, were now the advocates of conciliation.

There was some strange haggling over finances. When American Motors sent one expert to China to investigate some malfunctioning American parts, AMC suddenly asked Beijing Jeep to pay the man's hotel bills and advance him $2,000 for living expenses— even though the Americans had already assured their Chinese partners that AMC would take responsibility. AMC began delaying its payments to Beijing Jeep for the Cherokees it was buying for export. To the Americans working in Beijing, that seemed unfair: When the situation was reversed, Beijing Jeep had to pay AMC well in advance of shipment for the Cherokee parts kits.

St. Pierre tried to figure out what was happening. He thought perhaps everyone at AMC headquarters was trying to put everything into order before the Chrysler takeover was finalized. AMC executives seemed to be trying to make everything look good, to save their own individual jobs.

The Chrysler deal forced some of the Americans in China to worry about their own job plans. In the late spring of 1987 Ed Schulze had already lived in Beijing for nearly two years, and he was ready to go home. He had reached the point where the daily frustrations of trying to run the Cherokee assembly line outweighed the extra money he was getting paid to live in China. But after the takeover was announced, Schulze decided to stay in Beijing at least until the end of the year. There was so much confusion surrounding the takeover that it wouldn't be a good idea for an AMC employee to go back home right away.

St. Pierre seemed confident. He was firmly in charge at Beijing Jeep, and he had made some good friends in the Chinese government who might prove valuable to Chrysler. He figured that after the deal was completed, Iacocca would probably come to China to see Deng Xiaoping. St. Pierre hoped to be in the room for that meeting.

In late June St. Pierre ran into Zhu Rongji, the State Economic Commission official who by that time was virtually running the Chinese automobile industry. Wasting no time, St. Pierre asked Zhu what he would think of a major new Chrysler venture in China. Zhu said he was interested.

Recounting the conversation a few days later, St. Pierre grew excited. Zhu seemed to understand what St. Pierre was talking about: an automobile factory that would be up to international standards, with the sort of efficiency and high volumes found elsewhere. Maybe Chrysler and China could put an end to this special, only-in-China approach, St. Pierre thought, where 6,000 people did the work of 1,500 and the production level was ridiculously low.

As the hassles with AMC headquarters intensified, some of the Americans in China began saying, "Come on, Chrysler." AMC had only been a little car company trying to do the job of a big

company. For years, whenever there had been a fight with headquarters, the Americans working at Beijing Jeep had joked privately
that the real hardship was working for AMC, not the Chinese.

Oddly enough, amid the distractions and turmoil of the takeover,
the situation was steadily improving at Beijing Jeep. China was still
treating Beijing Jeep as a model joint venture. At a board meeting
in April 1987, the Chinese authorized a new dividend payment to
AMC of more than $600,000 from 1986 profits. The sum was pay-
able in dollars, and AMC was free to take the money out of China.
Combined with the $300,000 dividend the previous autumn, the
Chinese joint venture had paid back to AMC nearly $1 million of
its original $8 million cash investment.
  Cherokee sales were also picking up. Economic forces in China
—namely, a severe restriction on imported cars and, in the late
spring of 1987, a gradually increasing availability of foreign exchange—put the Chinese-made Cherokee in a favorable position.
Competitors like Toyota and Nissan weren't building cars in China
and found it increasingly hard to bring them in from Japan.
  At one conference in the spring of 1987, Zhu Rongji announced
that the Chinese government was prohibiting the importation of
all four-wheel-drive imported cars. Beijing Jeep, Zhu said, "now
supplies all our four-wheel-drive products in China."
  Beijing Jeep sold one block of 350 Cherokees to the Public
Security Bureau, the Chinese police agency. It sold another 150
Cherokees to the China Sports Federation. Other government units
began buying the Cherokees one at a time. By the summer of 1987
the Cherokees were becoming a status symbol. They were modern
and expensive—not quite a forbidden import, but not entirely
Chinese-made, either. Indeed, demand within China was so great
that those who wanted to order a Cherokee generally had to wait
one year for delivery. The Beijing Jeep factory increased Cherokee
production to 12 per day, or 3,600 per year.
  By international auto standards, the volumes remained low,
limited both by the restrictions imposed by the Chinese government and by the factory's inadequacies. Until Beijing Jeep installed
a new paint system, there would be no way to produce more than
20 or 22 cars a day, about 6,000 a year. St. Pierre thought that the
market in China for the Cherokees was probably 30,000 to 50,000

a year. Eventually Chinese cadres would no longer want the old-fashioned, uncomfortable BJ212's.

The Japanese cars bought in the binge of 1984–85 were already beginning to age under China's rough conditions. Either China would have to import more cars, or Chinese buyers would have to choose from among the modern cars being assembled in China: the Cherokees, the Volkswagens from Shanghai, the Peugeots being made in Canton. But these other joint ventures had faced at least as many frustrations as Beijing Jeep. They had no existing Chinese vehicle like the BJ212 to earn renminbi profits that could be converted into foreign exchange. In late 1986 Peugeot had to stop production on its assembly line in Canton because the rise in value of the French franc had made the importation of Peugeot parts kits into China much more expensive than the Chinese had expected.

None of this meant Beijing Jeep was in the clear. In the spring and summer of 1987 the Americans still had difficulty replacing American-made parts with ones made in China. That process, called localization, was going extremely slowly. In theory Beijing Jeep was supposed to produce a Cherokee whose content was 84 percent Chinese-made by the year 1990. St. Pierre estimated privately that Beijing Jeep would be lucky to reach a figure of 50 percent.

The Americans also had difficulty servicing and correcting a defect in the Cherokees. In April 1987 Chinese customers started complaining that the U.S.-made Cherokee engines rattled. Chinese mechanics at the plant noticed similar rattles in other Jeeps fresh off the assembly line. By June Beijing Jeep had 170 Cherokees at the factory with engine problems.

The result was a nasty dispute between the Chinese and Americans, which, although it was never publicized, nearly led to another shutdown of the Cherokee assembly line. The engines were fixable, but it was a time-consuming, costly process. Chinese officials understandably argued that the joint venture had paid for good engines and that American Motors should send experts over and pay all the costs of reworking the engines. AMC, then in its final months of existence, balked. At headquarters AMC experts couldn't understand what the problem was. The engines were the same ones used at home, and there had been no problems in the United States. Maybe the Chinese were imagining the rattle.

Finally Chen Xulin threatened to close the factory if AMC didn't fix the faulty engines. "I don't like to have this problem damage all the progress we have made," said Chen in late June. If the engine problem wasn't fixed, he said, it would "cause serious problems in the mind of the Chinese government" about the future of the joint venture. This time St. Pierre found himself siding with the Chinese, fighting with AMC headquarters to take the engine rattles seriously.

After a flurry of late-night phone calls, AMC relented. Over a period of more than six months, at a cost of roughly $100,000, American technicians, sometimes three at a time, worked at Beijing Jeep on the engine problem. It was slow, arduous work. At one point the technicians were fixing only four Jeeps per day, while at the same time three new Cherokees a day with engine problems were rolling off the assembly line. It was almost like running on a treadmill.

Much later St. Pierre acknowledged that the engines had probably been wrong for China: They had a structural weakness that was apparent only when the engines were run with the low-octane fuel commonly used in China.

Still, overall, as the time for the Chrysler takeover approached, both Chinese and American officials at Beijing Jeep seemed optimistic about the future of the joint venture.

By June Zhou Kaiying, one of the Chinese officials who had been in Detroit at the time the takeover had been announced, thought that Chrysler was probably good news for Beijing Jeep. After all, said Zhou, who was Beijing Jeep's sales and supply manager, Chrysler had more money and more advanced technology than American Motors. Maybe Chrysler could speed up the process of making parts in China.

Chen Xulin still wasn't too sure what Chrysler's arrival would mean. The Chrysler people talked only in very general terms, Chen told me in June, two months before the takeover. But Chen cautiously allowed that the takeover might provide Beijing Jeep with new opportunities.

That was exactly the message Chrysler—and AMC, in its final days—was trying to get across. From Detroit, Cappy, AMC's president, wrote to China, assuring Beijing Jeep's Chinese board members that the Chrysler takeover would not affect the joint venture;

in fact, Cappy said, Beijing Jeep might be able to get more help from Chrysler than it had from AMC. (After the takeover, Cappy went to work for Chrysler as group vice president in charge of the Jeep-Eagle division.)

In July 1987 Chrysler dispatched one of its star executives, Vice President Bob Lutz, to Beijing to ease lingering Chinese fears about the takeover. Lutz made the rounds of Beijing Jeep and Chinese automotive officials in Beijing. On behalf of Chrysler, he concluded a new deal to build an engine plant in the Manchurian city of Changchun, the site of one of China's biggest automotive factories. Throughout the trip Lutz provided reassurances that Chrysler was interested in China, that it would not abandon what American Motors had already created, that in fact big Chrysler had more to offer China than tiny, struggling American Motors could ever have given.

The Chinese finally went along. China never posed any legal challenge to the transfer of Beijing Jeep from American Motors to Chrysler. In August 1987 Chrysler swallowed up American Motors, including its Jeeps, its passenger cars, its employees, its factories, and its joint venture in the People's Republic of China.

23

Departures

In the early autumn of 1988, Tod Clare sat alone in the vacant nineteenth floor of the American Center, the silvery skyscraper on the outskirts of Detroit that had once served as the corporate headquarters for American Motors. Outside his office there was nothing but acres of worn carpet, empty desks, a single lonely secretary, a Xerox machine, bare wires, and a 360-degree expanse of glass windows. The Jeeps and other AMC products that had once proudly adorned the downstairs lobby were now gone. On the desk inside Clare's office, room 1960, lay a book on how to set up a business inside your home. His office walls still displayed large maps of Egypt and China, reminders of Clare's former career as AMC's vice president for international operations. He was a modern-day Ozymandias, a once mighty executive abandoned in the wreckage of a corporate takeover.

When the takeover had been completed the previous year, Clare had been one of the first AMC people to go. Chrysler had made it attractive for American Motors' top executives to leave the company: Those who were not offered a job with Chrysler with comparable responsibility and salary could resign with at least a full year's salary and two years of benefits, even if they subsequently landed another job. Even by the standards of the American auto industry, where benefits were good, this was a generous deal.

Clare quickly resigned. Others in the company felt he had been ousted. Chrysler had its own international division; it had been cut to the bone in the near bankruptcy of the late 1970s, but now, with AMC's Jeep to help out, the corporation had new global ambitions and certainly wasn't going to leave important decisions in the hands of outsiders from a stepchild company like AMC. Clare had been offered another management job with Chrysler, a job with somewhat vague responsibilities, but he decided he didn't want it. He felt a top-level Chrysler job wasn't worth fighting for. He had long dreamed of becoming an independent entrepreneur. It was time for him to do something else, he felt. For a while he avoided the office, where other AMC executives were spending their days trying to land other jobs. Friends saw him outside his home, cleaning his swimming pool and working on his Maserati.

Some of the lower-ranking people on AMC's China project were not treated as well as the six-figure executives. Those who happened to be working for AMC in Detroit at the time of the takeover, like Lauren Giglio, managed to move over to Chrysler. But several of the AMC people living in China found themselves out of work. While overseas they had lost both their positions and their contacts back home. From China, St. Pierre tried to help the Americans at Beijing Jeep to land good jobs with Chrysler, but with little success.

Bob Steinseifer returned from China to Detroit for eight months and then was told Chrysler had no jobs for him. He laughed. "You mean with twenty years' experience I can't even be a rookie industrial engineer?" he asked. No jobs at any level, Chrysler executives told him, and Steinseifer was forced to leave the company.

Ed Schulze came home to Kenosha, Wisconsin, just before Christmas in 1987, to find new Chrysler managers in charge of the old AMC factory there, managers who had never heard of him. They told him to wait for a new assignment at the plant. Schulze, by nature and profession a mechanic and tinkerer, found himself sitting at home with too much time to think. He read stories in the *Kenosha News* about Mikhail Gorbachev and wondered whether the resistance to change would be as great in the Soviet Union as he had found it to be in China. After a few months Chrysler found a new job for Schulze at the Kenosha plant, but it didn't last long. At the end of 1988 Chrysler closed the entire Kenosha factory, which had employed 5,500 people.

After a while Clare tried to put together some independent business deals. He was allowed to work out of his old office at AMC while Chrysler was in the process of moving out what was left of the AMC management team and absorbing it into Chrysler headquarters in Highland Park. Unrestricted by the old corporate dress codes, Clare dressed in an open-necked shirt, without a tie. He worked on one venture to modify American cars for sale to Europe. Clare didn't advertise it, but associates said he had also been quietly exploring some prospects for doing new business in China.

When Clare looked back on AMC's move into China, he had no big regrets. He continued to believe there were great future profits to be made by Western companies in China. He couldn't understand how anyone, at least any company of world stature, could afford not to have a China operation. For anyone who could keep his powder dry, the rewards would be there someday, perhaps twenty years from now. China would eventually become a huge market, he felt, and an automobile company would sell a hell of a lot of vehicles.

Clare's logic was simple. The volumes of cars sold in the United States were stable, about fifteen million or so a year. Western Europe was the same, a totally saturated market. In either place you could only sell more cars for your company by stealing someone else's share of the market. There wouldn't be any real growth. So where else would you go to sell cars? Latin America was dead broke, and Africa was worse. For Pakistan and India, the boat had sailed a long time ago, Clare felt. Very quickly, he said, you kept coming back to two huge countries, the only two markets in the world with real potential for huge growth in volume. One was the Soviet Union, and the other was China.

China just couldn't keep that domestic market for itself, Clare believed. No matter how much Chinese state enterprises wanted to protect their turf from the foreigners, they would be unable to do so. China would need new Western technology. In ten years the Cherokee would be outdated, and then China would have to build a replacement. There was just no way the Chinese could build a modern car by themselves, Clare thought. The day the Chinese built a jeep, or any other car, with 100 percent local (that is, Chinese) content was the day that vehicle became obsolete. They would continue to need smaller engines, better safety, other kinds of new technology, and they would have to get the know-how from foreigners.

China, and Beijing Jeep, remained an important part of Clare's life. Clare had directed the largest American manufacturing deal in China for nearly a decade, commuting from Detroit to Beijing regularly for negotiations, board meetings, crises, hand-holding, and hirings and firings.

Even after leaving AMC Clare kept in touch, particularly with his old friend Chairman Wu Zhongliang. It seemed to be a general principle of modern-day Sino-American relations that the pioneers, the first Americans in China, came to adopt attitudes of quasi-religious reverence toward the Chinese leaders and hosts with whom they had conducted their negotiations. Henry Kissinger—a man who often spoke with open contempt of American politicians and other world leaders—came to regard Chou En-lai with such awe that he depicted Chou in his memoirs as an almost supernatural being. So too Clare, who spoke bitterly of some of his former colleagues at American Motors, had nothing but warm feelings for his old friend Chairman Wu. He was a true gentleman, Clare felt, a man with a special demeanor, a particular dignity. Clare thought Chairman Wu always acted like an extremely wealthy man, the sort of person you would expect to be comfortable in the Louvre, to know good champagne from bad champagne. Chairman Wu was certainly not a farmboy, certainly not a peasant.

One night in the spring of 1988, Chairman Wu and some of the Chinese officials from Beijing Jeep, who had come to Detroit for a board meeting at Chrysler, took a night off to give a banquet for Clare and his wife. They went to the New Peking restaurant in Garden City.

Over dinner the Chinese brought Clare up to date on what had happened to the people he knew in China. Zhu Rongji, who had presided over Beijing Jeep's crisis negotiations in 1986, had just been named the mayor of Shanghai, one of the most powerful political positions in China. Other Chinese officials were also moving up the career ladder. Only Wu, who still retained the title of chairman at Beijing Jeep but had lost his more powerful job as head of the city's automotive industry, was being shunted aside.

"Everybody got promoted but me," said Chairman Wu.

"And me," replied Clare. Everyone laughed.

Don St. Pierre got one last lesson on where his own and other Western companies stood in China.

At the beginning of 1988 St. Pierre handed over the presidency of Beijing Jeep to Chen Xulin as part of the scheduled management rotation. It was an important victory for St. Pierre. Chen was the man he had groomed for the job, the man St. Pierre had schemed, lobbied, and maneuvered for Beijing officials to select. While re-

maining head of the American team at the joint venture, St. Pierre
assumed a new post of American vice chairman of the board.

A few weeks later, shortly after three o'clock on the afternoon
of February 8, 1988, a black limousine with the flag of the People's
Republic of China rolled to a stop in front of Beijing Jeep's body
shop. Out stepped Zhao Ziyang, Deng Xiaoping's protégé, formerly
China's premier and now general secretary of the Chinese Com-
munist Party. Zhao was making his first visit to Beijing Jeep. Chen
Xulin and Ji Chunhai, the Party secretary, headed the long line of
Chinese officials welcoming him.

Zhao had come to talk with the joint venture's Chinese officials. St. Pierre was in Hong Kong that day. No one told him before
he left that the highest-ranking official in China's ruling party was
coming to the factory. No other American was invited to sit in for
him; it was to be an all-Chinese affair.

The Chinese Communist Party was in the midst of one of its
recurring reappraisals of its policy toward foreign investment in
China. Although no Americans were present during Zhao's meeting, they were eventually able to find out what had transpired.
Chinese officials took written notes of the session, which was also
recorded on tape. Transcripts of the session found their way into
the hands of the Americans. A review of these internal records
indicated that Zhao went to extraordinary lengths to emphasize
the benefit to China of joint ventures like Beijing Jeep. More than
eight years after the regime had opened the way for foreign businesses to begin investing in China, it seemed, there were still many
cadres within the Communist Party who questioned whether foreign investment was of economic benefit to China.

Speaking at Beijing Jeep, Zhao explained that foreign investment was a cheap way of updating antiquated Chinese enterprises.
Generally, he said, the Chinese partner was investing only its existing plant and old equipment, while the Western company was
putting in new capital and modern technology. The result was to
increase the financial value of the Chinese shares in the enterprises. Through joint ventures China could modernize its industry
without having to spend too much money of its own.

Zhao acknowledged that people in China always said the for-
eigners were taking advantage of the Chinese. Relations between
Chinese and foreigners were an emotional issue, he said; some
Chinese people found it difficult to accept the way the Westerners

and their companies operated. If the foreigners sought something unreasonable, the Chinese should refuse to go along with it. But in general, Zhao went on, "if you want to learn, you have to put up with it."

The Communist Party secretary turned next to the problem of foreign exchange at the joint ventures and the difficulty of replacing imported components with those made in China. It wasn't necessary to produce a completely Chinese product and to replace every single foreign-made part, Zhao said. What counted was the economic principle of comparative advantage. Once a joint venture began producing or obtaining some low-cost Chinese parts, it could begin to trade these parts overseas for imported components. By exporting locally made parts, the joint venture would reduce the need for spending foreign exchange to obtain imported components, Zhao said. Achieving a balance in foreign exchange would be the key to success for the joint ventures.

Finally, Zhao had some words of praise for Beijing Jeep's Cherokees. The Cherokees were durable and spacious, certainly preferable to luxury imported vehicles. They would be good for use as taxis in small- and medium-size Chinese cities, he said. Needless to say, the cadres in Beijing Jeep were overjoyed to get such a glowing endorsement from the highest-ranking official in the Chinese Communist Party.

Zhao's visit to Beijing Jeep appeared to be aimed primarily at countering some new domestic criticism of the joint ventures. He seemed to be responding to people like Chen Zutao, the state official in charge of China's automotive industry, who had publicly criticized Beijing Jeep at a news conference three weeks earlier. Chen Zutao said China was considering changing to a new kind of automotive deal, which would start out by producing auto components such as axles and motors in China, rather than assembling finished vehicles from imported parts kits. China had been spending huge amounts of foreign exchange to keep projects like Beijing Jeep and the Volkswagen factory running, Chen said, yet the proportion of parts made in China remained very low.

"We will continue to support these projects, but the localization rate must be speeded up. I am not satisfied," Chen Zutao said. It was clear that Chen, who had helped negotiate the original contract with American Motors, had become increasingly disenchanted with the way things had worked out. A year earlier he had

lashed out at foreign carmakers who earned "double profits" by
first selling auto parts to China and then taking a share of the
earnings of the cars produced in China. Chen hadn't mentioned
American Motors or Volkswagen by name, but he left no doubt to
whom he was referring.[1]

Chen Zutao's attack on the joint ventures with foreign companies reflected more than his own personal views. He was said to
be aligned with the more conservative faction in the Communist
Party leadership, the faction aligned with Premier Li Peng. Indeed,
Americans like Tod Clare who knew Chen Zutao said that as a
youth in the 1940s, Chen's upbringing, education, and career were
personally guided by Chou En-lai and his wife, Deng Yingchao, just
as Li Peng's were. Like Li Peng, Chen was trained as an engineer in
the Soviet Union. Both men later ascended to power in the central
government bureaucracies in Beijing—unlike Zhao, who rose
through a series of posts in Chinese provinces. It is unclear whether
Chen Zutao and Premier Li Peng were personally close, but they
were certainly of the same generation and background.

Zhao's remarks at Beijing Jeep demonstrated that the Chinese
Communist Party, even in the late 1980s, remained preoccupied
with the question of whether or not foreigners were exploiting
China. Nearly a decade after the start of China's open-door policy,
the head of the Chinese Communist Party still felt obliged to defend some of the most basic elements and principles of that policy.
Moreover, Zhao's method of defending the policy against critics
was to couch it in terms of *reverse* exploitation: It wasn't the foreigners who were exploiting the Chinese, he said, but rather China
that was exploiting the foreigners.

It was an approach Zhao had learned from his crafty mentor,
Deng Xiaoping. When Deng greeted John J. Phelan, Jr., the chairman of the New York Stock Exchange, he asked if Phelan knew
why he and other Wall Street executives had been invited to China.
Phelan, looking baffled, groped for a reply. "The main purpose is to
exploit you," Deng said. "I think we have something to learn from
you." Phelan, suffering from the usual foreigners' disease of hopeless awe in the presence of Deng, found himself stammering,
"Well, it's a great honor to be exploited."

St. Pierre found Zhao's comments ironic. Either Zhao was deliberately overlooking the facts about Beijing Jeep, or he didn't realize what had been happening there. Zhao had talked about not

spending much Chinese money on joint ventures—and yet, under the secret deal that had been negotiated at Zhao's behest in May of 1986, China had guaranteed $120 million in foreign exchange to help keep Beijing Jeep alive. Also under the secret agreement of 1986, China was paying for new capital projects at Beijing Jeep. St. Pierre figured that the Chinese had contributed $70 million to modernize Beijing Jeep since the joint venture was formed. The American side had put in virtually no new capital at all since AMC's original $8 million investment.

The truth was that Beijing Jeep was not a particularly good example of the sort of deal Zhao envisioned. The joint venture couldn't have balanced its foreign exchange without help from the Chinese government. And it was the Chinese, not the Americans, who were putting up most of the money for modernizing the automotive factory.

Interviewed on Chinese radio programs shortly after Zhao's visit, St. Pierre quickly threw cold water on the Party secretary's idea of saving foreign exchange by trading Chinese-made components for foreign ones. We can't do that yet, St. Pierre told Chinese interviewers. The quality of Chinese parts isn't good enough yet, and the price isn't low enough.

For St. Pierre the end came quickly, more quickly than he had expected. When he became vice chairman of the board, he had intended to keep the job, while still living in China, for another nine to twelve months.

At the time, in early 1988, things were going well at Beijing Jeep. Sales of the Cherokee Jeeps were astonishing. The factory had produced 3,000 of the Cherokees in 1987, and they were all sold out. The 1988 production, set for 5,000, was also already sold out in advance at the beginning of the year. With imports of foreign cars still restricted, Chinese work units were lining up to buy vehicles produced by joint ventures inside the country. It was a seller's market.

Inside China there was a black market for the Cherokees: Dummy trading corporations would come up with the dollars to buy a Cherokee from Beijing Jeep and would then resell the vehicle for huge sums in renminbi to other Chinese customers. There were stories of Cherokees selling for 180,000 renminbi in south China— an amount that, even at the higher unofficial rates of exchange, was worth around $30,000. A Cherokee was a commodity: A Chinese municipality could buy it, then trade it for wheat or steel.

In Beijing St. Pierre did Chinese press interviews and served as the representative American businessman at Chinese meetings on foreign investment. Western visitors to Beijing came to see him at least two or three times a week, seeking advice on the prospects for doing business in China. He had become a regular participant at conferences on the future of China in places like Hong Kong and Hawaii.

Yet St. Pierre was working for a new management, Chrysler, and his position there was shaky. The Chrysler executives at headquarters had not lived either in China or through the crisis-filled early years of Beijing Jeep. St. Pierre was independent, outspoken, and nearing the end of his planned stay in China, but he was not yet an integral part of the Chrysler team.

In March 1988 St. Pierre accompanied a large delegation of Chinese officials from Beijing Jeep for meetings at Chrysler headquarters. One of the issues to be resolved was the price Beijing Jeep would pay Chrysler in 1989 for each kit of Cherokee parts: That was always one of the most important financial issues affecting the profitability of the joint venture to its U.S. shareholders. For nearly a year St. Pierre had been scheming in China to get a 6 percent increase, dropping hints to various Chinese officials to create a climate of acceptance for the raise.

St. Pierre believed he had been delegated by Chrysler to handle the negotiations over the price of the kits for the American company. He also thought he had the Chinese officials convinced they would have to pay the 6 percent increase. But one day in Detroit, Peter Badore, the executive in charge of the China project at Chrysler headquarters, had his own lunch with Chinese officials out of St. Pierre's presence. Following the lunch, the Chinese announced that Badore had accepted a Chinese offer of a smaller increase: a 2½ percent raise, with another 2½ percent in another six months.

St. Pierre was infuriated with Badore, the Chrysler official for whom he was supposed to be working. The two men didn't get along, and it rapidly became clear that there was no way St. Pierre would stay on in China, reporting to Badore, for the remainder of the year. St. Pierre would have liked to come back home to Chrysler in Badore's job, running the corporation's China operations, but he was never offered the post. Instead Chrysler offered St. Pierre a management job in business development, a position removed from any connection with China. Chrysler made plans to send an American expert in manfacturing to China to work under Chen Xulin as vice president of Beijing Jeep.

That spring St. Pierre began packing his bags in Beijing and, at the same time, exploring the prospects for new jobs. He soon found one he wanted as the Hong Kong–based director of China operations for FMC, the multinational corporation.

There was a long round of good-byes. St. Pierre had private lunches with vice mayors of the Beijing municipal government, a final banquet of the Chinese-oriented Joint Venture Club of Beijing, which St. Pierre headed; and a week-long series of dinners and farewell toasts with Beijing Jeep's management and trade union. There was even a sentimental farewell with Chairman Wu, with whom he had feuded on and off for nearly three years. Wu sent St. Pierre a framed picture, inscribed with a note saying that St. Pierre had contributed a lot to Beijing Jeep. Chairman Wu discovered—as he would later say with surprise—that St. Pierre was almost in tears before he left.

St. Pierre did a last round of Chinese press interviews, too. In one of the last ones, a reporter from the New China News Service, the official Chinese news agency, asked St. Pierre what he would most like to do in China that he hadn't already done. Never shy, St. Pierre said he would like to meet Deng Xiaoping. The reporter wrote down the request and said he'd pass it along. St. Pierre thought it might happen, but it never did.

On his last day, St. Pierre attended the annual Fourth of July party at the American embassy in Beijing, where U.S. Ambassador Winston Lord dressed up as a cowboy, and his wife, author Betty Bao Lord, appeared as an American Indian. It was a strange scene, utterly detached from the everyday realities of China, but perhaps a fitting one from which to head for the airport.

When St. Pierre made his first trip back to Beijing for his new company in the autumn of 1988, he went out to dinner with Chen Xulin.

They talked shop and old times. Chen complained that he was besieged with new duties. On the one hand, as Beijing Jeep's president, Chen discovered he had to perform many of the business tasks outside the walls of the factory that St. Pierre had once carried out. On the other hand, Chen said, he had been given new responsibilities within the factory by the Communist Party. Chen said he had recently been put in charge of guiding the thoughts (that is, the political indoctrination) of Beijing Jeep's work force.

There had been another new development, Chen told St. Pierre. Soviet officials had recently been visiting Beijing Jeep. The Soviets had been proposing a new idea—a joint venture between Beijing Jeep (of which China still controlled 69 percent of the shares) and the Soviet Union. The goal would be to transfer the new American Jeep technology from China to the Soviet Union. The proposal amounted to history coming full circle: Three decades earlier, China had obtained the design for its first jeeps from the Soviets.

Chen and St. Pierre had worked alongside one another for most of the previous three years. St. Pierre had come to know Chen, his protégé, better than any other Chinese official at Beijing Jeep. Chen had visited St. Pierre's luxurious apartment at the Lido-Holiday Inn Hotel. They had talked a lot, confided in one another, prided themselves on their close relationship. St. Pierre taught Chen about American business, and Chen taught St. Pierre about China.

Yet throughout his entire three years in China, St. Pierre never once saw the inside of Chen Xulin's home. Chen never invited him, and St. Pierre never pushed it.

24

A Very Long Haul

Once Chrysler had acquired Beijing Jeep, it seemed inevitable that Lee Iacocca, the Chrysler chairman and American legend, would make a trip to China, which he had never seen. Within a half year after the takeover, Chrysler officials began preparing for the Visit. Chrysler's advance and public relations men began arriving in China to lay the groundwork. Special consultants were paid for their expertise and contacts. Michel Oksenberg—the insightful University of Michigan sinologist who, while serving on President Carter's National Security Council, had helped work out the establishment of diplomatic relations with Beijing—was brought in for advice. Hill & Knowlton, the multinational public relations firm, was employed to make arrangements for an Iacocca banquet. The trip was scheduled, postponed, and finally rescheduled for October 1988. Iacocca was to spend his sixty-fourth birthday in China.

The Chrysler chairman was already a reasonably well-known figure in China. Iacocca's autobiography had attracted the attention of some Chinese economists and intellectuals interested in American business practices. The Chinese had their own unique perspectives on the book. On December 10, 1986, for example, the *Economic Daily*, China's rough socialist equivalent of *The Wall Street Journal*, had published a front-page commentary marveling at Iacocca's firing by Henry Ford and his subsequent ascension to power at Chrysler.

"What would have happened if Iacocca were in China?" the newspaper asked. It offered its own answer: Iacocca would have had to accept his "unlucky fate" in being disliked and eventually ousted by his boss at Ford. In China individual workers were at the mercy of their leaders, the commentary noted; there was no job mobility, no opportunity for talented people to choose their own jobs, to switch jobs, to quit and start anew. There was little room in China for a personality conflict, even with a quirky boss: You had to learn to coexist with him for years, perhaps forever. "Iacocca's biography tells us that it is important to create the social conditions under which strong people can exist and develop," the Chinese newspaper said.

In the year between the takeover of American Motors and Iacocca's visit, Chrysler had held out the prospect of big new plans for China. In the summer of 1987 Chrysler's vice president Bob Lutz had signed the deal with the First Automotive Works in Changchun under which Chrysler sold new engine technology to China. Chinese officials were also talking to foreign auto companies about the possibility of manufacturing passenger cars in Changchun, and Chrysler also hoped to land that contract. Top Chrysler executives, such as Gerald Greenwald, head of the Chrysler Motor division, traveled to China in pursuit of the passenger car deal.

At the same time, Chrysler officials began talking with authorities in Beijing about the possibility of a major expansion of Beijing Jeep. There was talk of having the Beijing joint venture start manufacturing trucks, a project of which American Motors had once dreamed. Some Chinese officials also suggested Beijing Jeep might move from Cherokees into passenger cars, although the factory didn't even have the front-wheel-drive technology necessary for a modern car. At one point the Chinese suggested that Chrysler should invest as much as $80 million to $100 million in new capital for the expansion of Beijing Jeep. For their part, Chrysler executives let it be known that some new money for China might be in the offing; American Motors was a small company, and Chrysler had more financial resources, more people at its disposal.

But nothing worked out. Despite Chrysler's efforts, the First Automotive Works of Changchun gave the contract for passenger cars to Audi, a subsidiary of Volkswagen. Meanwhile, in the first year after the takeover, Chrysler officials moved cautiously on the idea of expanding Beijing Jeep, avoiding any commitment to invest new money in the joint venture.

During the period before Iacocca's visit, the tide seemed to be running against the Americans in China. There had been a prolonged, nasty foreign policy dispute over China's arms sales in the Middle

East: in 1987 President Reagan's national security advisor, Frank Carlucci, had publicly lambasted China for selling Silkworm anti-ship missiles to Iran, and in 1988 U.S. officials subsequently discovered to their surprise that China had also sold intermediate-range missiles to Saudi Arabia. The Chinese regime was irked when the U.S. Congress passed a resolution denouncing China's human rights policies and was infuriated when members of Congress expressed sympathy for the cause of independence for Tibet.

China's foreign policy and its foreign trade were beginning to move in new directions. The fascination with the advanced world of Japan, the United States, and Western Europe of the early 1980s was now beginning to recede. Japan, of course, was in a class by itself: at the beginning of the decade a model for emulation, but by now often the object of Chinese hostility and fear. With the Americans and the West Europeans, the problem was one of incompatibility. The American, German, French, and British companies seeking to do business in China didn't come cheaply, and neither did their products. Doing business with them required huge amounts of foreign exchange. At the beginning of the decade, the inclination of Chinese officials had been to go out and buy the best technology in the world. Now, many of these officials were having second thoughts.

One place for China to look was the East bloc. Trade with the Soviet Union and Eastern Europe might not provide the most advanced technology, but it was conducted in barter and therefore required no spending of hard currency. Soviet and Chinese foreign policy were changing in ways so that the two countries could begin to accommodate one another. In his very first speech as Communist Party general secretary in 1985, Soviet leader Mikhail Gorbachev declared that improving relations with China would be one of his highest priorities. Under Gorbachev, the Soviet Union had offered territorial concessions to China in their long-running border dispute and began to withdraw some Soviet troops from Mongolia near the Chinese border. The Soviet Union's trade with China increased dramatically, and the Soviet Union quickly became China's fifth-largest trading partner, well ahead of such major Western nations as Britain, France, or Italy.

In Shanghai, the birthplace of the Chinese Communist Party, newly arrived Soviet diplomats restored and reopened one of the choicest pieces of real estate in the city—the old Soviet consulate along the Bund, the waterfront area by the Huangpu River. The building, constructed under Czar Nicholas II in 1914, had been closed during the Sino-Soviet split a quarter century earlier, and since then the Chinese had been using it as a seamen's club. By the end of 1987 articulate Soviet diplomats like Valery I. Biryukov were moving back into the consulate and preaching the virtues of a new Sino-Soviet friendship.

"I believe that China and the Soviet Union have passed that period of their childhood when there were arguments about who was the leader of the socialist movement," said Biryukov. "We have grown up. Both of our countries can concentrate on economic development. We understand their problems."

Despite Biryukov's suggestion, China's opening to the Soviet Union was based on more than ideology. For China it was a matter of money, diversification, and foreign policy. China was seeking to save foreign exchange, to prevent relying too much on the advanced nations of the West, and to increase its own political influence in the world.

At the same time that China was upgrading ties with the Soviet Union and Eastern Europe, it was also moving in an entirely different direction—toward the newest economic stars in the capitalist firmament, South Korea and Taiwan. From the founding of the People's Republic in 1949 through the first half of the 1980s, political obstacles had prevented China from doing business with either of these countries. Taiwan's Nationalist Party had prohibited any trade or, indeed, contacts, with the mainland; and China's ties with its Communist neighbor in North Korea had prevented it from doing business with Seoul.

In the last years of the 1980s economic factors managed to overcome these political barriers. In both South Korea and Taiwan businessmen were pressuring their governments to help them win access to the China market. China was even more alluring to the businessmen of Seoul and Tapei than it was to their counterparts in Western Europe or the United States, because it was so close by. From China's perspective, Taiwan and South Korea offered new sources of investment, technology, and management expertise. The businessmen from Taiwan and South Korea were fellow Asians, yet not the feared Japanese; furthermore, their products weren't as expensive and the businessmen themselves weren't as wasteful as their counterparts from the United States and Western Europe.

. . .

In the fall of 1988, on the eve of Iacocca's trip, the political climate in China turned against Zhao and his policies of market-oriented reforms.

Early that year Zhao urged the Chinese leadership to pursue an economic strategy of developing the regions along China's eastern coastline as export centers in hopes that they would follow along the lines of Pacific Rim economies like South Korea and Taiwan. But Zhao's proposal produced a backlash among Party leaders in China's huge inland provinces, who feared that their areas would receive less money and fewer resources from the central government.

Meanwhile Zhao pressed ahead with the centerpiece of his entire economic reform program, the effort to free up state-controlled prices. For years Zhao and his economic advisers had argued that unless China moved to a system where prices were determined by market forces rather than set by the state, its economy would remain fettered.

In making changes in the pricing system the focus of their entire economic policy, Zhao and those Chinese reformers supporting him echoed the views of Western economists and, indeed, Western governments. The CIA, in its official public report to Congress on the Chinese economy in April 1988, concluded: "Without price reform, China's attempts to make enterprises more responsive to market signals—and to hold them accountable for poor investment, production, and personnel decisions via the initiation of bankruptcy proceedings—will fall short."

On several prior occasions, the regime had begun to lift the lid on state-controlled prices, but then pulled back in the face of inflation. In the spring of 1988, at a time when inflation was already running at levels of around 10 percent, Zhao pressed the cause of price reform once again, harder than ever before, arguing that China couldn't stop halfway, that it had to keep moving on price reform. The result was a level of inflation unprecedented since the final years of the Nationalist regime of Chiang Kai-shek four decades earlier. Demand was too high, bank credit too easy, government spending out of control, and wasteful state-owned enterprises still secure from the ultimate sanction of bankruptcy.

By autumn the overall cost of living in Chinese cities had jumped by 31 percent from the previous year, by China's own official statistics, and some economists estimated that the actual rate was 40 percent or higher. Once again the Chinese engaged in hoarding and panic buying. There were runs on banks in several cities, and the regime began to impose limits on the amount of savings that could be withdrawn from bank accounts.

The results were damaging to Zhao's own political future. After the annual summer meetings of China's top leaders in the seaside retreat of Beidaihe, Zhao was forced to hand over authority for economic policy to Premier Li Peng, the cautious, Soviet-trained leader who had spent virtually his entire career in China's government bureaucracy and central-planning apparatus and had sought repeatedly to restrict the extent of change in China's existing economic system. China announced it would start a two-year period of "readjustment," in which the price reforms would be either slowed down or brought to a halt.

And what would this new "readjustment" mean for foreign companies in China? At first the Chinese leadership maintained that there would be no changes at all. At one point Li promised visiting business delegations from the United States and Japan that China would carry out all the contracts that had been signed with foreign companies. Within less than two months, however, that pledge was being qualified. "Some joint ventures with heavy Chinese investment will be postponed," a senior Chinese official told *The Wall Street Journal*.[1] Once again, it seemed, foreign companies were about to be caught in the spend-and-freeze cycles of China's domestic economy. In periods of retrenchment, China always seemed to reevaluate the commitments previously made to foreign companies.

When Iacocca landed in China in October 1988, his reception was astonishingly cool. He and his aides had expected to be received by China's top leaders, including Deng, Zhao, Li, and Chinese President Yang Shangkun. Yet despite all the months of preparations and the fact that he remained in China for nearly eight days, Iacocca was able to land only a single dinner session with one of these top four leaders, Li Peng. The other three Chinese leaders were said to be too busy; the heads of state of Finland and Rumania were in town. (In the mid-1980s, by contrast, Deng and Zhao had regularly found time to meet with visiting American board chairmen or chief executive officers from Fortune 500 companies.)

During his session with the Chinese premier, Iacocca said he felt China had made a mistake in choosing to link up with the German Audi, rather than Chrysler, for production of the passenger cars. The premier did not press Iacocca for additional investment by Chrysler in China.

When Iacocca hosted a banquet in Beijing, not a single high-ranking Chinese leader or minister came. The only Chinese figure of prominence was Deng's son, Deng Pufang, the head of the Chinese Welfare Fund for the Handicapped. Although Chrysler officials didn't seem to realize it, Deng Pufang's appearance was hardly an unmixed blessing; Deng Pufang was, at the time, under a political cloud. His own welfare organization was fighting off accusations of improper business dealings, and in general the power and wealth enjoyed by the children of high-level officials was becoming an increasingly sensitive issue in China.

Iacocca had flown to China on his own corporate jet, a Gulfstream 4. The plan was for him to fly from Beijing to Xian for a bit of tourism and up to Changchun for a visit to Chrysler's engine project at the First Automotive Works there. But despite what Chrysler officials believed they had been told during the advance preparations, after Iacocca arrived in China Chinese officials announced that he would not be permitted to fly to these two cities in his personal jet.

The Xian leg of the trip had to be scrubbed. Chrysler officials chartered a Chinese jet to transport Iacocca to Changchun, but that trip was postponed at the last minute when Chinese officials in Beijing said that there was bad weather in Changchun. (When Chrysler officials called up Changchun to give word of the delay, they were told the weather there seemed fine.) Eventually Iacocca succeeded in getting out of Beijing for a quick one-day visit to Changchun.

Meanwhile Chinese officials took Iacocca's personal jet out for a spin over Beijing. They asked for permission first, and Chrysler officials gave their assent, making sure that Chrysler's own pilots were aboard for the ride.

With so much unexpected time on his hands in Beijing, Iacocca played tourist, seeing all the sites. He also visited Beijing Jeep, which had been carefully scrubbed and cleaned before his arrival.

Iacocca is not one to hold back from voicing his own blunt opinions, and in China he lived up to his reputation for plain speaking. During his visit to Beijing Jeep, in his meetings with Chinese officials, and in interviews and at a press conference, he pressed two themes: first, that China should increase the volume of Cherokees produced at Beijing Jeep; and second, that Chinese enterprises would have to improve the quality of their products before they could begin to export.

These views, of course, furthered Chrysler's own interests. Higher production volumes at Beijing Jeep meant more profits for Chrysler on the sale of Cherokee parts kits to China. Complaints about the low quality of Chinese products would help to reduce pressures on Chrysler to arrange for the export of Chinese-made Cherokees—which Chrysler preferred to sell, for greater profit, inside China's domestic market. Iacocca also volunteered the opinion that China's auto factories had too many people working in them.

Although he was unable to see Deng Xiaoping or Communist Party Secretary Zhao Ziyang, Iacocca did meet with leaders from the Beijing city government. After his return to the United States, the Chrysler chairman turned down my request for an interview about his impressions of China. A spokesman, John Guiniven, said Iacocca's inability to see Deng had not been a big disappointment to Iacocca himself, although, Guiniven conceded, it was a disappointment "at the staff level."

The spokesman said Iacocca had been impressed by the increasing openness and progress in China. However, he said, the Chrysler chairman also believed that modernizing China's auto industry would take time. Iacocca's verdict on China, he said, was this: "It's a long haul, a very long haul."

25

Exodus

For the Americans at Beijing Jeep, 1989 began like any other year. Progress was slow, and there were the usual headaches of doing business in China.

In March Beijing Jeep almost shut down its Cherokee production line again because of a nasty customs dispute. Officials at the customs bureau in Tianjin suddenly announced a hefty increase in the duties on the parts kits Chrysler was shipping to China, a rate so high that Chrysler calculated it would lose money on every Cherokee it built in China. The American company enlisted the help of Beijing city officials and even suggested it might close the factory and air its complaints publicly, much as St. Pierre and American Motors had done three years earlier. Finally, after a series of negotiations, the customs officials backed down.

Chrysler also discovered a growing backlog of money Beijing Jeep was owed for the sales of the BJ212's. Chrysler's Chinese partner, Beijing Auto Works, collected the money and was supposed to turn it over to the joint venture. But by March 1989, BAW owed Beijing Jeep 33 million renminbi (at official rates, more than $8 million). Privately Chrysler officials grumbled that BAW was using Beijing Jeep as its private banker. With interest rates in China running at about 15 percent for short-term loans, BAW was in effect borrowing free money by delaying its payments.

The political demonstrations for democracy started in mid-April, following the death of former Communist Party General Secretary Hu Yaobang. Students, coming mostly from the universities in the northwest part of Beijing, streamed into Tiananmen Square to protest the Party leadership's failure to honor Hu and his efforts to reform China's political system. At first these events had little impact on Beijing Jeep, which lies to the southeast, far away from the main thoroughfares of political action.

But by the week of May 15, when Soviet President Mikhail Gorbachev visited China, the demonstrations in Beijing swelled to nearly a million people, and the crowds started to affect Beijing Jeep's production. The streets were so jammed that workers had difficulty getting to and from the factory. To bicycle the distance of three-quarters of a mile from the Beijing Auto Works apartment complex to the Beijing Jeep factory sometimes took two hours.

By this time some of Beijing Jeep's younger Chinese workers began to take part in the demonstrations. They would leave at the 5:30 P.M. closing hour and head for Tiananmen Square. A group was observed in the demonstrations carrying a "Beijing Jeep" banner. One worker from the joint venture, who was eventually arrested, joined a revolutionary motorcycle group called the "Flying Tigers," which served as the student demonstrators' messenger service and their modern-day Paul Reveres. Some Chinese cadres at the factory responded by issuing strict warnings: No workers were supposed to leave the factory grounds before the end of their shifts, and no one was to bring Beijing Jeep property to the demonstrations.

In the days after Chinese Premier Li Peng and President Yang Shangkun declared martial law on the morning of May 20, getting work done at the factory became even more difficult. Residents of Beijing began barricading the streets in hopes of protecting themselves from the army, which was poised on the outskirts of the city. Beijing Jeep, which only keeps small stockpiles of materials on the premises, was on the verge of shutting down until the Chinese troops temporarily pulled back and the barricades were removed. Still, Beijing Jeep officials, both Chinese and American, were proud of their achievement: During the month of May, despite the massive political demonstrations, production at the factory ran at close to 90 percent of the planned levels.

As soon as martial law was declared, Chrysler sent its dependents to Hong Kong. However, within ten days the Chrysler executives brought their families back to Beijing. The traffic was moving, the food stalls were reopening, and the protesters at Tiananmen Square had dwindled to a few thousand. At the end of May the situation seemed to be returning to normal.

Several families of Chrysler executives flew back from Hong Kong to Beijing on May 30. That same day, however, the students in Tiananmen Square put up their famed statue, the Goddess of Democracy, an imitation of the Statue of Liberty. Four nights later Chinese troops, tanks, and armored personnel carriers launched an assault on downtown Beijing.

On the evening the troops launched their offensive, Kerry Ivins and his wife and two children were watching a videotape in their apartment in the Lido-Holiday Inn. Ivins, an Australian, was the deputy finance director for Beijing Jeep. He had worked in China for twenty months; next to St. Pierre, who stayed three years, Ivins held the record for longevity among all the Chrysler employees at Beijing Jeep.

Ivins heard the news when a fellow businessman called him Sunday morning. Chinese troops had opened fire on civilians, killing hundreds, perhaps thousands. Ivins was stunned. The top Chrysler official in China, Beijing Jeep Vice President Richard Ott, had been in the United States throughout most of the month, and during his absence Ivins had been responsible for reporting to Chrysler on the political situation. Ivins believed the Chinese government had too much at stake to kill large numbers of people. On that Saturday night, like countless others in Beijing, he was proven wrong.

Early Sunday morning Ivins joined a small group of Western businessmen who were discussing what they and their companies should do. The sessions started in the office of the Bechtel Corporation, the American engineering and consulting firm, and then moved to an IBM conference room at the Lido-Holiday Inn. When the talks started, there were eight participants. By late afternoon there were thirty.

On the streets downtown, Chinese troops were patrolling and firing, and some angry resisters were trying to set fire to abandoned armored personnel carriers. The businessmen were trying to decide whether it was safe to travel around the city or whether they should stay inside the hotel. What should they tell their home offices, their Chinese partners, their embassies? How was the food supply in Beijing? There was talk in Beijing of a general strike.[1] They calculated that if a strike shut off the electricity to the Lido-

Holiday Inn, the hotel's backup generator could supply forty-eight hours of full power. After that the electricity and the water supply would be at risk.

Ivins believed that at the back of all their minds was the thought of clearing out, although for the moment the businessmen seemed eager to convince one another that they were still safe.

Later that morning the six foreign executives of Chrysler in Beijing met. Ott, who had returned to China the previous week, was in charge. Ivins thought the tone was different in these sessions. The issue was how many should leave, and how soon. Each Chrysler person was given his own task: Some tried to gather information about the situation around Beijing, while others worked on getting plane tickets.

At first Ivins wanted to remain in Beijing for a few more days at least. He thought that Chrysler should fly out the families and some of the foreign executives, but that he and perhaps Ott should stay behind to demonstrate that Chrysler was not abandoning Beijing Jeep.

Ott and Chrysler officials in Detroit disagreed. They wanted everyone from Chrysler, including Ivins, to get out of China. It was a question of safety. On Sunday afternoon, as Ivins stood by, Ott talked with Peter Badore, the head of Chrysler's China operations in Detroit. I'm not ordering you all to get out of China, Badore had said, but I'd certainly like you out of there.

Ivins looked at Ott. "Are you sure Chrysler wants us to just walk out of this place?" he asked. "To leave, to risk wiping out our whole investment?"

"Yep. We're out," Ott replied.

Ott and Ivins wandered down to a small office of the Civil Aviation Administration of China (CAAC), the Chinese government airlines, inside the Lido-Holiday Inn. To their amazement, they found people working at the ticket counter—even though it was a Sunday afternoon and the city was in turmoil. No one else seemed to have noticed the airline office open its doors, and as the Chrysler executives purchased plane tickets to leave Beijing on the next day's flights, a long queue formed behind them.

The Chrysler executives and their families, after packing what they could, headed for the airport before dawn Monday. The straight, tree-lined road from the Lido-Holiday Inn to the Beijing airport, usually peaceful and boring, was dotted with armored personnel carriers. China seemed on the verge of civil war.

The airport was surprisingly empty. Chrysler was among the first Western companies to pull its employees out of Beijing. With relief, Ivins watched his wife and two children leave on a flight to Hong Kong, from which they would return home to Australia. Along with the rest of the Chrysler team—five executives, four wives, six children—he boarded the flight to Tokyo. Ivins didn't have a first-class ticket, but he sat in the mostly empty first-class compartment anyway, guessing that the Chinese crew would never check on him. During the flight, he wondered whether he and Chrysler had made the right decision to pull out so quickly.

A few weeks later Ivins admitted Chrysler had been right. Almost as soon as they left, Chinese troops had begun firing into foreigners' homes and offices. By evacuating relatively early, the Chrysler team had saved itself the trouble of dealing with a rush for plane tickets and a jammed airport as virtually every other Western businessman in Beijing deserted the city.

On Monday morning, June 7, 1989, Beijing Jeep was in the hands of its Chinese staff. For the first time in more than five years, there wasn't a single American Motors or Chrysler executive in Beijing.

Some Chrysler executives stayed in Tokyo. There they checked in with Chrysler's Japan office, spoke to Detroit, and spent hours reading newspapers and watching television scenes of the chaos in Beijing. Phoning Beijing Jeep, they discovered that production at the factory had virtually stopped during the week after the massacre. The factory was all but empty. One Chinese employee said he had had to duck bullets during his bicycle ride to work.

Seeing the reports that thousands had died in Beijing, Don St. Pierre immediately sent out urgent inquiries to his old friend Chen Xulin, wanting to know whether Chen and his family were safe. A faxed response arrived a few days later at the Hong Kong office of St. Pierre's company. Chen and his family were in good shape, and it appeared that others at Beijing Jeep were safe, too.

But at that time not everyone had been counted. Within two weeks some Chinese officials quietly passed the word that a low-level Communist Party cadre in the factory's chassis shop had been killed during the massacre. There may have been one or two other deaths as well among Beijing Jeep's four thousand Chinese employees, they suggested. The reports remained unconfirmed. A month later a Chrysler spokesman in Detroit insisted that none of the Chinese workers had died.

In the weeks after the army assault, as Chinese security forces arrested several thousand people on charges related to the political demonstrations, armed soldiers raided the Beijing Auto Works (BAW) factory and led off from ten to fifteen workers.[2] There were no reports of arrests at Beijing Jeep itself.

Once Beijing Jeep resumed operations in mid-June, the Chinese team was able to run the Cherokee assembly line on its own. But the absence of the Chrysler team inevitably slowed down the introduction of new automobile technology, such as programs to manufacture axles and engines in China instead of importing them from the United States.

Thus, within weeks after the massacre Chrysler, like hundreds of other companies, was deluged with phone calls, fax messages, and telexes urging the company to send its employees back to China. The political situation had stabilized, said Chinese officials. Everything was safe. One telex to Chrysler from Beijing Jeep Board Chairman Wu Zhongliang repeated the phraseology used by Chinese leader Deng Xiaoping: the "counterrevolutionary rebellion" had ended.

In Detroit Chrysler officials found themselves in the midst of political controversy. One day in late June Chinese students from the University of Michigan and other schools in the Detroit area demonstrated outside Chrysler's main gate to urge the company to close down its China operations. A couple of Chrysler's American vendors—small companies supplying parts to Beijing Jeep—called the company to say they had no desire to do business in China anymore. Chrysler officials also discovered in the weeks after the massacre that some shipping companies were unwilling to carry cargoes to China.

Chrysler refused to go along with the protesters' requests. Setting up the China operation had taken years of effort and millions of dollars. The company might slow down or stop any new investment in China, one executive said, but it was not going to stop what was already in the works. Things were too far down the road.

Just as Chrysler had been one of the first Western companies to flee from China, it also became one of the first firms to announce its intention to return.

Within a month after the massacre, Ott returned to China, and Ann Lalas, a company spokesman, said other Chrysler executives would soon be sent back to the factory. "We feel what we're doing is consistent with the policies of the United States," Lalas said.

After waiting in Tokyo for nearly two weeks, Kerry Ivins went home to Australia. Chrysler officials had talked with him about the possibility of resuming work at Beijing Jeep. Ivins's tour of duty in China was scheduled to last until the end of 1989.

Ivins wasn't sure he wanted to go back. His wife had no desire to return to China. Moreover, as a matter of principle, Ivins wasn't sure Chrysler should rush back into China. The Australian government, he pointed out, was urging businesses not to return.

American Motors and Chrysler had put a lot of work into getting a business established in China, Ivins acknowledged. And at Beijing Jeep itself, the Chinese he worked alongside seemed to be decent people. On the other hand, Ivins didn't understand how his company could just head back into China after the massacre and say that everything was normal again.

"Who wants to do anything? Who wants to do business with them?" Ivins asked. "We know now that we're working under such a murderous regime, under people that we feel are corrupt, people we know so clearly now are against our principles and values and how we feel about human life. None of us will ever be the same."

Conclusion

By mid-June 1989 the Western enclaves of Beijing, Shanghai, and Canton were virtually empty. Hotels for foreigners—such as C. B. Sung's Great Wall Hotel in Beijing—seemed like ghost towns, occupied primarily by visiting journalists assigned to cover China's political upheavals. Newly built office buildings for Western businesses were similarly deserted. Air travel to China was so light that United Airlines reduced the number of weekly flights into and out of Beijing from three to one, and Northwest Airlines halved its weekly flights to Shanghai.[1]

In the wake of the June 4 massacre, Zhao Ziyang was dismissed from his job as general secretary of the Chinese Communist Party. He was accused of encouraging the student demonstrations and of fostering divisions within the Party. Throughout the 1980s, first as China's premier and then as leader of the Communist Party, Zhao had served as the nation's leading champion of the importance of attracting foreign investment and of gradually integrating China into the world economy. He had proven no more acceptable to the Party elders than his predecessor Hu Yaobang; for the second time in little more than two years, the octogenarians of the Long March generation intervened to force out the Party's general secretary, its titular leader. In both instances, the Party leaders were said to have gone astray by encouraging Westernization too rapidly; by identifying themselves with advocates of political change in China; and by challenging too forcefully the authority and privileges of the established order.

China's assault on Tiananmen Square and its use of lethal force against the protesters brought about a marked change of attitudes in the West concerning the prospects for foreign businesses in China. Former U.S. Ambassador to China Winston Lord, for example, who two years earlier had told visitors about China's improving investment climate, now advised American companies to hold off on putting any new money into China. "People are going to be worried about the long-term security of their investment. . . . [The June massacre] has dealt a body blow in the near term" to China's efforts to transform its economy, he said.[2]

Many Western companies would eventually return to China. The massacre of 1989 did not mean the end of all business activity between China and the outside world. Beijing Jeep would keep operating, and Chrysler would send executives back to the auto factory.

But the political turmoil did mark an end to the Western illusions about the chances for doing business in China. The popular image of a China that was steadily modernizing and of a sagacious leadership dedicated to economic advancement was shattered. In 1984 China was portrayed in magazine articles and newspaper columns as a nation abandoning Marxism.[3] After the 1989 assault on Tiananmen Square, the Chinese leadership was commonly perceived as more Stalinist than that of the Soviet Union.[4]

Throughout the second half of the 1980s, Western companies had become more dubious about their original expectations for China. The American Motors dispute of 1986 had prompted Western companies to begin to air publicly their grievances, although their complaints had little effect. The ouster of Party Secretary Hu Yaobang and the brief campaign against "bourgeois liberalization" the following year had produced a new wave of skepticism about China's commitment to modernization.

The optimistic Western assumptions that had held sway throughout the 1980s—that China had put political chaos behind it and had set out on a course of steady progress—gave way in 1989 to new pessimism. As China faced the certainty of disorder, it was thought that perhaps the country would never change in the ways Western companies had hoped.

China should not be judged by images alone. Optimism and pessimism, dreams and disillusionment, are by themselves subjective terms. It might be unfair to draw conclusions about Western companies in China based solely on the increasingly negative attitudes of the executives who did business there.

Yet there are objective standards as well. When Western companies and governments came to China in the early 1980s, they made specific forecasts about their prospects in China. These predictions turned out to be wrong.

When American Motors signed the contract for its joint venture in China in May 1983, W. Paul Tippett, the company's board chairman and chief executive officer, asserted that the China deal gave the company "a low-cost manufacturing base from which to compete with the Japanese in Southeast Asia."[5] He said Beijing Jeep would phase out the old Chinese jeeps and replace them with new American-style Jeeps, at least a quarter of which would be exported to other Asian countries. Other company executives and AMC press releases made similar predictions. Those claims—which helped produce a dramatic rise in the value of the company's stock—remain unrealized.

When President Reagan visited China in April 1984, an administration spokesman told the White House press corps that Western businesses would earn "megabucks" in China. Within five to seven years, the spokesman said, U.S. investment in China's oil industry would be between $10 billion and $15 billion. He was wrong by a factor of ten: By 1989 U.S. investment in China's oil industry was approximately $1.02 billion. So, too, the Reagan administration in 1984 held out the prospect that China would purchase twelve nuclear power plants within the next few years; by 1989 it appeared that China would build only two or at most three nuclear plants. During Reagan's trip to Beijing, on nationwide television, National Security Advisor Robert McFarlane told the American public that "perhaps hundreds of thousands of Americans and other Westerners" would be going to work in China. Five years later, before the mass exodus from China caused by the violence at Tiananmen Square, the total number of American business personnel in China —including their spouses, children, and other dependents—added up to 6,100.[6]

Such examples could be repeated for other companies and for other Western governments. Their forecasts for the commercial possibilities in China were often extraordinarily inaccurate. Their numbers and business projections were overly optimistic.

The question that remains is why. How did it come about that Western corporate executives, trained to be tough-minded and skeptical, misjudged their prospects in China?

· · ·

One reason was the unpredictability of working within a Communist system.

The Western companies in China represented the cutting edge of a new phenomenon: that of capitalist management operating extensively under the centralized state planning of a Communist economy. The foreign business executives were dealing with something they had never faced before, at least not on the same scale as in China. They were promised that China's economic system would change, but they had no way of knowing how far the changes would go.

As it turned out, the economic changes brought about under Deng Xiaoping, while startling when judged against the standards of Mao Tse-tung's China, also had their limits. They never went as far as Chinese reformers like Zhao Ziyang had hoped or as far as Western executives had been promised during the early 1980s. The reforms did not change the fundamental nature or structure of China's economic system. China did not succeed in transforming itself into a market economy, and the state planning apparatus remained firmly in place.

Many of the difficulties Western businesses faced in China could be found in other Communist countries. The businesses generally found themselves working with state-owned enterprises. The business plans for their China operations were subject to the central government's National Economic Plan. Joint ventures like Beijing Jeep had annual production quotas set by state planners, and they obtained many of their resources from and sold most of their output to the state. Any foreigner who started a business in China believing that the country had already "gone capitalist" was sooner or later stripped of his illusions.

The private Western businessmen and -women discovered that Chinese factory managers spent much of their time on welfare problems and had little independent decision-making authority. The real power, they learned, lay with cadres in the municipalities, in government ministries, or in the Party leadership. The Western executives placed the highest possible value on economic efficiency, even if it led to differentials in income or unemployment; by contrast, they found that Chinese state enterprises were more willing to tolerate inefficiency for the sake of equality of income, full employment, and social order. A similar conflict of values might well be found if Western companies start up joint ventures in Moscow or Leningrad. These problems are not necessarily unique to China. They are, rather, part of the political process of capitalism mixing with communism.

A second explanation is rooted in Chinese culture and history. The experiences of the private businesses inside the Middle Kingdom in the 1980s have amounted to a new chapter in the long-running saga of frustrated Westerners in China, a saga that began more than a century before the Chinese Communist Party came to power.

The Western business representatives who settled into Beijing, Shanghai, and Canton over the past decade have run up against many of the same cultural and bureaucratic obstacles that stymied Christian missionaries trying unsuccessfully to convert Chinese souls a century ago. They confronted the same proud Chinese nationalism as the agents of Josef Stalin, who failed to turn the Chinese Communist Party into a clone of the Soviet Communist Party.

From the outside China has always seemed malleable; from inside it seems intractable, endlessly capable of frustrating change. The Western businessmen arrived in China with their new management techniques and marketing skills, only to discover that China was not quite as receptive as they had expected.

The Western businessmen and -women who came to live in China found a country quite different from the one presented to illustrious short-term visitors such as their own board chairmen and chief executive officers. What transpired daily at their China operations did not often match the government pronouncements of change, the rosy descriptions in China's official press, or the bland assurances that had been given to their own bosses. Yet Chinese leaders were so remarkably skillful at entertaining visitors, promising improvements, and overlooking unpleasantness that Western business executives abroad often clung to the view that the prospects for their China operations were more hopeful and encouraging than their own representatives inside China believed them to be.

In a sense, this phenomenon, too, amounted to a revival of an old tradition in Western dealings with China. The prospects for China usually look more promising to Westerners overseas or visiting China than to those living and working inside the country.

The British traders at Canton in the 1830s had argued with their bosses back home at the East India Company in London. During World War II, General Joseph Stilwell, in China, had come to conclusions about Chiang Kai-shek quite different from those of President Roosevelt in Washington; and, similarly, *Time* magazine's China correspondent Theodore White had a famous falling-out with Henry Luce, his editor in New York, over the merits of Chiang's Nationalist regime.

So it was, once again, with the Americans involved in Beijing Jeep. Executives in Detroit such as Tod Clare continued to believe that China would become a huge market for Western businesses someday. The businessmen who lived in China and worked at Beijing Jeep, such as Don St. Pierre, came to different conclusions.

The historical cycle in Western attitudes toward China—of romance and attraction giving way to disillusionment and fear—is so firmly established that it may never be broken. The chances are that businessmen, like others in the West, may follow along the same circular path again and again.

There are several possibilities over the next few years. On the one hand, it is at least conceivable that the Chinese leadership will be able to rekindle the flame of Western desire for China's vast market. That was the hope of the Communist regime in the immediate aftermath of Tiananmen. While campaigning against "bourgeois liberalization" (Western political and cultural trends), the Chinese Communist Party quickly proclaimed its desire to keep its doors open to the outside world and to continue attracting foreign investment from the West. Yet the Western revulsion with political events in China, the country's growing economic problems, the difficulties encountered by foreign businessmen in China through the 1980s, and the comparative attractiveness of other East Asian countries for investment make it unlikely that this effort to keep the old romance alive will succeed.

A second possibility is that a new group of Chinese leaders will strike up a different romance with the West. Perhaps, over the next decade, the Chinese movement for democracy will prevail and, like Solidarity, the Polish workers' movement, gain at least a share of power. The Chinese democracy movement has touched a deep wellspring of sympathy overseas, raising hopes that the world's most populous country might someday have a Western-style political system. Just as Western businessmen had a few years earlier dreamed of China embracing capitalism, so Western human rights activists dreamed of China turning to democracy. Chinese students and intellectuals proved just as adept at cultivating Western public opinion as Deng Xiaoping had been in courting the business community. The plaster-and-Styrofoam Goddess of Democracy erected in Tiananmen Square during the demonstrations of 1989 served as an alluring symbol of China's potential for political change, just as the opening of Maxim's, Chinese golf courses, and a Kentucky Fried Chicken had earlier served as symbols of the potential for economic change.

In each case China's huge size, its enduring culture, its national pride, and its intractable problems ensured that the actual change would fall well short of Western expectations. Western hopes of creating a China in its own image have always failed. Still, a new Chinese leadership disposed to bring about democratic reforms, whether it succeeded or not, would almost certainly revive Western commercial interest in China.

The third and most likely possibility is that there will be no immediate new romance between China and Western businesses. If the Chinese leadership continues to resist political change, the cycle may move once again toward Western disillusionment with, or fear of, China. For its part, China might turn inward once again or, as in the era of Mao Tse-tung, might start to portray itself to the world as an alternative both to Western capitalism and to Soviet-style communism.

In the late 1980s there were early signs of such an estrangement when the United States began to denounce China's efforts to sell arms and missiles at cut-rate prices on the international market. China, it seemed, was reverting to a more assertively independent foreign policy, engendering Western mistrust in the process. If this estrangement were to deepen and if the Chinese leadership continues to rule out any political liberalization, it is even possible to envision a time in the future when the United States and European countries begin to close their markets to low-priced Chinese goods, perhaps citing as justification the exploitation of Chinese workers by their government.

And what of the fabled China market? Is the West forever doomed to play what Tod Clare once called a game of blindman's buff with China? Perhaps not. Modern communications make

China more accessible to the West, and Western goods and ideas more accessible to China, than they ever were before. Nevertheless, Western hopes of a stable and increasingly affluent China, buying huge quantities of foreign products, seem more remote today than they did a decade ago.

China is likely to remain a relatively poor country for a long time. Moreover, there will always be limits on what foreign businessmen may do, and sell, inside China. If there ever is truly a huge, unified China market, it will likely be captured not by the foreigners who have been pursuing this commercial dream for more than a century, but first of all by the Chinese themselves.

Epilogue

December 15, 1996

More than seven years have passed since the events described in *Beijing Jeep*. The turmoil of Tiananmen Square in 1989 has been replaced by an enforced orderliness. The disgruntlement and the fears of the foreign business community in Beijing have given way to a renewed, sometimes militant belief that the world's leading corporations should, indeed *must*, start up operations in China.

It is worth trying to put the story of *Beijing Jeep* into some historical perspective. What has changed in China and what has not? What is the significance of American Motors' and Chrysler's experience in the 1970s and 1980s for companies seeking to do business in China in the late 1990s or in the new century? What has happened to foreign businesses in China in the 1990s and why?

In many ways, many of the underlying dynamics are still the same. *Beijing Jeep* serves as a case study, an example of the cultural conflicts that crop up and the feelings, beliefs, and pressures foreign business executives confront when companies from abroad start up operations in China.

In order to do business in China, a company needs to negotiate a contract, just as Tod Clare did for American Motors in the early 1980s. To be sure, the atmosphere is different now. The sense of innocence and adventure is gone. In Chapter 2 of this book, Tod Clare and his aide Jeff Trimmer borrowed a typewriter to type up a contract in the antediluvian Beijing Hotel. Nowadays, visiting executives come to China armed with lawyers and laptops to negotiate in the air-conditioned comfort of deluxe hotels. In 1983, when Tod Clare escorted a wide-eyed Chinese delegation to see American Motors' factory in Egypt, few Chinese officials outside the Foreign Ministry had ever been out of the country before. Now, in the late 1990s, chances are that the Chinese counterparts with whom an American executive is negotiating will be well traveled and sophisticated.

Yet many aspects of modern-day negotiations are the same as they were in Tod Clare's day. In the never-ending dance between China and foreign investors, the Chinese of the 1990s still seek to obtain as much foreign technology as possible, while the visitors from abroad try to obtain permission to sell as much as possible in the Chinese market. In negotiations, Chinese leaders still play off one company against another and one country against another—just as they did in Chapter 4 of this book, when officials from Westinghouse and Framatome were kept on different floors of the same hotel in Beijing for weeks.

So, too, concessions or "final" offers from a seemingly immovable Chinese negotiator are still sometimes volunteered only after an exasperated Western board chairman or CEO is on the way to the airport to leave the country.

Once a contract is finally signed, the company starting up business in China still discovers, as Clare and Don St. Pierre did, that the process of negotiating has only started. Operating in China still usually requires the permission of ministries and local governments. Inside joint-venture factories, meanwhile, the cultural divide still exists, just as it did in Chapter 16 of this book. Chinese workers still believe the foreign executives are overpaid; while Western managers complain that the Chinese leaders have to spend too much time on social problems, such as housing, that have little to do with production.

It is clear now that the events of *Beijing Jeep* took place quite early in the process of China's opening to the outside world. In retrospect, the business dealings of the 1980s were merely the opening act in a decades-long drama.

During the 1990s, foreign investment flooded into China at a speed and scope that had seemed unimaginable only a few years earlier. The amounts of money China was attracting increased to levels nearly twenty times as high as in the previous decade.

In 1985, the year American Motors began producing its Cherokee Jeeps in Beijing, foreign companies signed new contracts worth a total of $5.9 billion for new investment in China. That was, as it turned out, the most active year for foreign investors in the entire decade of the 1980s. But in the early 1990s, foreign investment began to increase geometrically. In the single year of 1991, approximately $12 billion in new contracts were signed; in 1992, over $58 billion, and the following year, contracts worth $111 billion (see Table E.1). By the mid-1990s, China had come to rank second in the world, behind the United States, as a host country for foreign investment.[1]

What had happened to produce this extraordinary upsurge in investment in China in the 1990s?

To some extent, the business executives of the world were simply following the reasoning of Tod Clare in Chapter 23 of

TABLE E.1   Foreign Direct Investment in China 1979–1995

	New Contracts	Value of New Contracts (Millions of $)	Investment Actually Utilized (Millions of $)
1979–82	922	4,608	1,771
1983	470	1,731	916
1984	1,856	2,650	1,419
1985	3,073	5,931	1,956
1986	1,498	2,834	2,245
1987	2,233	3,709	2,647
1988	5,945	5,297	3,740
1989	5,779	5,600	3,774
1990	7,273	6,596	3,410
1991	12,978	11,977	4,366
1992	48,764	58,124	11,008
1993	83,437	111,437	27,515
1994	47,549	82,680	33,767
1995	37,011	91,282	37,521
TOTAL	258,788	394,455	135,215

Sources: Chinese Ministry of Foreign Trade and Economic Cooperation (MOFTEC); U.S.–China Business Council.

this book. In the late 1980s, Clare argued that there were only two large markets in the world where an international company could find the potential for significant growth: the Soviet Union and China. By the early 1990s, the Soviet Union had disintegrated, and its successor states, including Russia, were in economic turmoil. That left China.

Moreover, there were four new phenomena underlying the accelerated business rush to China in the 1990s. Each of these factors reinforced the others and compounded the desire of international investors to put new investment funds into China. Each one represented a change from the way that business had been conducted in China during the 1980s.

These factors were 1) the Asianization of the foreign business community; 2) the victory of pro-growth forces in China's domestic politics; 3) the widening of access to China's domestic market; and 4) the easing of foreign-exchange problems for foreign businesses in China.

Asianization

During the 1980s, when Beijing Jeep was starting up, China was looking primarily to the West and to Japan for outside investment, technology, and management skills. Although many Hong Kong investors, advisers, and middlemen were doing business in China, otherwise the number of Asian companies doing business in China was relatively modest during the era covered in this book.

Until the late 1980s, political obstacles kept Taiwan and South Korea out of China. Taiwan's Nationalist government did not allow Taiwan companies to invest in China, and South Korean firms were hampered by the lack of diplomatic relations between Seoul and Beijing.

The situation changed dramatically near the end of the decade. In 1988, Taiwan opened the way for its companies to invest in the mainland. Soon, Taiwan business executives were streaming to the southeastern Chinese coastal areas to set up factories where they could make use of China's lower wage rates. Meanwhile, China began to court South Korean investors, who set up factories both in southern China and along the northern coastal areas, like Shandong Province, that are nearest to South Korea. Beijing and Seoul established formal diplomatic relations in 1992.

It is worth pointing out that for China, these new links to Taiwan and South Korean businesses served both political and economic objectives. Politically, they helped China win new friends and supporters in the region: South Korea turned from China's adversary to a friend and partner in Asian diplomacy. Taiwan's commercial links to the mainland became a factor of growing importance in the diplomacy between Taipei and Beijing.

Economically, Taiwan and South Korea served as new sources of investment capital. Moreover, in the late 1980s, at just the time when China was becoming disillusioned with the high costs of Western management and technology, the new visitors from Taiwan and South Korea often provided their services at lower costs and in ways that were less disruptive to daily life in China. Americans and Germans had to be lodged at the biggest and most expensive hotels in Beijing or Shanghai; the Taiwanese and South Korean businessmen settled into the more modest hotels that had once been built for overseas Chinese.

For companies in Taiwan and South Korea, China proved a godsend. By the late 1980s, the wage rates in those countries were rising and workers were becoming scarce. The new business links with China meant that those Taiwan and South Korean firms could shift the production of materials like shoes and textiles to the Chinese mainland. So much Taiwanese investment streamed into China that in the year 1993 alone, Taiwan signed contracts for about $10 billion in new investments in China, an amount larger than the sum of investments of the United States ($6.8 billion) and Japan ($3.0 billion) for that year.

In the wake of the Tiananmen Square upheavals of 1989, while the United States, Western European governments and Japan were shunning high-level contacts with Beijing, China shifted the focus of its diplomacy to Southeast Asia. Chinese officials established diplomatic relations with Singapore for the first time since 1949, and restored the ties with Indonesia that had been broken off in 1965. By the early 1990s, Southeast

Asian investors from Indonesia, Malaysia, and Singapore, many of them overseas Chinese, were pouring unprecedented sums of money into China, too.

The cumulative effect was to increase dramatically the amount of investment capital available to China. Moreover, the flood of new money from within Asia gave China new leverage in dealing with foreign investors. Chinese officials were no longer quite so hard-pressed to obtain investment capital from American, European, and Japanese companies; they could be more confident that investment capital would come, if not from one company or country, then from another. The influx of Asian capital also meant that Chinese enterprises and consumers had more money to spend. By the time in the early 1990s when Western and Japanese companies were ready to invest in China again, they found a far more competitive environment. China had a stronger hand.

China's Domestic Politics

Throughout the 1980s, the Chinese Communist Party leadership was divided over the wisdom of pursuing high rates of economic growth. Economic reformers were generally willing and eager to stimulate the Chinese economy; more conservative leaders sought to hold down growth, in order to keep the country under a greater degree of control. The Chinese government's problems in managing the economy in the 1980s helped to reinforce the arguments of conservative forces. High growth rates usually led to a sharp increase in inflation, and whenever this happened, the leadership in Beijing sought to clamp down on the economy.

During the two years after the Tiananmen Square crackdown, the Chinese leadership kept the economy under wraps. The Chinese economy grew by only 4 to 5 percent in the 1989–90 period, the lowest levels in the decade. But in January 1992, in what was probably the last memorable act of his long political career, Deng Xiaoping made a highly publicized journey to southern China and pressed for a rapid expansion of the Chinese economy once again.

In retrospect, that trip by Deng set the course of the Chinese economy for the 1990s and, in the process, virtually ended the intra-party debates over how fast the Chinese economy should expand. During the period from 1992 to 1995, China began to grow at rates of from 10 to 14 percent a year, faster than any other nation in the world. Moreover, Chinese leaders seemed to be able to keep inflation under control even in the midst of this rapid expansion.

The effect on foreign investors was dramatic. The high rates of growth, of course, were attractive for their own sake: they meant that China had new money to spend and that it needed more goods and capital from abroad in order to continue to grow. Moreover, China's ability to maintain this growth without the boom-and-bust cycles of the 1980s meant that foreign companies doing business in China were less subject than before to the sort of prolonged freezing of economic activity that Don St. Pierre faced at Beijing Jeep during the retrenchment of 1986.

Access to China's Market

During the decade of the 1980s, China still clung to what might be called the "Tianfu Cola" model of the China market. As described in Chapter 3 of this book, when Coca-Cola first opened bottling plants in China, it was required to sell Coke only to tourists and other foreigners, not to Chinese. At the same time, a Chinese-made imitation, Tianfu Cola, began to appear, the product of a Chinese factory in Sichuan Province. Chinese consumers were told that Tianfu Cola looked and tasted the same as Coke, but that it had a different formula, one that would help the Chinese liver and spleen.

That approach usually didn't work. Even if the Chinese imitator could duplicate Coca-Cola, itself a questionable proposition, Tianfu Cola couldn't compete with the brand name. More and more Chinese were traveling overseas, where they were learning the names of the leading consumer products in the world. Meanwhile, China began to open up to advertising and promotion. Chinese officials found that there was no small amount of money to be made by allowing companies like Coca-Cola to hawk their wares by advertising on Chinese television or by promoting Chinese sports events.

Thus, in the 1990s, China began to grant a much greater degree of access to its consumer market. Not only Coca-Cola, but also countless other foreign companies began to sell brand-name products like Tide, Marlboro, Hitachi, and Panasonic inside China.

China's dream of the 1980s had been that foreign companies would bring in their capital and technology and make products almost exclusively for export, rather than domestic sale. By the 1990s, China had decided to let companies sell their goods inside the country, as long as they could work out a deal that provided benefits for China or at least for some Chinese partners.

Often, the bargain was that the foreign company would have to buy its parts for the China operations locally, as Chrysler and other auto manufacturers were required to do. Sometimes, the deal hinged on the foreign company's being required to bring in technology from abroad. In still other cases, Chinese officials or business partners would have to be given some sort of financial incentives. Sometimes, the deal was a combination of all these factors. But one way or another, the Chinese leadership was letting consumer goods from abroad be sold inside China to a greater extent than in the past.

As a symbol of the changes of the new decade, in 1994 Tianfu Cola itself sold 60 percent of its factory and the Tianfu name to Pepsi-Cola. It was the seventh of eight Chinese cola companies to sell a controlling interest to a foreign firm.[2] Like other Chinese companies, Tianfu Cola had discovered that, rather than try to eradicate the foreign competition entirely, it could profit by entering into a partnership with its competitors from abroad. The very Chinese brand that had been set up to counteract competition from abroad wound up doing business with and for a foreign company.

Foreign Exchange

Some of the changes of the 1990s are ones of degree and are, at least to some extent, reversible. But in one respect, the business climate in China has been transformed since the events of *Beijing Jeep*. The problem of obtaining foreign exchange, the continuing preoccupation of foreign companies doing business in China in the 1980s, has been virtually eliminated.

During the late 1980s, the Chinese government set up what were called "swap centers" around the nation. At these centers, foreign companies could take the renminbi they were earning inside China and trade them for dollars or other foreign currencies. At the outset, the exchange rates were worked out by the parties themselves.

These swap centers provided a way for companies from the West, Japan, and the rest of Asia to obtain the foreign exchange required to bring parts and supplies to factories in China. The swap centers also enabled these foreign companies to take out of China the profits that had been earned in renminbi. For some Chinese enterprises, meanwhile, the swap centers provided a means of obtaining renminbi at times when credit was tight and the Chinese banks were holding down on their loans.

By 1994, China took the next step by creating a unified, nationwide foreign-exchange market, so that the rates of exchange at all the swap centers were the same.[3] Gradually, China was moving through the 1990s toward a system in which its currency would be fully convertible on world markets.

In theory, China at this writing still maintains some control over foreign-exchange transactions by foreign businesses. Joint ventures in China are required to submit to the government their plans for balancing foreign exchange. If there were some sudden, drastic change in the Chinese economy, such as a drop in foreign reserves, it is possible that China would once again seek to restrict foreign-exchange transactions. In practice, however, foreign companies doing business in China say that obtaining foreign exchange is no longer the preoccupation it was during the 1980s.

This does not mean that foreign companies can run their operations in China without interference from the government. The Chinese leadership has many other means of controlling what these companies do: old methods, like state-planning restrictions on resources and output; and new ones, like industrial policies aimed at strengthening and protecting Chinese enterprises. But the method used in the 1980s, a crimp on foreign-exchange transactions, now seems to have been discarded.

In at least a few important respects, then, doing business in China has improved since the 1980s.

The underlying dynamics haven't changed. The negotiations are endless, and so is the pressure on foreign companies to transfer technology to China. Yet the many companies starting up business in China in the 1990s are finding that they have a better chance of trying to sell their products in the domestic Chinese market than they had a decade earlier. Moreover, they are able to exchange their Chinese earnings for foreign currency in ways that seemed unimaginable throughout most of the 1980s.

The final chapter of *Beijing Jeep* was written in 1989, within months after the bloody crackdown on the Tiananmen Square demonstrations. Some of its conclusions were overly pessimistic about the prospects for foreign businesses in China. As it turned out, China was indeed able to rekindle the flame of the desire for the China market. Businesses have short memories, especially when it comes to politics. The revulsion over political events in China subsided within two or three years, at least in the corporate boardrooms of North America, Europe, and Japan. The desire to sell to China overcame all inhibitions, whether economic or political.

Nevertheless, by the late 1990s, the prospects for these foreign companies in China remained uncertain. Many of the fundamental questions about where China was heading were left unanswered through the first half of the 1990s.

At this writing in late 1996, China stands at a crossroads. The era of Deng Xiaoping is over, but China's future political leadership probably won't be clear for a few years after the death of Deng. China's economic course is equally in doubt, in ways that could affect foreign business operations in China.

The core economic question China must confront is what to do about its state enterprises, the huge entities that are both the core of China's socialist system and yet also the biggest drag on its economy.

In the late 1990s, state enterprises still employed about two-thirds of all the workers in Chinese cities. It is from these enterprises that most of the residents of urban China obtain not only their salaries but also their pensions, housing, health care, child care, and even schooling. These enterprises are losing large and increasing amounts of money, requiring ever-greater subsidies from the government, draining more and more loans from state banks to keep afloat.

In some cases, to be sure, these state enterprises are losing money because they are supposed to. They are serving as the welfare system that buttresses the more successful parts of the Chinese economy. Indeed, there is a sleight-of-hand aspect to the supposed dichotomy between thriving private companies and failing state enterprises. In some instances, Chinese officials have stripped the money-making operations out of a state enterprise, then set it up as a government-controlled "private" company—leaving the money-losing clinics, housing, and nurseries in the state enterprise.

To take one example, Sinopec, the huge Chinese petroleum ministry, created Shanghai Petrochemical, a private stock company, out of its profitable Shanghai operations. Shanghai Petrochemical is one of China's blue-chip stocks, trading on the Hong Kong and New York stock exchanges. The hospitals and clinics left in Sinopec, the state enterprise, lose money. And yet Sinopec (that is, the Chinese government) owns 61 percent of the stock of Shanghai Petrochemical.[4]

In many other instances, however, the state enterprises have little or nothing profitable to salvage. China has been keeping these enterprises alive primarily as a means of ensuring that the residents of its cities have jobs, housing, and health care.

During the 1980s, China began to talk about the idea of letting the most unprofitable of these state enterprises go bankrupt. As mentioned in Chapter 18 of this book, authorities experimented with a "model" bankruptcy, a single case meant to demonstrate how the phenomenon would work.

A decade later, there has been little progress. Only a few small enterprises have been forced to close. The leadership has been unwilling to risk the consequences of rising unemployment and discontent. At the end of 1996, Chinese leaders were still talking about the need to try to merge failing enterprises with more successful ones rather than letting them go bankrupt.

The issue of bankruptcy has been, so far, too sensitive. The implicit bargain the Chinese leadership struck with its people after the Tiananmen Square upheavals was that China would maintain and improve living standards if ordinary people would stay out of politics. Throwing people out of work would jeopardize that bargain. It is easier to try to keep failing enterprises alive somehow. Yet in doing so, the regime faces the prospect that the debts will continue to mount. By 1994, more than 40 percent of all state enterprises in China were losing money.

For foreign businesses in China, the fate of these state enterprises is important in a number of ways. In the broadest sense, China's future prosperity hinges on what happens to them. If the leadership is unwilling to reform or close down the most unprofitable state enterprises, they could drain the economy to such an extent that the rapid growth rates of the early 1990s will fade.

Moreover, the failing state enterprises create a strong constituency for Chinese protectionism. If the Chinese regime's aim is to protect these enterprises at all costs, then the regime cannot possibly lift tariffs on the products from abroad that would compete with these Chinese enterprises.

Finally, most companies entering the China market have done so through a partnership with some Chinese state enterprise or another. Few if any large-scale joint ventures are with truly private entities. American Motors' and Chrysler's partner in Beijing Jeep, for example, was the state enterprise, Beijing Automotive Works. It is these state enterprises that often require foreign companies to help build housing and health care facilities for Chinese workers, and that require Chinese factory managers to play the noneconomic role Tod Clare once compared to a summer camp director.

At this writing, China has begun to acknowledge the importance of setting up other systems—unemployment compensation, social security, municipal housing, and health care—to supply the benefits that until now have been provided by state enterprises.[5] But the systems are only in their earliest stages.

Once these welfare funds are available to provide an alternative form of social safety net, the Chinese leadership may be more willing to let failing state enterprises go bankrupt. Foreign companies doing business in China will be required to help pay into these funds, to help offset the costs of their workers' benefits. From the standpoint of a foreign business in China, making these contributions is probably better than being asked to build housing or help operate a hospital.

By treating these state enterprises so gingerly, China has so far avoided the unemployment and economic dislocations experienced in countries like Poland. The ultimate question is whether this gradual approach will work or whether China is merely postponing the inevitable.

On November 10, 1996, Chairman Wu Zhongliang—the first Chinese chairman of Beijing Jeep, who had, eleven years earlier, fled in horror from American Motors' raucous dealer show in Las Vegas—died after a heart attack in Beijing. Chairman Wu had stepped down from the auto venture for health reasons two years earlier.

A handful of Beijing Jeep representatives attended his funeral. Even an old antagonist from the battles of the 1980s, Don St. Pierre, sent flowers. After leaving Beijing Jeep and Chrysler, St. Pierre had worked in Taiwan for another American company, FMC, a Chicago-based defense contractor. In 1994, he moved back to China to run a new venture aimed at setting up auto parts ventures in China. He even assembled some of his old team from Beijing Jeep—men like Ed Schulze, Kerry Ivins, Dennis Noonan, and Bob Steinseifer—to work with him. But the project, funded by a group of American investors, quickly became embroiled in a series of management disputes, and St. Pierre left within a year. He stayed on in Beijing, working on various ventures to sell wine and golf equipment in China and, for a time, to sell Chinese-made guns in the United States.

By 1996, seven years after the upheavals of Tiananmen Square, Beijing Jeep was beginning to operate like a modern automobile factory. It was producing about 80,000 vehicles a year—more than three times as many as it had a decade earlier, yet still a modest figure when compared with other car plants around the world.

The once-antiquated Beijing Jeep factory had been modernized with new axle and engine shops and a foundry operation. Its work force of 8,000 was being increasingly filled with younger, better-educated, better-skilled Chinese personnel. According to Chrysler officials, the average wage for these workers in 1996 was 1,500 renminbi or about $180 per month. That made Beijing Jeep's wages per worker the second-highest in Beijing, behind a Panasonic venture for the production of television sets. By contrast, government workers in Beijing were being paid wages of about $50 per month.

In the decade of the 1990s, Chrysler still confronted many of the dilemmas of dealing with workers within the confines of China's repressive political system. In 1994, Beijing Jeep briefly vaulted into the headlines once again when it attempted to fire Gao Feng, a worker in its stamping shop who had not shown up at the factory for more than a month. Gao claimed to be a member of an underground Christian organization, and he said he hadn't been able to come to work because Chinese security officials had been detaining him to prevent him from holding a religious commemoration for people who had died in the Tiananmen Square crackdown. In the United States, human rights groups protested directly to Chrysler Chairman Robert Eaton just as he was preparing to accompany Commerce Secretary Ron Brown on a trip to China. Chrysler eventually relented and permitted Gao to return to work.[6]

The problems with foreign exchange that had so preoccupied St. Pierre and American Motors a decade earlier were, by 1996, merely a memory. The secret deal of 1986, guaranteeing Beijing Jeep the right to exchange its Chinese renminbi for dollars, had become all but irrelevant. Beijing Jeep was still required to submit its plans for obtaining and spending foreign exchange to

Chinese authorities. But on the whole, joint ventures throughout China found that they were able to get the foreign exchange
they needed. Zhu Rongji, the Chinese official who had brokered
the secret deal, became in the 1990s a member of the Politburo
standing committee, one of the leading officials in China.

Nevertheless, Beijing Jeep, like other joint ventures, was still
subject to a variety of Chinese government restrictions. It was,
to say the least, still not operating in anything resembling a
free-market economy. The car venture was obliged to draw up
both a long-range plan and a five-year plan, and get the approval
of various ministries for its efforts. Chinese authorities required
Beijing Jeep to get official authorization not only for its levels of
output and its spending of foreign exchange but also for its profits. Both foreign enterprises in China and domestic state enterprises were required to show the government their plans for
making a profit.

Even more significantly, China in 1994 imposed a series of
new restrictions on joint ventures like Beijing Jeep by formally
adopting an industrial policy for automobiles in China. The in-
dustry-wide rules imposed limits on how many automobile assembly projects would be allowed in the country. They banned
all imports of CKD (complete knock-down) kits, like the ones
that American Motors had used a decade earlier for assembling
Jeep Cherokees in China; this rule forced foreign car companies
to move toward the purchase of Chinese-made parts. The 1994
regulations forced car companies to set up research-and-devel-
opment facilities in China. And the rules required any new automobile ventures established after 1994 to produce at least
100,000 cars in their first year of operation, and to begin exporting some of the cars made in China.

These rules for autos were reminiscent of the industrial policies that had earlier been used by other countries, such as Japan,
to nurture along domestic manufacturers and to protect them
from too much foreign competition. China's industrial policy
made clear that despite the steps the regime has taken to open
up the economy further in the 1990s, it intends to keep foreign
companies under strict limits.

By the middle of the decade, Chrysler was one of several car companies from the United States, Western Europe, and Japan jockeying for the right to set up new car factories inside China. The fact that Beijing Jeep had been one of the earliest joint ventures in China proved to be of little help. In 1995, Chrysler lost out to Mercedes in a competition for the right to produce Chinese minivans. The deal fell through when Chrysler refused to go along with a Chinese demand that it transfer all the technology for the van to China, and then let China sublicense the design for the van and sell it in the rest of Asia.[7]

"Our Beijing Jeep is starting to be a halfway decent little company," Eaton, the Chrysler chairman, told one magazine reporter in 1995. But he went on to say that "there are going to be lots and lots of ups and downs in that country [China]." By the mid-1990s, Chrysler officials had concluded that the fastest-rising business opportunities for the company in Asia lay not in China, but in Vietnam.[8]

The days when Tod Clare peered across the border from Hong Kong into China had long passed by. After two decades of trial and error, tribute and tribulation, American businesses were still in China. Many of them now considered China an obligation. Few of them had yet found it the answer to their dreams.

Notes

Introduction

1. Initially, U.S. officials put the death toll at three thousand to five thousand, based in part on a thorough examination of shell casings and other physical evidence in Tiananmen Square after the massacre. See *Los Angeles Times*, June 30, 1989, p. 1. Officials at the Chinese Red Cross initially put the figure at 2,700, based on hospital estimates; the Chinese organization later retracted this figure, probably under pressure from the Chinese government. The lowest Western estimates, based on deaths specifically witnessed or recorded at Chinese hospitals, were that seven hundred people had been killed. Chinese officials continued to insist that no more than two hundred Beijing residents died. See *Washington Post*, July 1, 1989. p. 11.

2. *New China News Service*, July 3, 1989.

3. Teng and Fairbank, *China's Response to the West*, Harvard University Press, 1979, page 54.

Chapter 1

1. See Thomas J. McCormick, *China Market: America's Quest for Informal Empire 1893–1901*, Quadrangle Books, 1967, pp. 114–119.

2. *Far Eastern Economic Review*, May 6, 1954.

3. *Far Eastern Economic Review*, May 20, 1954.

4. Information concerning the formation of the National Council for U.S.-China Trade is based on the council files in the Gerald R. Ford Library in Ann Arbor, Michigan.

5. Figures taken from memorandum from secretary of commerce to President Gerald R. Ford, "Background Material Regarding Commercial Relations for Your Visit to China," November 21, 1975, included in files at Gerald R. Ford Library.

6. Bauer, *China Takes Off*, University of Washington Press, 1986.

7. For Kissinger memo to Ford concerning Bush, see White House Central Files in Gerald R. Ford Library, Ann Arbor; for Goldwater ultimatum, see files of Jack Marsh in the Gerald R. Ford Library.

8. See J. Lelyveld, "In China, Funeral Wreaths Tell of the Politically Living," *New York Times*, May 6, 1974.

Chapter 3

1. "How Bloomingdale's Is Selling China," *New York Times*, September 7, 1980.

2. *Newsweek*, September 22, 1980.

3. *Wall Street Journal*, December 28, 1978.

4. Teng and Fairbank, *op. cit.*, p. 39.

5. "U.S., China Jointly Track Firings of Soviet Missiles," *Los Angeles Times*, June 19, 1981.

6. "Hard Sell for a Soft Drink," *China Daily*, April 1, 1986.

7. Quoted in McCormick, *China Market: America's Quest for Informal Empire, 1893–1901*, Quadrangle Books, 1967, p. 129.

Chapter 4

1. See China: Lieberthal, K., "The Politics Behind the New Economics," *Fortune* magazine, December 31, 1979.

2. See Linda Mathews, "China Puts Development on Hold," *Los Angeles Times*, May 1, 1980; and "China Runs Short of Cash," *Los Angeles Times*, August 22, 1980.

3. Michael Parks, "Despite Project Cutbacks, U.S. Fares Better Than Other Nations in China Trade," *Los Angeles Times*, February 10, 1981.

4. *Beijing Review*, November 4, 1985.

5. Richard H. Solomon, "China: Friendship and Obligation in Chinese Negotiating Style," in *National Negotiating Styles*, Foreign Service Institute, 1987.

6. Lucian Pye, *Chinese Commercial Negotiating Style*, the Rand Corporation, 1982.

Chapter 5

1. *Beijing Review*, November 4, 1985.

2. *Wall Street Journal*, May 6, 1983.

Chapter 6

1. *Automotive News*, July 9, 1984.

Chapter 7

1. Lucian Pye, *Chinese Commercial Negotiating Style*, pp. 78–9.

Chapter 8

1. In 1988 China enacted its first bankruptcy law, opening the way under certain limited conditions for failing Chinese enterprises to be declared bankrupt.

2. Michael Parks, "Taking China to China: Key Issue for Reagan Trip," *Los Angeles Times*, April 12, 1984, p. 1.

3. When President Bush visited Beijing in February 1989, he rankled the Chinese leadership by inviting a leading dissident, the scientist Fang Lizhi, to his banquet. Chinese security officials barred Fang from attending. On the other hand, Reagan had no inclination to be daring in his guest list. At the time of Reagan's 1984 visit, the only known dissidents in China were those who had taken part in the 1979 Democracy Wall campaign, and many of them were in jail. Fang Lizhi grew to prominence during a series of student demonstrations in 1986.

Chapter 9

1. Once, while I was based in China, a visitor from the United States called an operator at the Beijing Hotel seeking the local phone number for the *Los Angeles Times*. The operator seemed to understand and went off, leaving the visitor on hold for a full fifteen minutes. Finally she returned and replied, "You want the Los Angeles time? Twelve o'clock, midnight."

2. See *Los Angeles Times*: "Prices Soaring in China—But Just for Foreigners," May 24, 1980; "Costs

of Doing Business in China Keep Soaring," March 22, 1985.

3. At the time, in September 1987, China, with a population of 1.1 billion, had reported a total of six AIDS cases. One was a foreign tourist, one was a Chinese citizen returning from ten years in the United States, and four were hemophiliacs who had had transfusions with blood products from abroad.

4. See "I Was Peking's Guinea Pig," *South China Morning Post,* December 8, 1981.

Chapter 10

1. See the series of articles by American journalists on the Nixon trip: William M. Ringle, "How Now, Mao?", *Nation's Business,* May 1972; J. F. ter Horst, *Detroit News,* February 23, 1972; William M. Ringle and James A. Michener, "China Diary," *Reader's Digest,* May 1972. See also Ringle, "Bonus Plan Helps Beijing Jeep Factory," page H-1, *Washington Post,* June 2, 1979.

2. For shorthand, I have used the term *Americans* to describe the American Motors employees assigned to China. It should be noted that, in fact, a few of the American Motors personnel were not U.S. citizens but Australian or British nationals.

3. Confidential board of directors minutes, August 27, 1983.

4. Confidential board of directors minutes, December 7, 1983.

5. Contract for Beijing Jeep Corporation, May 1983, appendix 7.

6. See Neal Ulevich, "Firecrackers Pop as AMC Makes Jeeps with Chinese Automaker," Associated Press, January 15, 1984.

Chapter 11

1. See Michael Parks, "China's Economy Growing, But Not Enough to Meet Consumer Demand," *Los Angeles Times,* February 21, 1984, part IV, p. 3.

2. See R. K. Jain, *China and Japan 1948–1980,* Humanities Press, Atlantic Highlands, 1981; also "The West and Trade with China," published in *Far Eastern Economic Review,* February 14, 1957.

3. See Mathews, "China Seeks to Emulate Japan," *Los Angeles Times,* October 30, 1978.

4. See *Business Week,* April 22, 1955, p. 32; *China Daily,* October 7, 1985; and *Far Eastern Economic Review,* August 1, 1985, p. 46.

5. Quoted in *China Trade Report,* June 1985, p. 12.

6. New China News Service, August 17, 1985.

7. See *Nihon Keizai Shimbun,* September 2, 1985; and *International Herald Tribune,* November 26, 1985.

8. Cappy, who later became president of AMC, declined through a Chrysler spokesman to be interviewed for this book. His $500-a-car offer is contained in the board of directors minutes of Beijing Jeep for the meeting of February 6, 1985.

Chapter 12

1. See "Joint Venture: Success Speaks for Itself," in *Beijing Review,* November 4, 1985, p. 21.

2. Another AMC official, Charles Johnson, the head of the special team sent in to launch the new Cherokee, was put temporarily in charge of the Americans in Beijing.

Chapter 14

1. A *Business Week* reporter, Dori Jones Yang, spoke with a cooperative St. Pierre at about the same time St. Pierre met with O'Neill.

   American Motors' problems in China had received one earlier airing in the press, which was not generated by St. Pierre. In late February AMC president Joseph Cappy told reporters in Detroit that a shortage of foreign currency had caused a sharp cutback in production plans for Beijing Jeep. However, Cappy did not mention the money the Chinese units were withholding from BJC. Nor did Cappy raise the possibility that the Chinese venture might halt production or that AMC might pull out of China—the two key elements added in the interviews granted by St. Pierre.

2. Hawke, whose name is now Hulan Saren, later moved back to the United States and at this writing works on China business ventures for General Motors. In an interview she declined to name the Chinese intermediary who passed on St. Pierre's letter to Zhao, pointing out that if that person's identity were disclosed, it would be harder to get such a message through in the future.

3. See *Washington Post,* April 11, 1986, p. B-8.

Chapter 15

1. See *Time,* June 2, 1986, p. 40; *Washington Post,* April 11, 1986, p. B-8; *International Herald Tribune,* June 10, 1986; *Wall Street Journal,* July 17, 1986.

2. See "Guangzhou Firms Reach Crisis Point," *South China Morning Post,* June 14, 1986.

3. Memo, "Beijing Jeep Corporation," obtained from U.S. Department of Commerce under Freedom of Information Act.

4. Memo, "U.S. China Joint Commission on Commerce and Trade," Department of Commerce, obtained under Freedom of Information Act.

5. Quoted by Associated Press, June 12, 1986.

Chapter 16

1. In 1988 the Americans sought further increases to $300,000 for each of its employees at Beijing Jeep. The Chinese, after objecting furiously, finally agreed on a figure of $273,000.

Chapter 17

1. Chen Zutao declined to be interviewed for this book. A scheduled interview in 1988 was canceled at the last minute when a spokesman for Chen said he had to attend an important meeting. His views were obtained from others who took part in the talks.

2. China obtained one additional concession. AMC agreed that the 2,000 Cherokees for 1986 would include the 1,008 units that had been boxed up and were awaiting shipment to China since the previous fall. In other words, more than half the 1986 production would go to clear away the old backlog.

3. See Report of Joint Commission on Commerce and Trade, obtained from U.S. Commerce Department under Freedom of Information Act.

Chapter 19

1. See "Beatrice Advice for Investors in China: 'Don't Wait for Guidelines,' " *South China Morning Post,* October 16, 1984.

2. "Food Company's Challenges and Surprises," *China Daily* supplement, April 8, 1987.

3. "Export Hopes Fade for Food Venture," *South China Morning Post*, September 28, 1986.

4. E. E. Bauer, *China Takes Off*, University of Washington Press, 1986.

5. Another important Asian economy, Hong Kong, had its currency pegged to the U.S. dollar and so also benefited from the 1985 currency changes. But Hong Kong's ability to attract new investment was not as great as that of Taiwan and South Korea because of concern over the agreement transferring Hong Kong back to Chinese sovereignty in 1997. Much of the new investment in Hong Kong in the mid-1980s came from China itself.

6. See New China News Service, June 5, 1986, and August 7, 1986.

7. *People's Daily*, August 29, 1986; *Economic Daily*, August 13, 1986.

8. Story recounted by Roger Sullivan, president of the U.S.-China Business Council.

Chapter 21

1. See "Talk of Political Reform Begins to Flower in China," *Los Angeles Times*, June 23, 1986.

2. In theory Hu outranked Deng, China's acknowledged leader, within the forty-four-million-member Communist Party. However, Deng held the crucial post of chairman of the Communist Party's Central Military Commission, the Party group that supervises the People's Liberation Army.

3. *China Television News*, January 22, 1987.

4. See "China's No. 2 Man Resigns in Dispute," *Los Angeles Times*, January 17, 1987; and "Chinese Reports from United States Reflect Negative Propaganda Campaign," February 5, 1987.

5. *Beijing Daily*, May 27, 1987.

6. "Monthly Highlights Report," People's Republic of China, December 1986, prepared by commercial section of U.S. embassy in Beijing.

7. "Foreign Economic Trends and their Implications for the United States: People's Republic of China," U.S. Department of Commerce, October 1986.

8. Herbert Liu's name is a pseudonym, the only one used in this book. He spoke with a reporter on the condition that neither his real name nor the computer company for which he worked in China would be identified. Liu said he feared that the company might retaliate against him and that public identification could jeopardize his job prospects and career.

9. "China: Economic Policy and Performance in 1987," report by the Central Intelligence Agency to the Joint Economic Committee, April 21, 1988.

10. See "China Expels Reporter for French Wire Service," *Los Angeles Times*, January 27, 1987.

11. See *Los Angeles Times*, January 16, 1987; and *South China Morning Post*, February 26, 1987.

12. See "Statistics for 1987," issued on February 23, 1988, by the State Statistical Bureau of the People's Republic of China.

13. U.S. Department of Commerce report, People's Republic of China, 1988.

14. "Monthly Highlights Report," People's Republic of China, January 1987, prepared by commercial section of U.S. embassy in Beijing.

Chapter 22

1. "AMC Accepts Sweetened Bid for Chrysler," *The Wall Street Journal*, May 21, 1987, page 8; "Chrysler Corp. Says It Hopes to Complete American Motors Corp. Acquisition by Aug. 15," *The Wall Street Journal*, May 22, 1987, page 12.

Chapter 23

1. For Chen's public remarks, See Reuters News Agency, January 21, 1988; New China News Service, November 14, 1986.

Chapter 24

1. Adi Ignatius, "China to Postpone Some Joint Ventures with Foreigners in Bid to Cool Economy," *Wall Street Journal*, December 7, 1988, p. A-11.

Chapter 25

1. During the nighttime assault by Chinese troops on Tiananmen Square, some Beijing residents began shouting *"Ba gong! Ba gong!"*—a call for a general strike. The strike never materialized. Indeed, in the terror that followed the massacre, many Beijing residents risked their lives bicycling through gunfire in order to appear for work.

2. Report from confidential source in Beijing.

Conclusion

1. See, for example, "Rerouting Asian Trips Away from China," *New York Times* Travel Section, July 9, 1989, p. 3.

2. See "10-Year Effort to Transform Backward Economy 'Dealt a Body Blow,' " *Washington Post*, June 10, 1989, p. A-14. Lord's earlier beliefs taken from interview with author in Beijing, June 1987. Lord stepped down as U.S. ambassador to China in early 1989.

3. See, for example, "Capitalism in the Making," *Time*, April 30, 1984, p. 26. See also William Safire's column "Great Leap Forward," *New York Times*, December 10, 1984, p. 23: "When it comes to world history . . . the big event of 1984 was surely the rejection of Marxism and embrace of capitalism by the government of a billion Chinese."

4. See, for example, newspaper column by Jeane Kirkpatrick, *Washington Post*, June 26, 1989, p. A-11; and editorial in *The New York Times*, June 13, 1989, p. A-26, "Stalinism is supposed to be a spent force, but the news has not yet reached Beijing."

5. Tippett, now the president of Springs Industries, said in a 1989 interview with the author that he did not intentionally mislead anyone through these public statements. "We said, 'We hope this is the basis for a low-cost venture in Asia,' and, well, some things happened in the meantime," Tippett explained. "When oil prices dropped like a stone, they [China] had hard-currency problems. Those are the kinds of things, when you deal overseas, that are always risky."

6. Figure supplied by U.S. State Department, July 1989. The department estimated that, before the evacuation of June 1989, there

had been 9,800 private citizens with American passports living in China. Of these, 3,700 were students, missionaries or tourists on long-term stays. The remainder were business personnel and their dependents.

Epilogue

1. See U.S.-China Business Council, *Forecast '96*.
2. Steven Mufson, "All the (Foreign) Tea in China Causing Tempest for Economic Nationalists," *Washington Post*, May 19, 1996.
3. See "Monetary and Exchange System Reforms in China," International Monetary Fund, September 1996.
4. Jim Mann, "Is China Really 'Going Capitalist'? A Close Look Shows That It's Not," *Los Angeles Times*, June 12, 1995.
5. Anne Stevenson-Yang, "Revamping the Welfare System," *China Business Review*, January 1996.
6. Steven Mufson, "For U.S. Firms in China, a Struggle over Rights and Roles," *Washington Post*, Aug. 25, 1994; interview with Franc Krebs, president of Beijing Jeep.
7. "How Mercedes Trumped Chrysler in China," *Business Week*, July 31, 1995.
8. See Marshall Loeb, "Empowerment That Pays Off," *Fortune*, March 20, 1995, p. 146.

Index

About the Book and Author

When China opened its doors to the West in the late 1970s, Western businesses jumped at the chance to sell their products to the most populous nation in the world. Yet, over the decade leading up to the bloody events in and around Tiananmen Square, that experiment produced growing disappointment on both sides, and a vision of capturing the world's largest market faded.

In this updated version of *Beijing Jeep*, Jim Mann traces the history of the stormy romance between American business and Chinese communism through the experiences of American Motors and its operation in China, Beijing Jeep, a closely watched joint venture often visited by American politicians and Chinese leaders. He explains how some of the world's savviest executives completely misjudged the business climate and recounts how the Chinese, who acquired valuable new technology at virtually no expense to themselves, ultimately outcapitalized the capitalists.

Jim Mann served as the Beijing bureau chief for the *Los Angeles Times* from 1984 to 1987, then returned to China in 1989 to cover the democracy uprising.